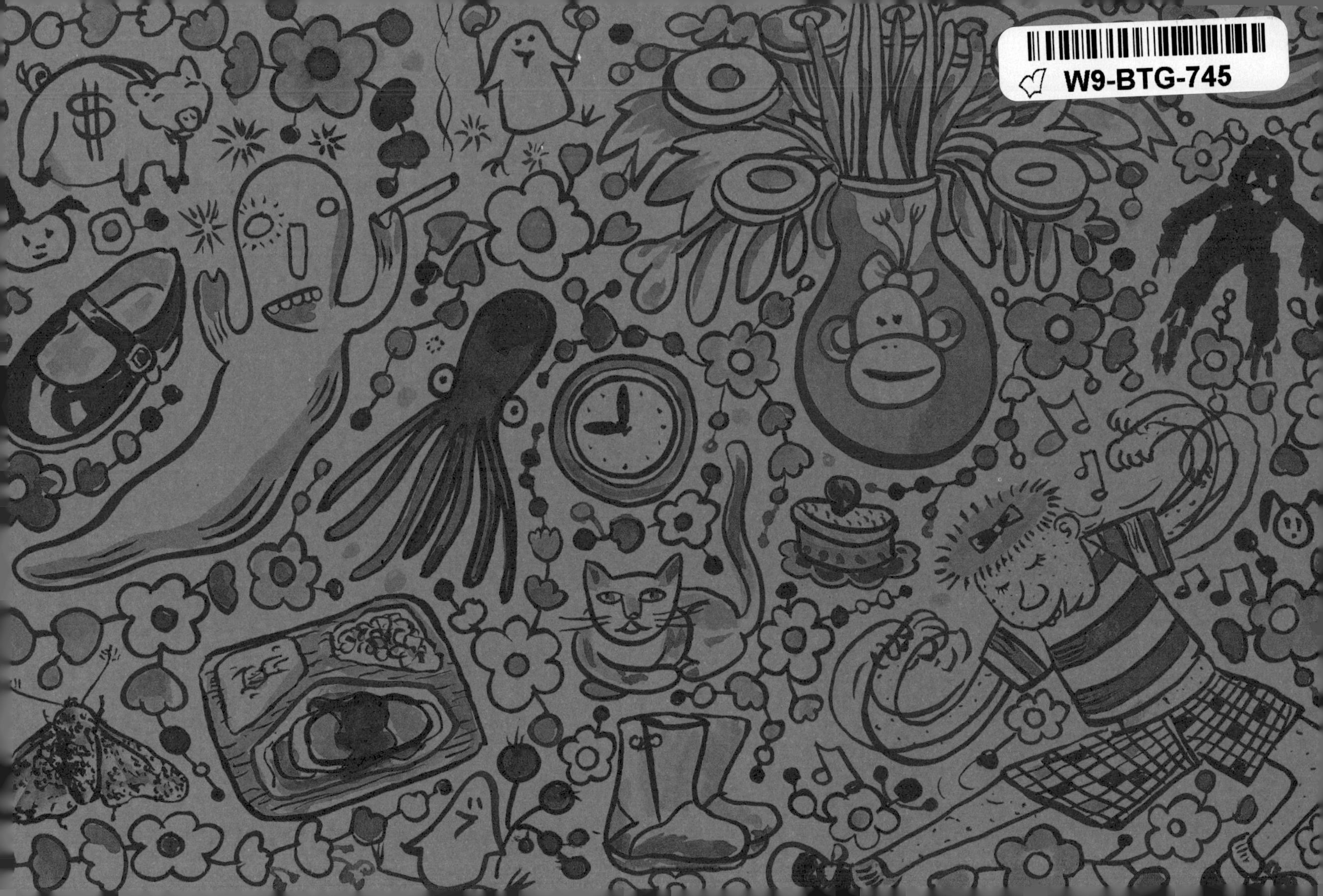

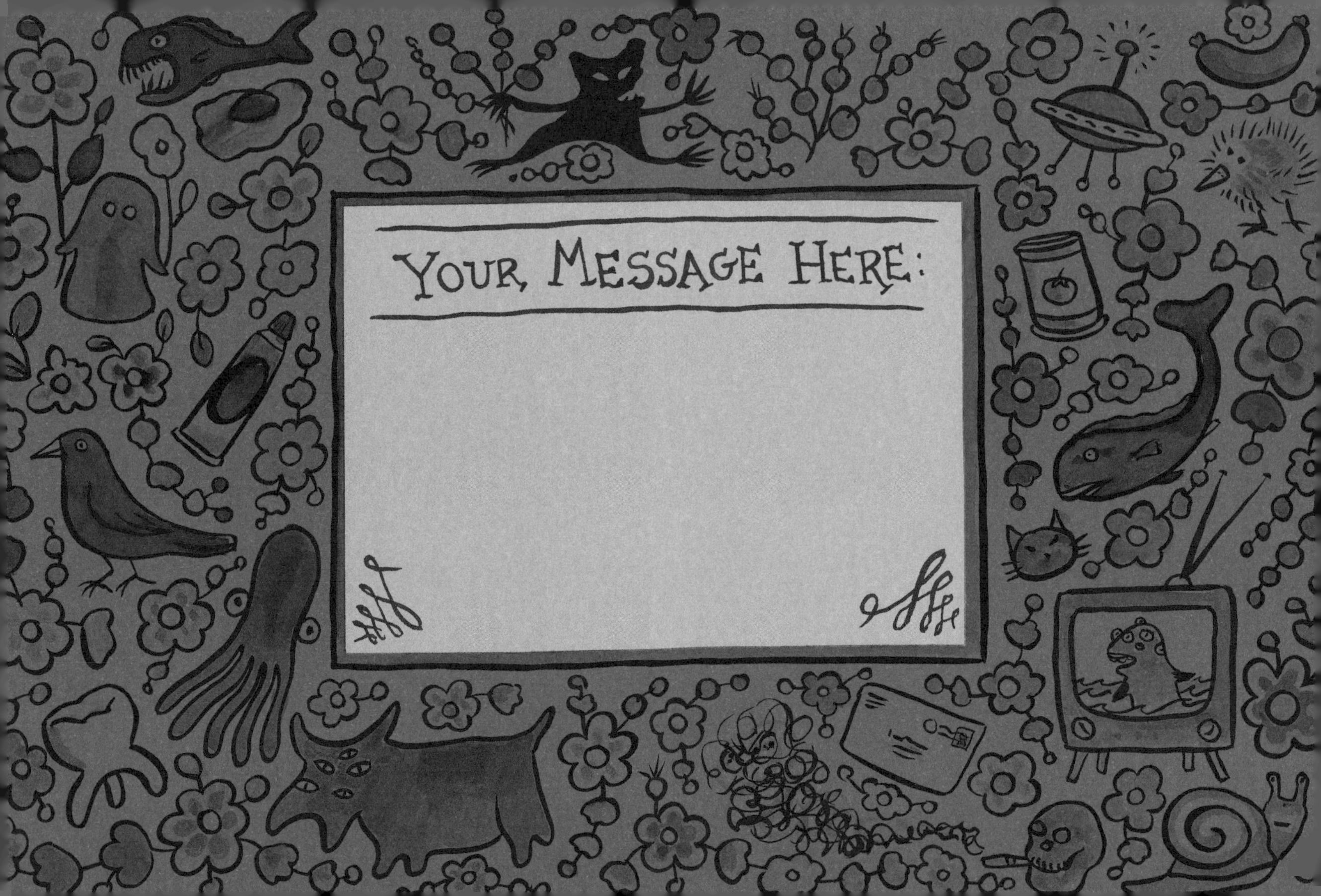
YOUR MESSAGE HERE:

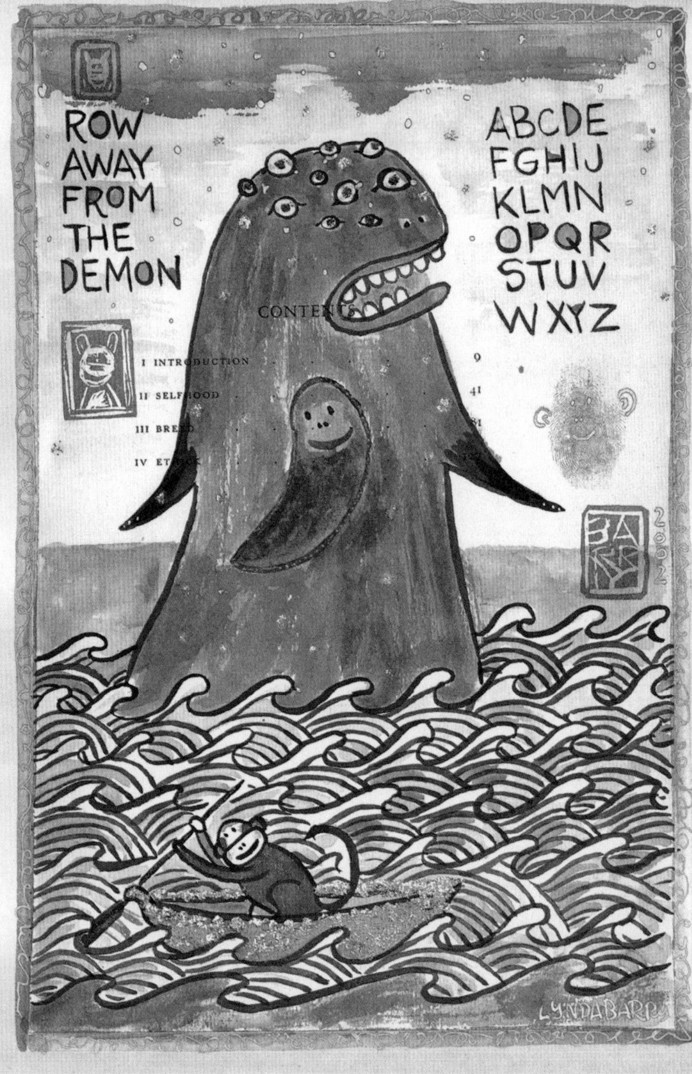
ROW AWAY FROM THE DEMON
ABCDE
FGHIJ
KLMN
OPQR
STUV
WXYZ
I INTRODUCTION 9
II SELFHOOD 41
BARRY 2002
LYNDABARRY

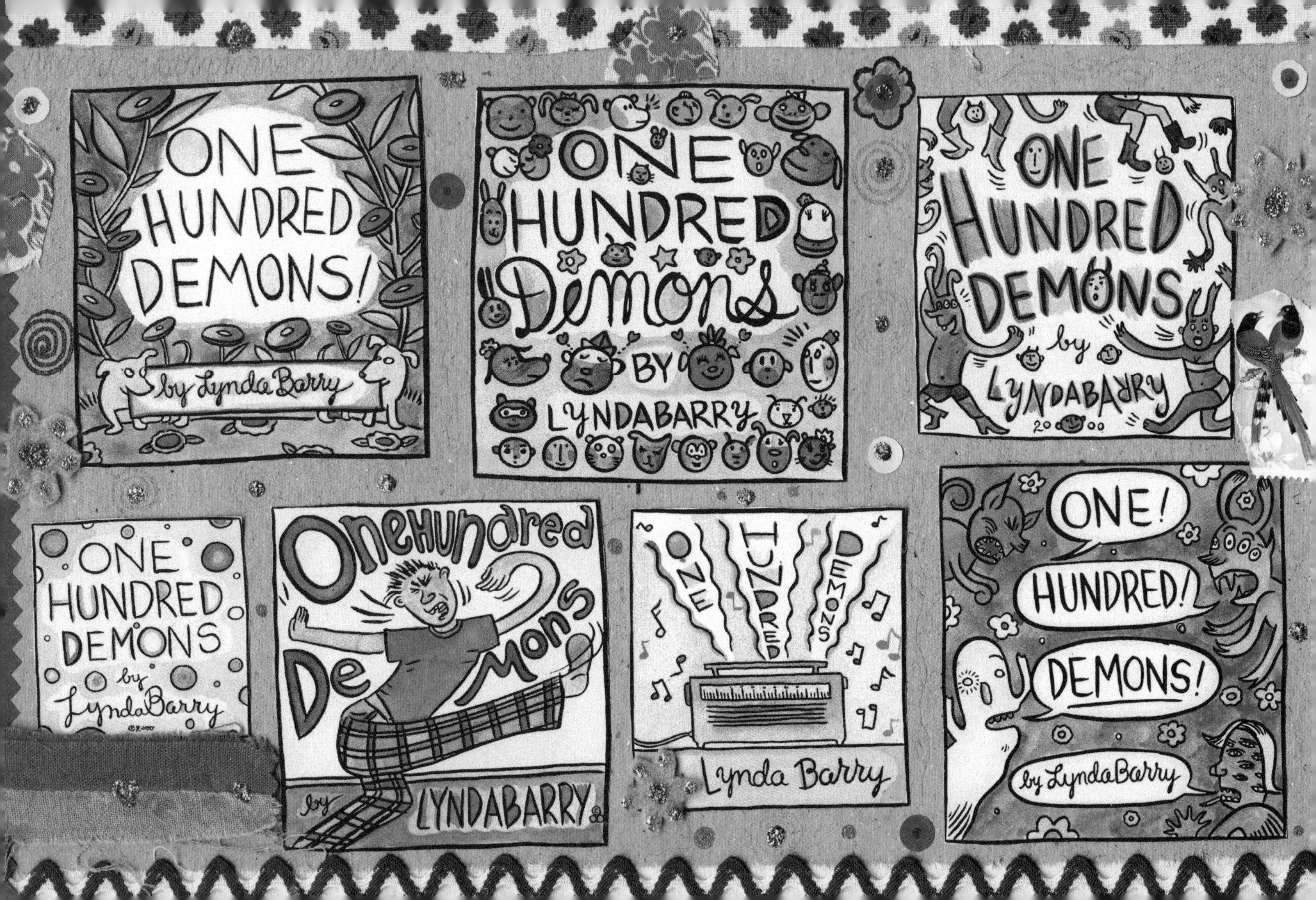

ONE HUNDRED DEMONS!
by Lynda Barry
ONE HUNDRED Demons
BY LYNDABARRY
ONE HUNDRED DEMONS
by LYNDABARRY
2000
ONE HUNDRED DEMONS
by LyndaBarry
©2000
OneHundred DeMons
by LYNDABARRY
ONE HUNDRED DEMONS
Lynda Barry
ONE!
HUNDRED!
DEMONS!
by LyndaBarry

For Jennifer Sweeney

a 4 ONE

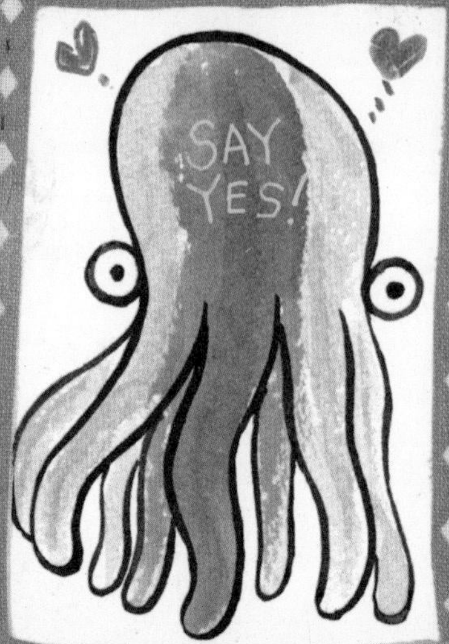
SAY YES!

SpecialThanks
L.C.KevinKawula,LizDarhansoff,JenniferSweeney&Staff@Salon.com,GaryLuke&Staff@SasquatchBooks,YingXingWang@Acornplanet.com,TomThumbHobbiesandCrafts,Evanston,Ill,andespeciallytoAmieZGleedandTomGreensfelderwhoworkedsohardonthisdangbook.P.S.MattGisstillFunkLordofUSA
Also thank you Daniel at marlysmagazine.com

Please NoTE: THIS IS A WORK OF AUTOBIFICTIONALOGRAPHY

Book Design Team:
Amie Z. Gleed
Lynda Barry
Tom Greensfelder
watercolor help and contributing demon illustration:
Kevin Kawula

these comic strips first appeared on Salon.com!

Sasquatch Books
615 Second Ave
Seattle, WA 98104
(206) 467-4300
www.SasquatchBooks.com
books@SasquatchBooks.com

printed in HONG KONG
Published by Sasquatch Books
Distributed by Publishers Group West

Library of Congress Cataloging in Publication Data
Barry, Lynda, 1956–
One hundred demons / Lynda Barry.
p. cm.
ISBN 1-57061-337-0
I. Title: 100 demons. II. Title.
PN6727.B36 O54 2002
741.5'973—dc21 2002021657

06 05 04 03 02 7 6 5 4 3 2

Table of Contents

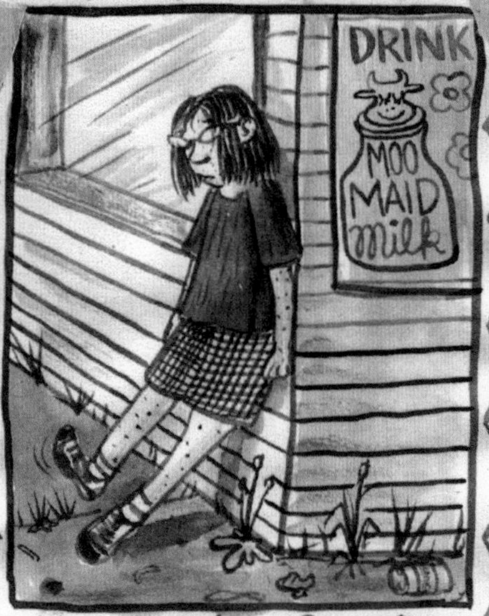
DRINK
MOO MAID milk

autobifictionalography

are these stories

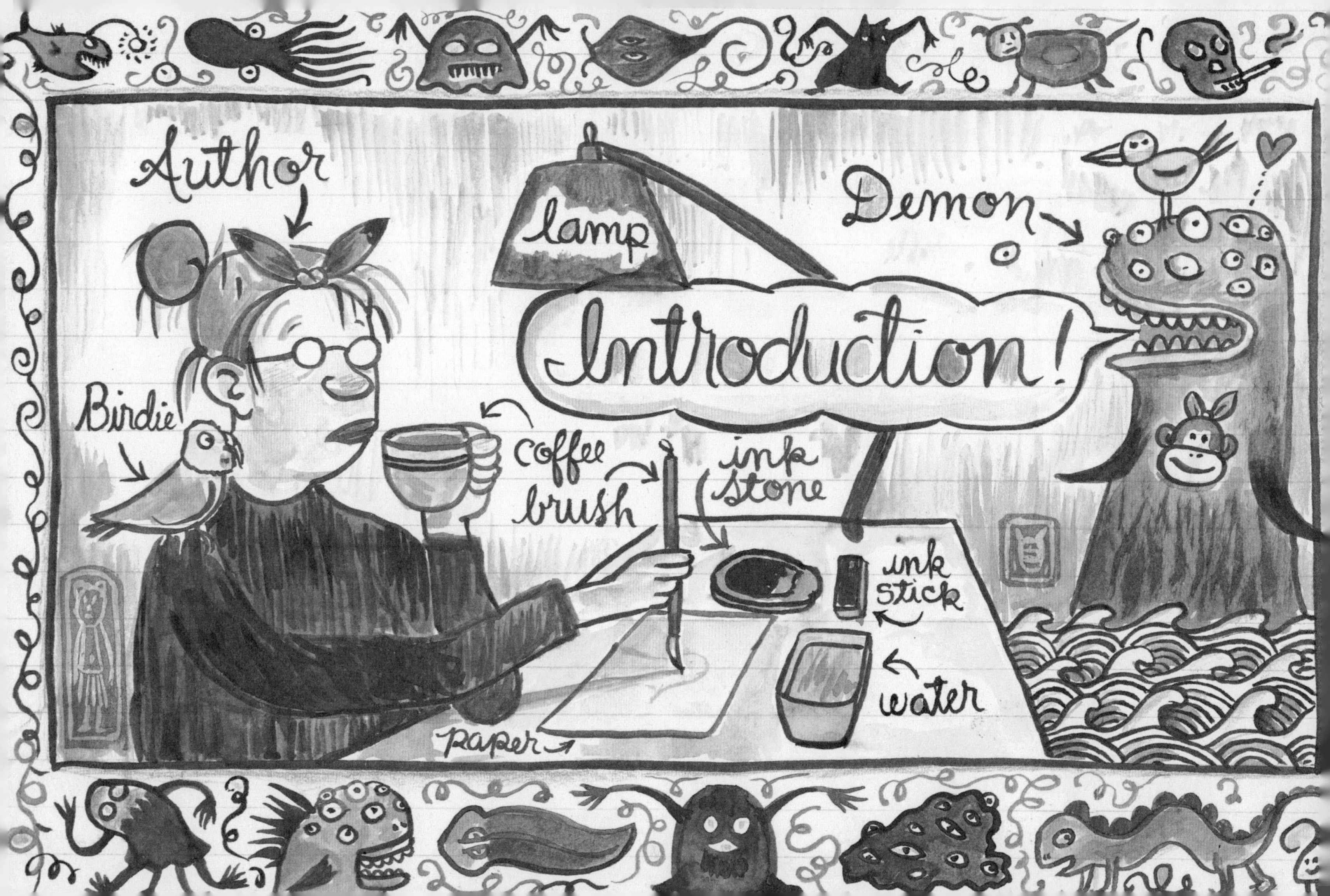
Author
lamp
Demon
Introduction!
Birdie
coffee
ink
stone
brush
ink
stick
water
paper

Is it autobiography if parts of it are not true?
Is it fiction if parts of it are?

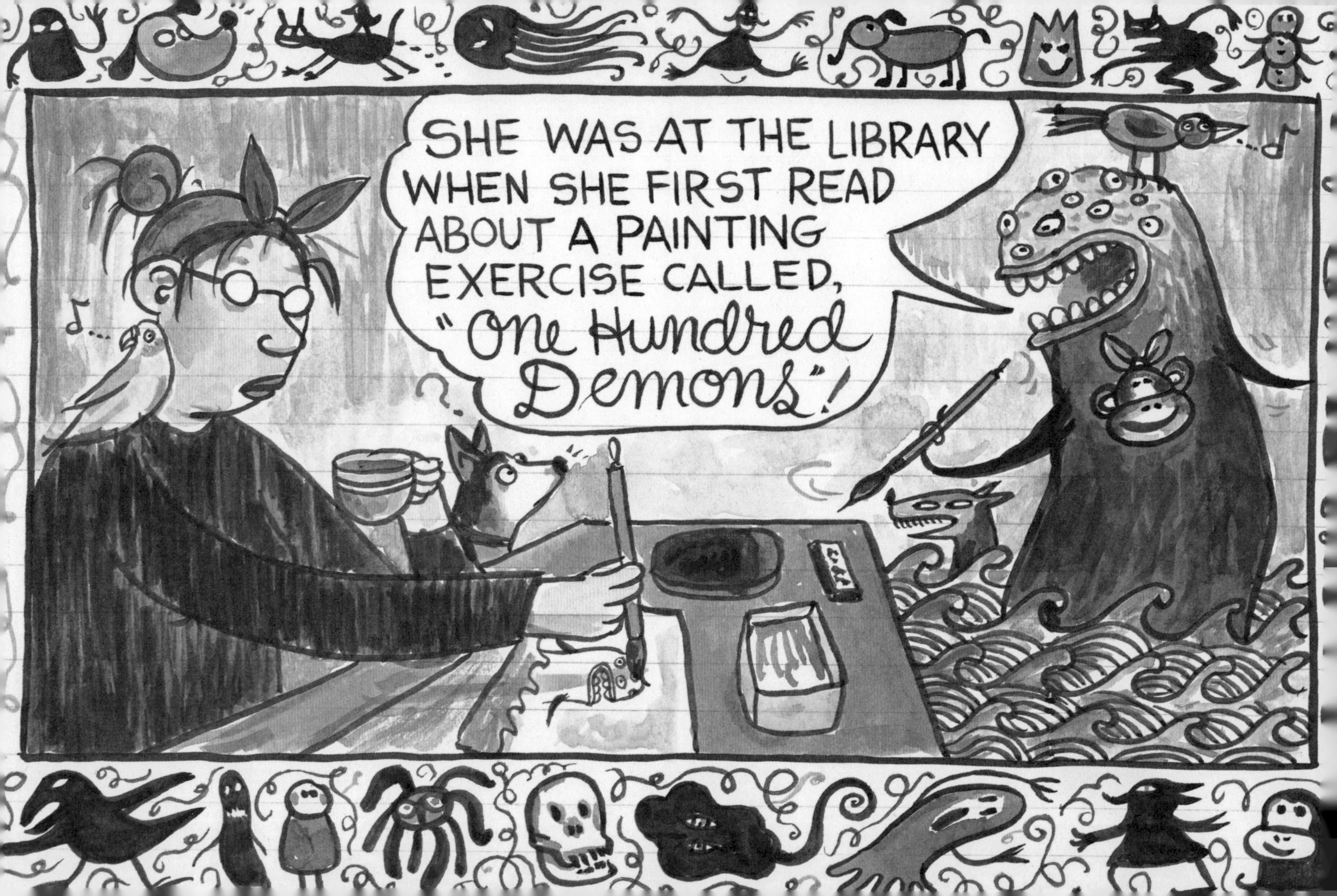
SHE WAS AT THE LIBRARY WHEN SHE FIRST READ ABOUT A PAINTING EXERCISE CALLED, "One Hundred Demons"!

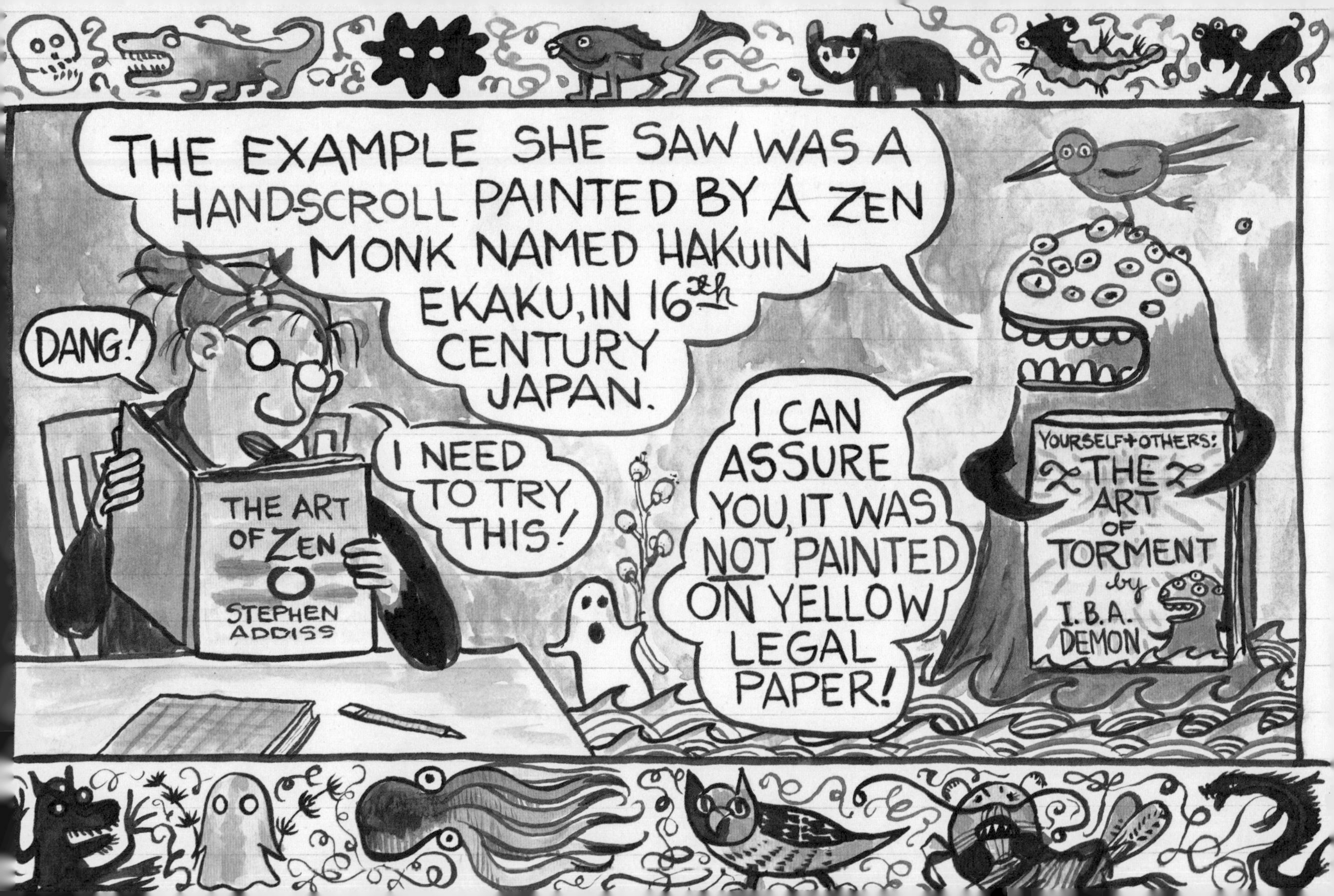

THE EXAMPLE SHE SAW WAS A HAND-SCROLL PAINTED BY A ZEN MONK NAMED HAKUIN EKAKU, IN 16th CENTURY JAPAN.
DANG!
I NEED TO TRY THIS!
I CAN ASSURE YOU, IT WAS NOT PAINTED ON YELLOW LEGAL PAPER!
THE ART OF ZEN
STEPHEN ADDISS
YOURSELF + OTHERS: THE ART OF TORMENT by I.B.A. DEMON

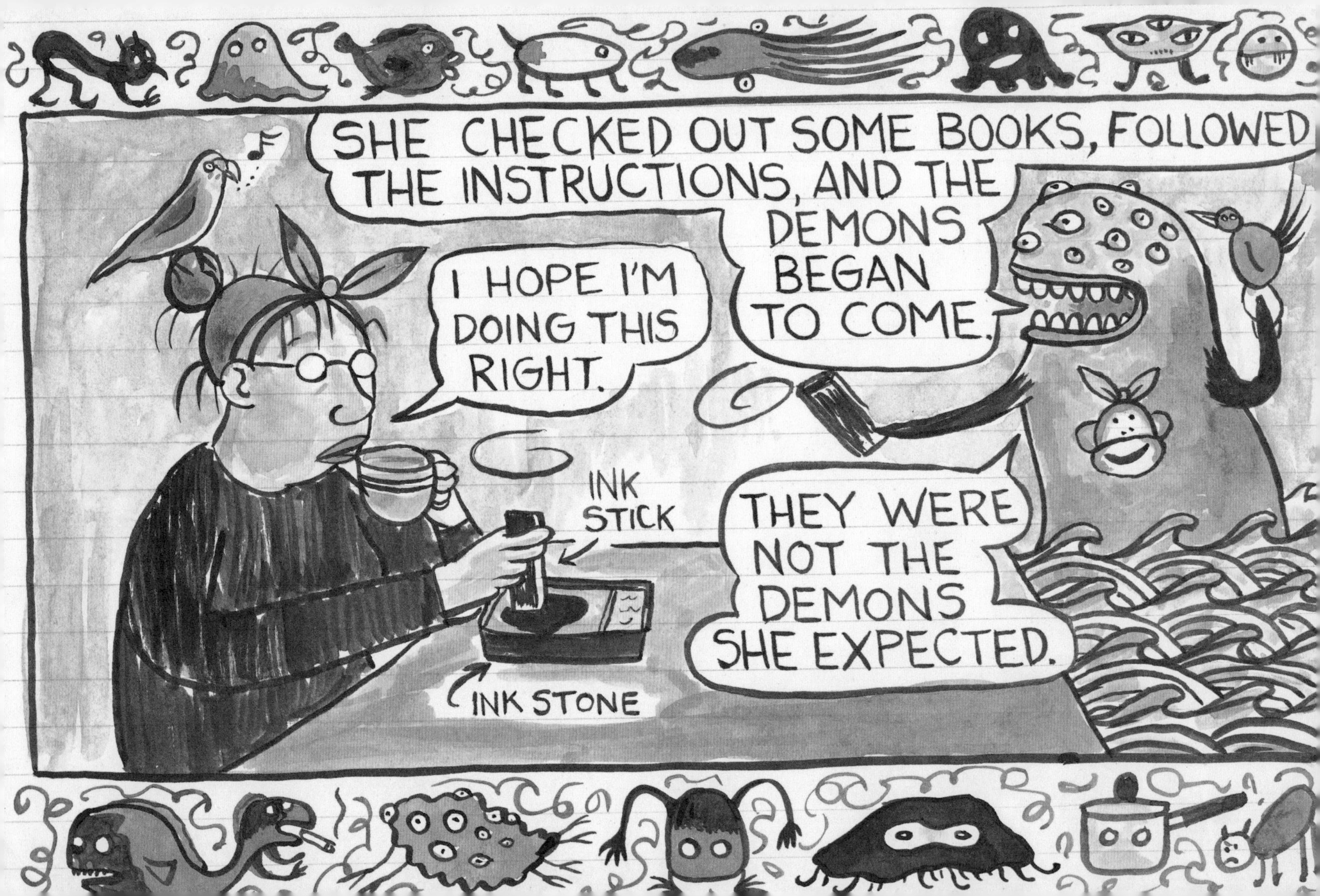
SHE CHECKED OUT SOME BOOKS, FOLLOWED THE INSTRUCTIONS, AND THE DEMONS DEMONS BEGAN TO COME.
I HOPE I'M DOING THIS RIGHT.
INK STICK
INK STONE
THEY WERE NOT THE DEMONS SHE EXPECTED.

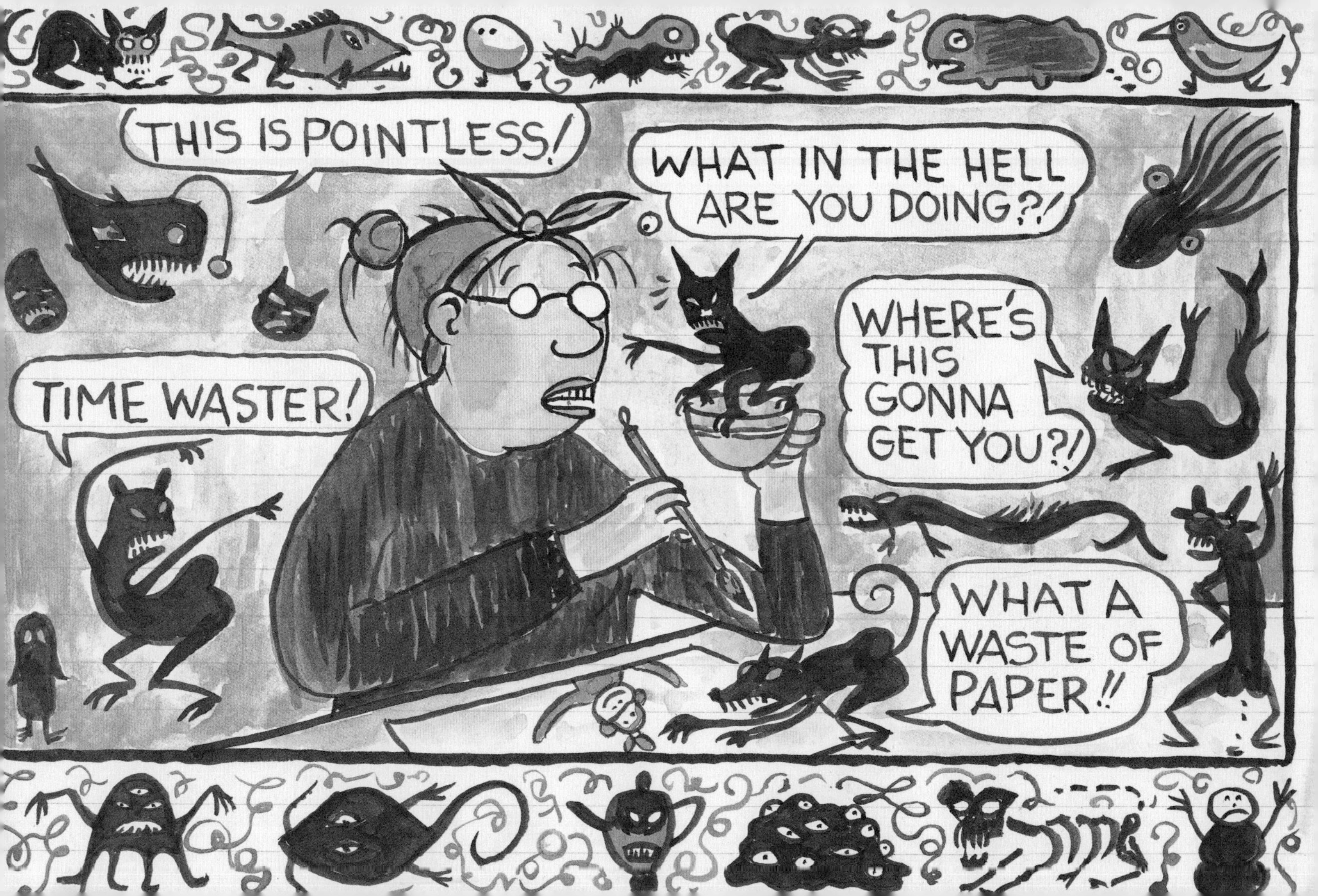
THIS IS POINTLESS!
WHAT IN THE HELL ARE YOU DOING?!
TIME WASTER!
WHERE'S THIS GONNA GET YOU?!
WHAT A WASTE OF PAPER!!

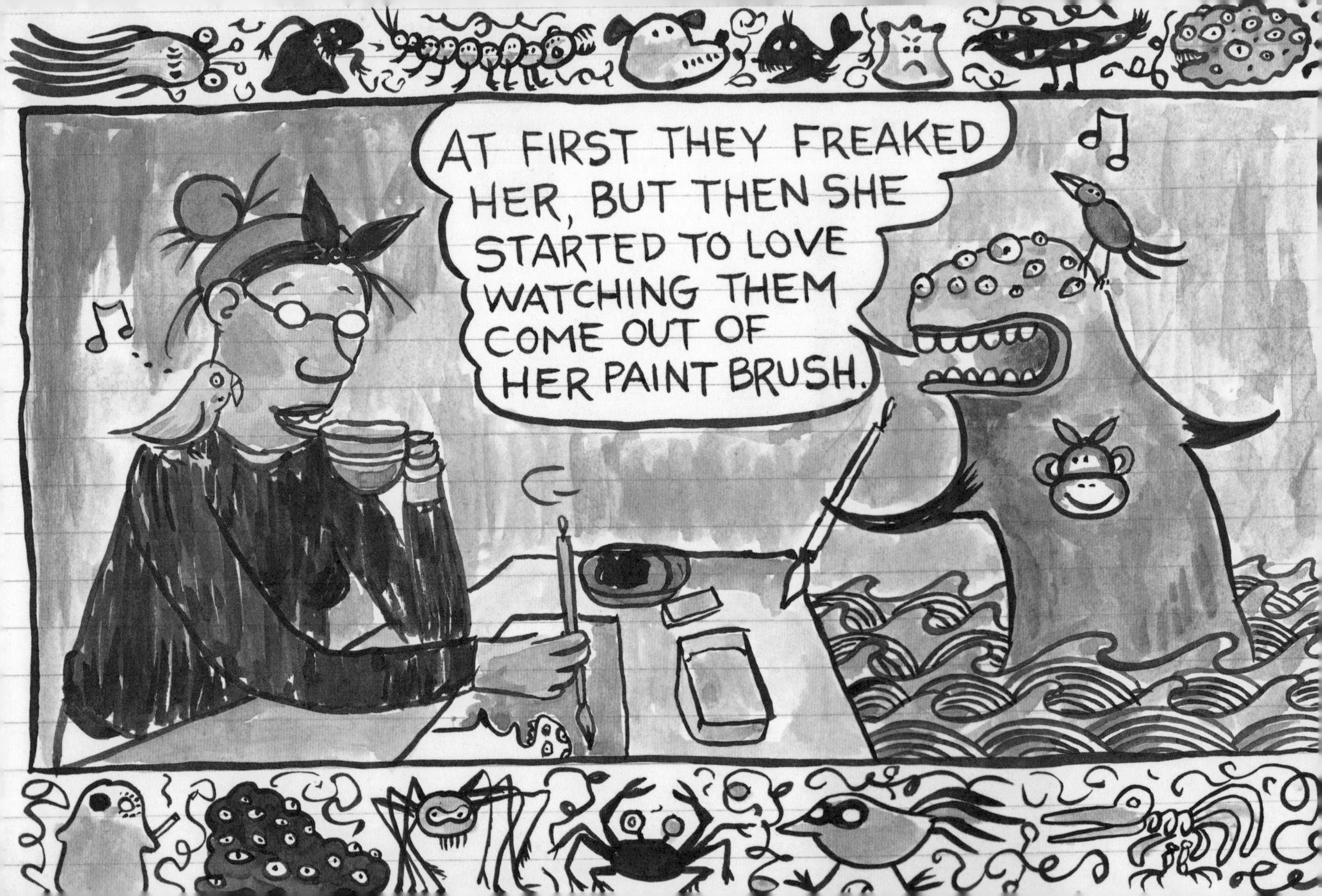
AT FIRST THEY FREAKED HER, BUT THEN SHE STARTED TO LOVE WATCHING THEM COME OUT OF HER PAINT BRUSH.

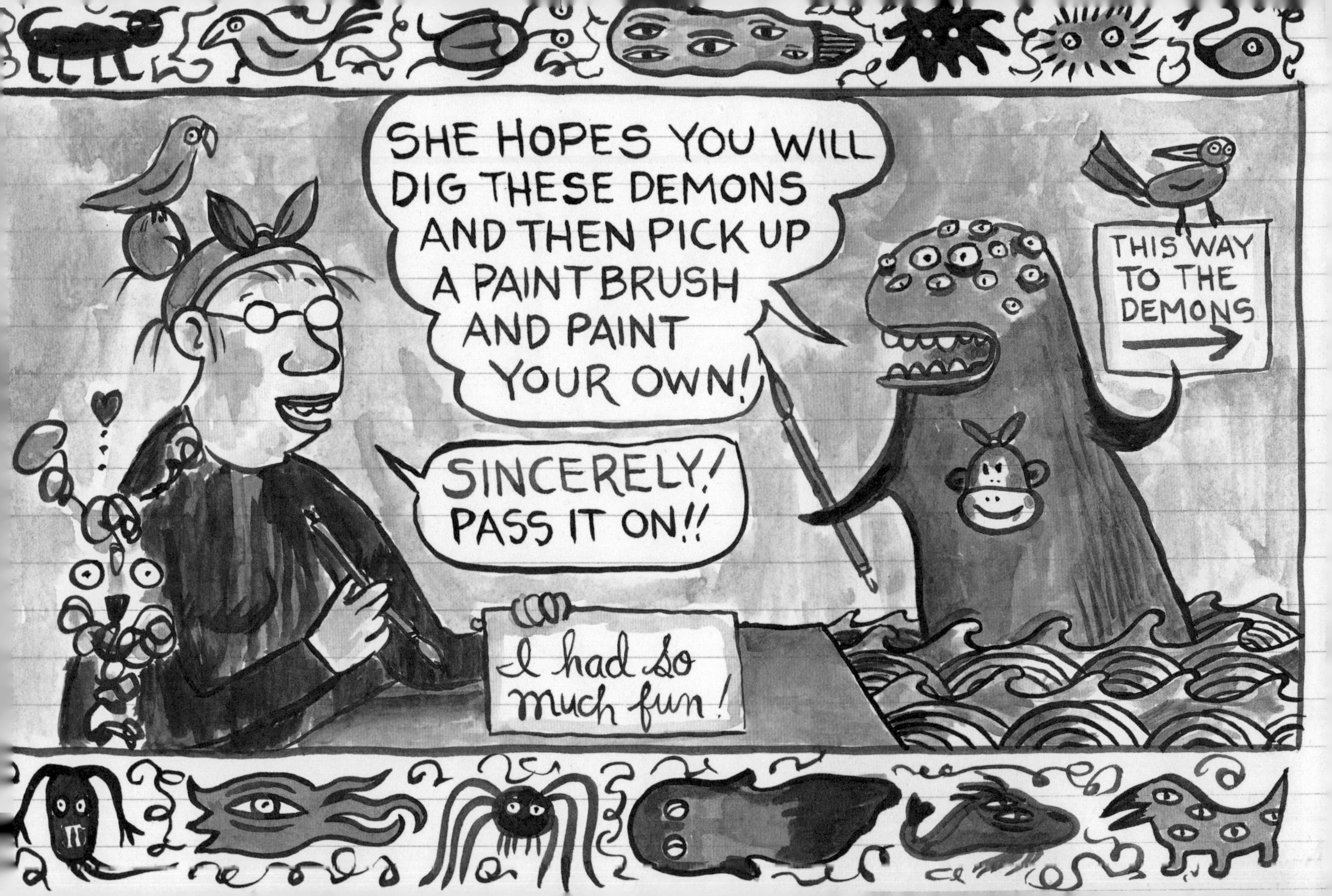
SHE HOPES YOU WILL DIG THESE DEMONS AND THEN PICK UP A PAINT BRUSH AND PAINT YOUR OWN!
SINCERELY! PASS IT ON!!
THIS WAY TO THE DEMONS
I had so much fun!

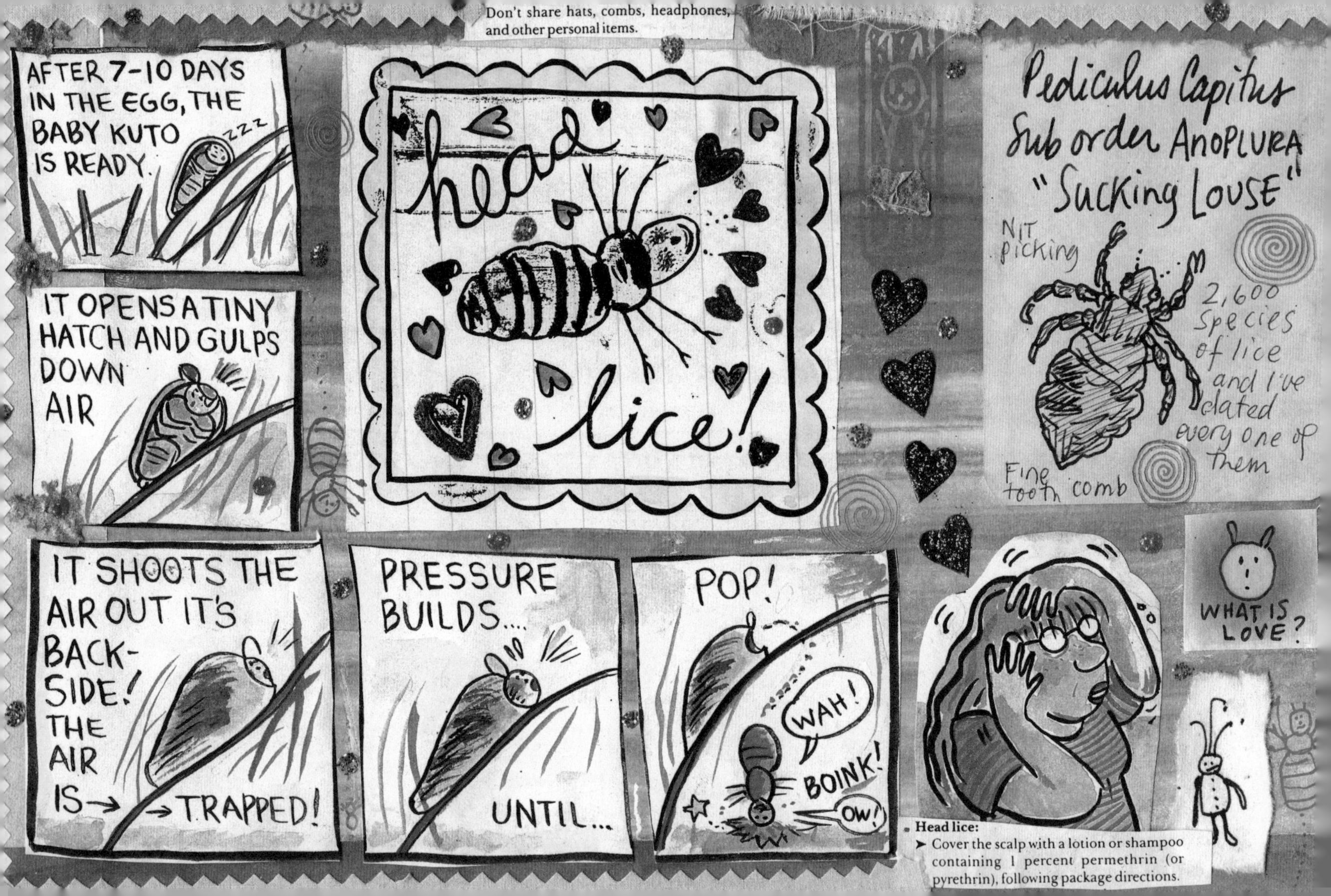
Don't share hats, combs, headphones, and other personal items.
AFTER 7-10 DAYS IN THE EGG, THE BABY KUTO IS READY.
ZZZ
IT OPENS A TINY HATCH AND GULPS DOWN AIR
IT SHOOTS THE AIR OUT IT'S BACK-SIDE! THE AIR IS→ →TRAPPED!
PRESSURE BUILDS....
UNTIL...
POP!
WAH!
BOINK!
OW!
head lice!
Pediculus Capitus
Sub order ANOPLURA
"Sucking LOUSE"
NIT picking
2,600 species of lice and I've dated every one of them
Fine tooth comb
WHAT IS LOVE?
Head lice:
➤ Cover the scalp with a lotion or shampoo containing 1 percent permethrin (or pyrethrin), following package directions.

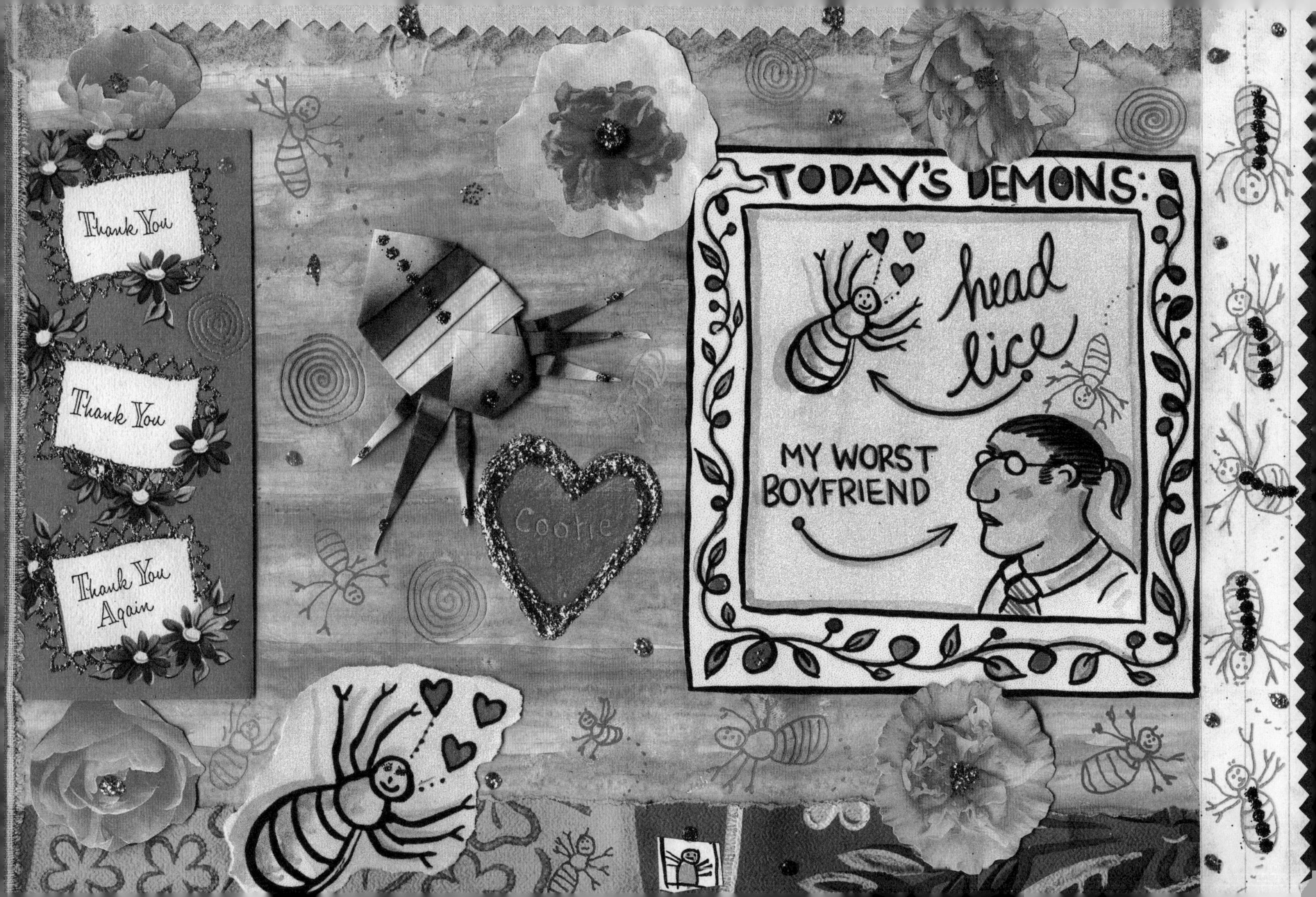
Thank You
Thank You
Thank You Again
Cootie
TODAY'S DEMONS:
head lice
MY WORST BOYFRIEND

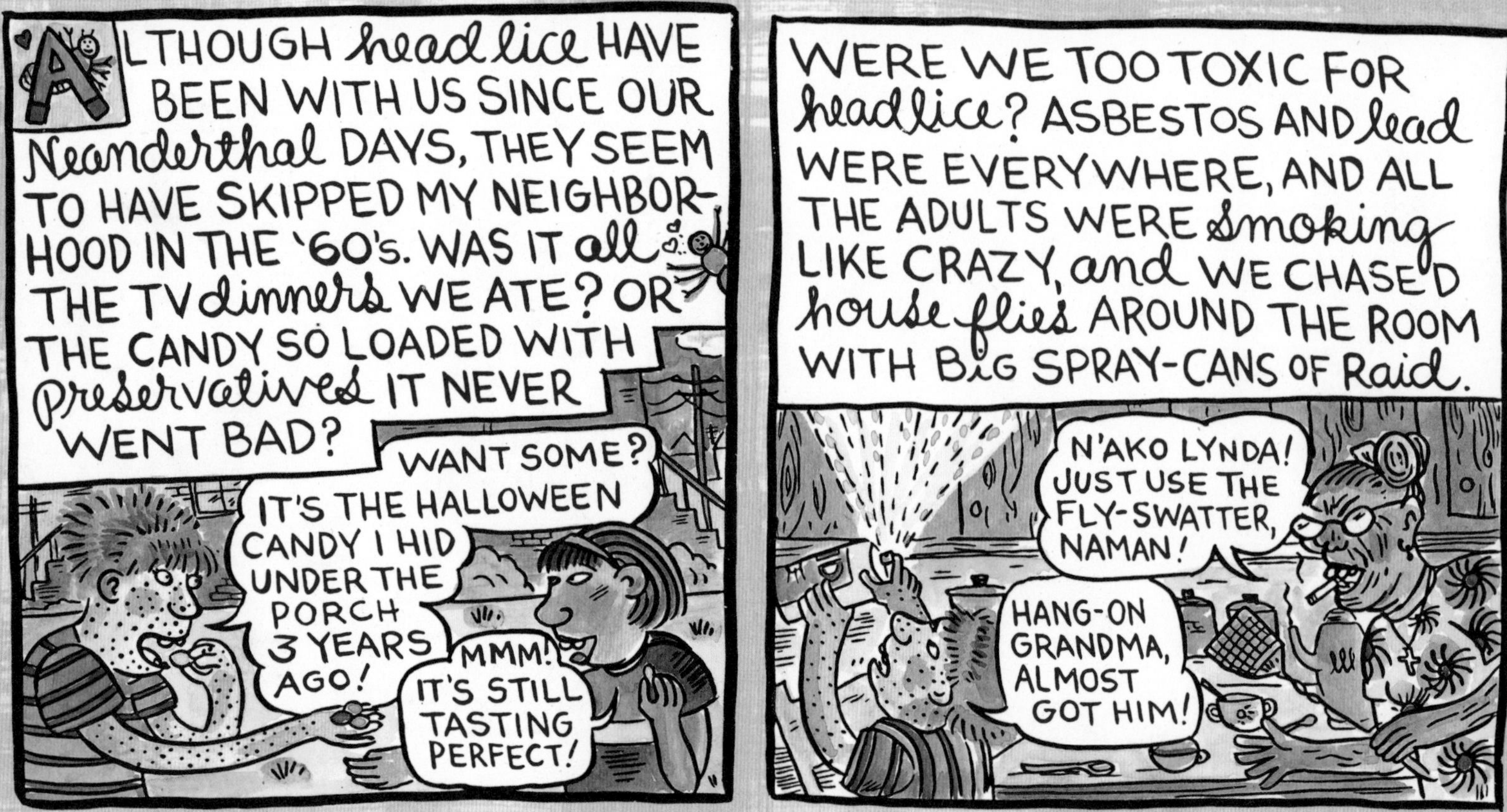
ALTHOUGH head lice HAVE BEEN WITH US SINCE OUR Neanderthal DAYS, THEY SEEM TO HAVE SKIPPED MY NEIGHBORHOOD IN THE '60's. WAS IT all THE TV dinners WE ATE? OR THE CANDY SO LOADED WITH preservatives IT NEVER WENT BAD?
WANT SOME?
IT'S THE HALLOWEEN CANDY I HID UNDER THE PORCH 3 YEARS AGO!
MMM! IT'S STILL TASTING PERFECT!
WERE WE TOO TOXIC FOR head lice? ASBESTOS AND lead WERE EVERYWHERE, AND ALL THE ADULTS WERE smoking LIKE CRAZY, and WE CHASED house flies AROUND THE ROOM WITH BIG SPRAY-CANS OF Raid.
N'AKO LYNDA! JUST USE THE FLY-SWATTER, NAMAN!
HANG-ON GRANDMA, ALMOST GOT HIM!

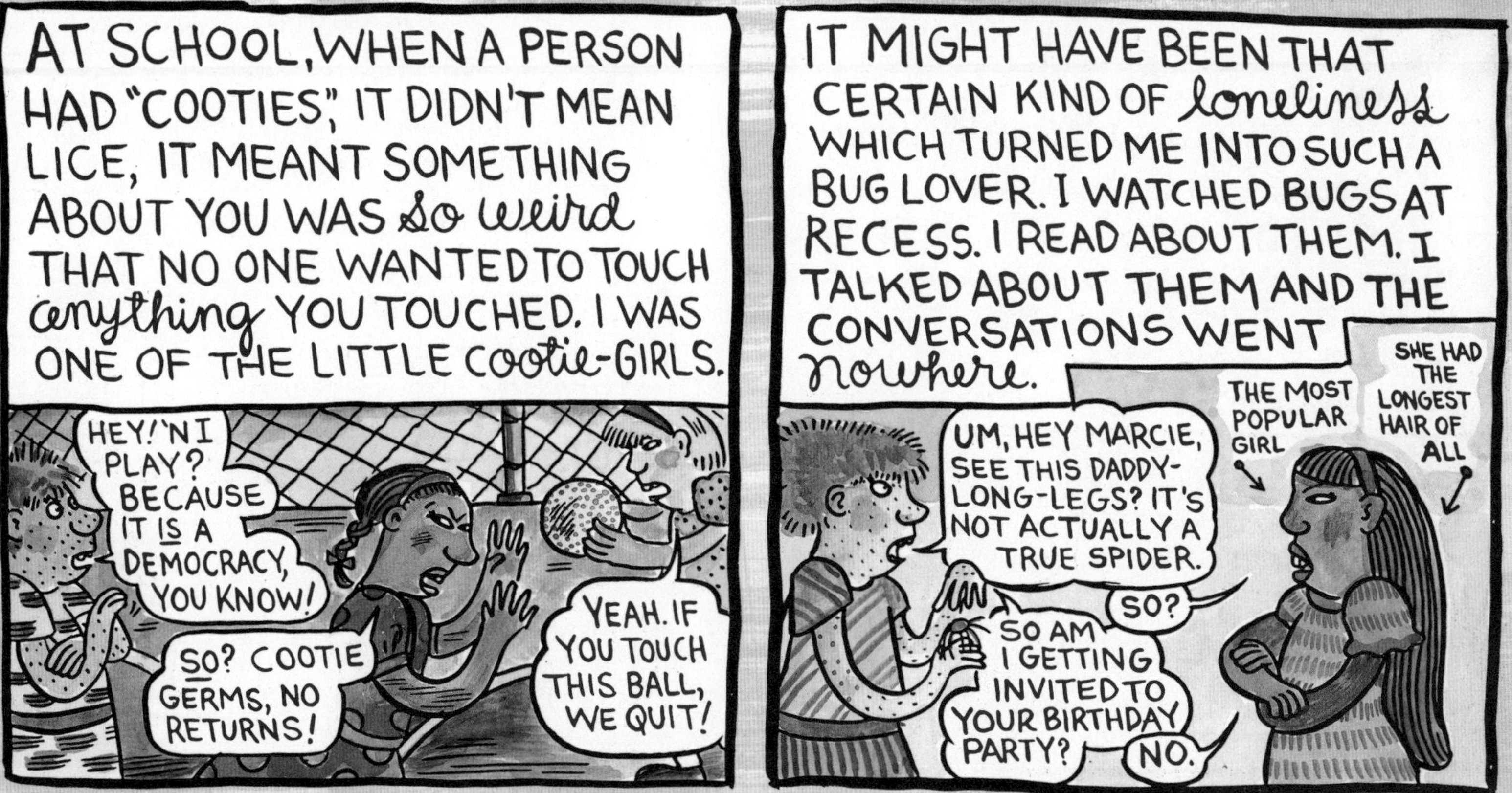
AT SCHOOL, WHEN A PERSON HAD "COOTIES," IT DIDN'T MEAN LICE, IT MEANT SOMETHING ABOUT YOU WAS *so weird* THAT NO ONE WANTED TO TOUCH *anything* YOU TOUCHED. I WAS ONE OF THE LITTLE *cootie*-GIRLS.
HEY! 'N I PLAY? BECAUSE IT IS A DEMOCRACY, YOU KNOW!
SO? COOTIE GERMS, NO RETURNS!
YEAH. IF YOU TOUCH THIS BALL, WE QUIT!
IT MIGHT HAVE BEEN THAT CERTAIN KIND OF *loneliness* WHICH TURNED ME INTO SUCH A BUG LOVER. I WATCHED BUGS AT RECESS. I READ ABOUT THEM. I TALKED ABOUT THEM AND THE CONVERSATIONS WENT *nowhere*.
THE MOST POPULAR GIRL
SHE HAD THE LONGEST HAIR OF ALL
UM, HEY MARCIE, SEE THIS DADDY-LONG-LEGS? IT'S NOT ACTUALLY A TRUE SPIDER.
SO?
SO AM I GETTING INVITED TO YOUR BIRTHDAY PARTY?
NO.

IN THE SUMMER OF THE 5TH GRADE WE WENT TO VISIT RELATIVES IN THE PHILIPPINES. I *was* SURPRISED TO *make* FRIENDS SO EASILY WITH TWO OF THE KIDS THERE WHO WERE QUITE *interested* IN MY RED HAIR. THEY HEARD WHITE PEOPLE HAD WHITE-COLORED LICE AND WANTED TO *see* THEM.

HERE WE CALL THIS INSECT "KUTO." AS MY SKIN IS BROWN, SO MY KUTO ARE BROWNISH. AS YOUR SKIN IS LIKE IVORY SOAP, YOUR KUTO WILL BE THE COLOR SOAPISH.

WHAT IF I DON'T GOT NONE?

N'AKO! EVEN THE HOLY VIRGIN HAD KUTO!

ALTHOUGH IT SOUNDS FAR-FETCHED *to think* DIFFERENT COLORS OF PEOPLE COULD HAVE DIFFERENT *colors* OF *head lice*, IT TURNS OUT TO *be* TRUE. IN CERTAIN EVOLUTIONARY *ways*, LICE ARE GENIUSES. IT'S ALSO TRUE THAT THEY WERE PRESENT AT *the birth* OF EVERY RELIGION, THOUGH WHEN I *mentioned* THE THING ABOUT THE HOLY VIRGIN *to* MY MOTHER, SHE SLAPPED ME.

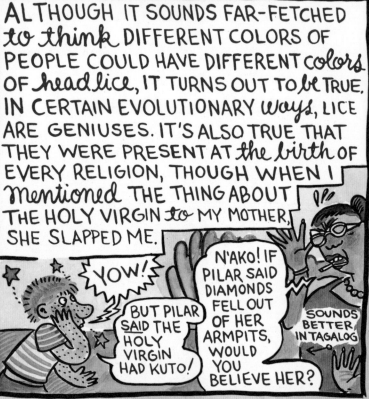

YOW!

BUT PILAR SAID THE HOLY VIRGIN HAD KUTO!

N'AKO! IF PILAR SAID DIAMONDS FELL OUT OF HER ARMPITS, WOULD YOU BELIEVE HER?

SOUNDS BETTER IN TAGALOG

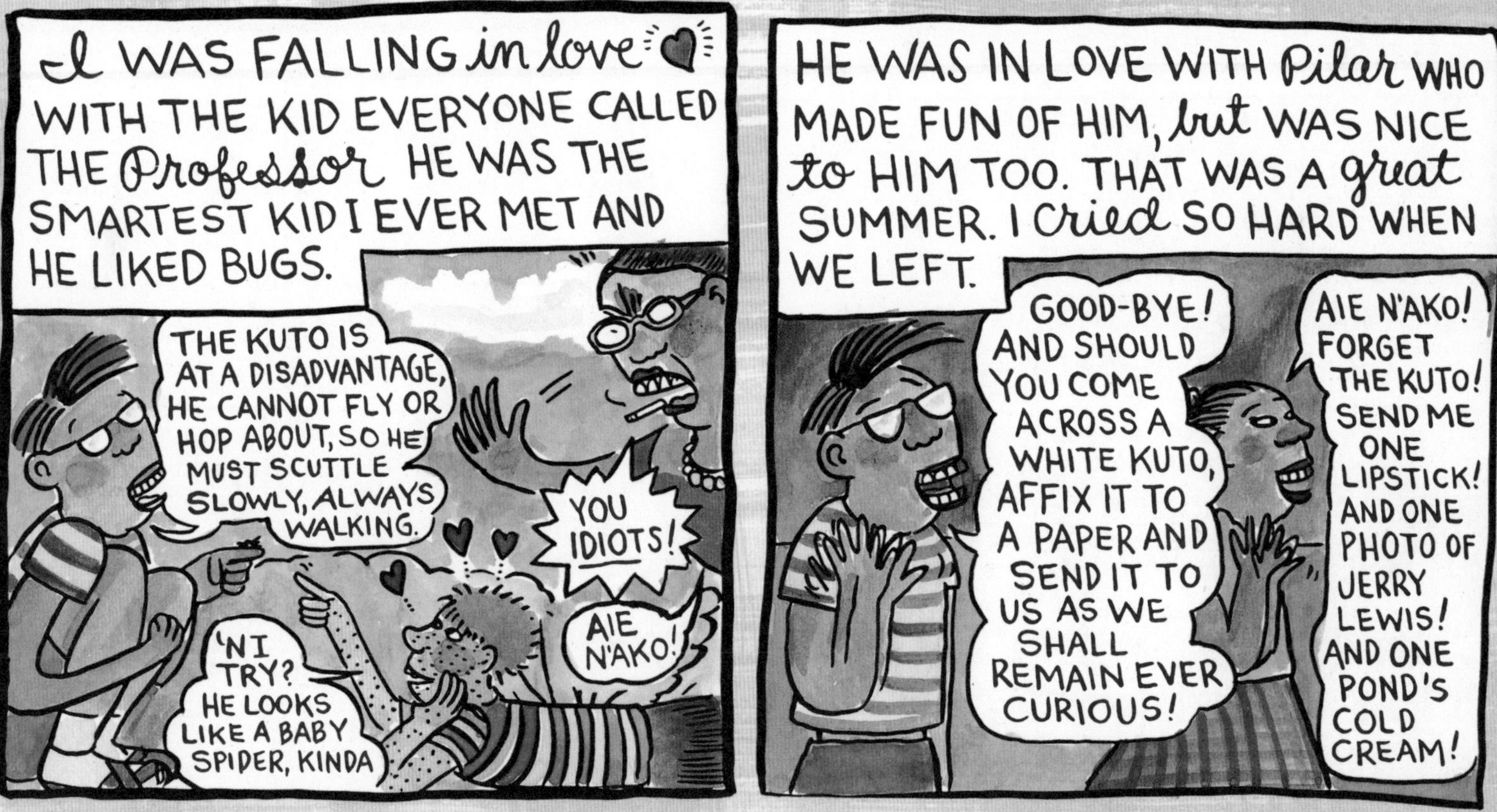
I WAS FALLING in love WITH THE KID EVERYONE CALLED THE Professor HE WAS THE SMARTEST KID I EVER MET AND HE LIKED BUGS.
THE KUTO IS AT A DISADVANTAGE, HE CANNOT FLY OR HOP ABOUT, SO HE MUST SCUTTLE SLOWLY, ALWAYS WALKING.
'NI TRY? HE LOOKS LIKE A BABY SPIDER, KINDA
YOU IDIOTS!
AIE N'AKO!
HE WAS IN LOVE WITH Pilar WHO MADE FUN OF HIM, but WAS NICE to HIM TOO. THAT WAS A great SUMMER. I Cried SO HARD WHEN WE LEFT.
GOOD-BYE! AND SHOULD YOU COME ACROSS A WHITE KUTO, AFFIX IT TO A PAPER AND SEND IT TO US AS WE SHALL REMAIN EVER CURIOUS!
AIE N'AKO! FORGET THE KUTO! SEND ME ONE LIPSTICK! AND ONE PHOTO OF JERRY LEWIS! AND ONE POND'S COLD CREAM!

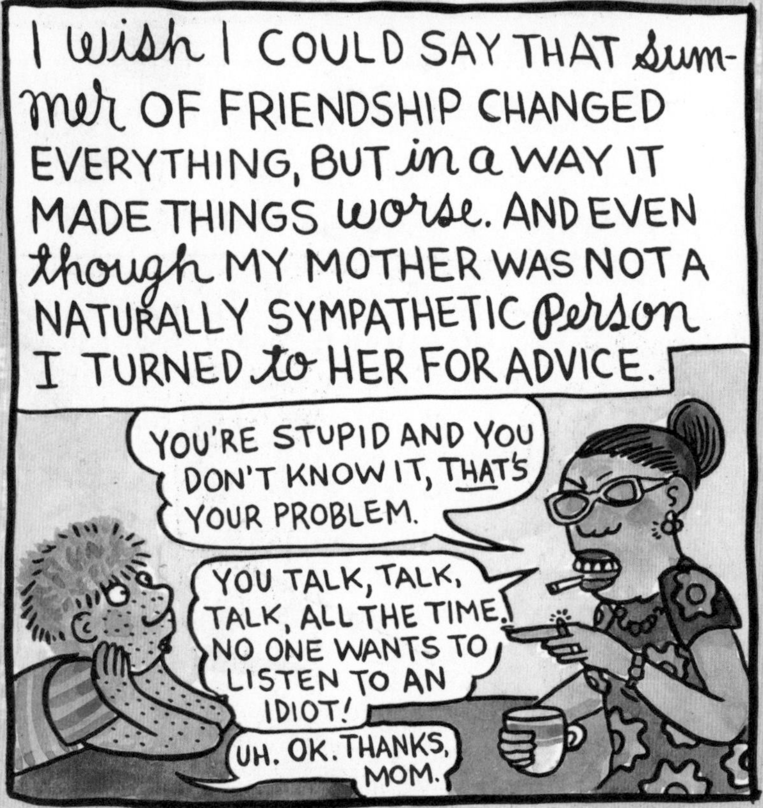
I WISH I COULD SAY THAT SUMMER OF FRIENDSHIP CHANGED EVERYTHING, BUT IN A WAY IT MADE THINGS WORSE. AND EVEN THOUGH MY MOTHER WAS NOT A NATURALLY SYMPATHETIC PERSON I TURNED TO HER FOR ADVICE.
YOU'RE STUPID AND YOU DON'T KNOW IT, THAT'S YOUR PROBLEM.
YOU TALK, TALK, TALK, ALL THE TIME. NO ONE WANTS TO LISTEN TO AN IDIOT!
UH. OK. THANKS, MOM.
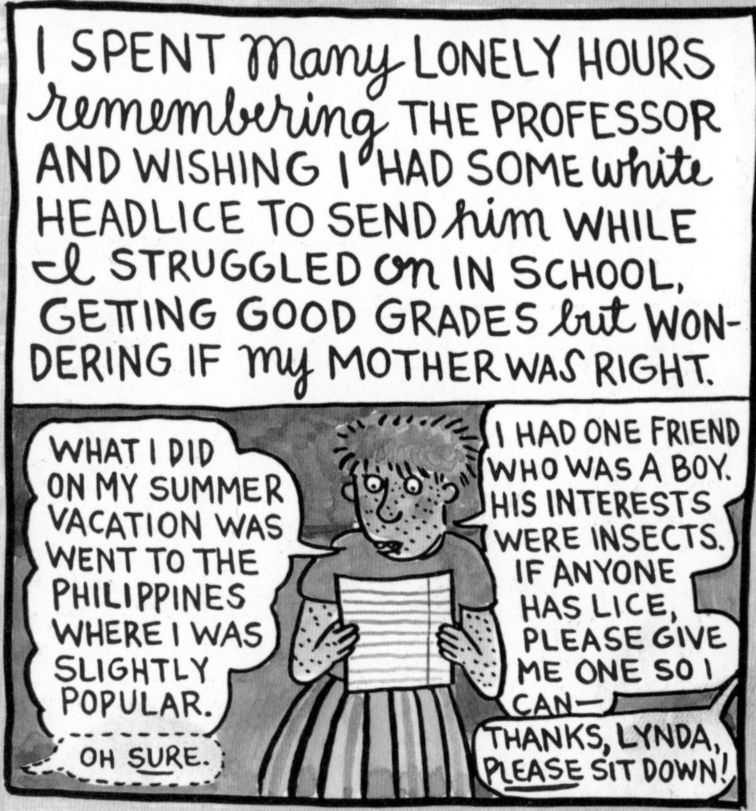
I SPENT MANY LONELY HOURS REMEMBERING THE PROFESSOR AND WISHING I HAD SOME WHITE HEADLICE TO SEND HIM WHILE I STRUGGLED ON IN SCHOOL, GETTING GOOD GRADES BUT WONDERING IF MY MOTHER WAS RIGHT.
WHAT I DID ON MY SUMMER VACATION WAS WENT TO THE PHILIPPINES WHERE I WAS SLIGHTLY POPULAR.
I HAD ONE FRIEND WHO WAS A BOY. HIS INTERESTS WERE INSECTS. IF ANYONE HAS LICE, PLEASE GIVE ME ONE SO I CAN—
OH SURE.
THANKS, LYNDA, PLEASE SIT DOWN!

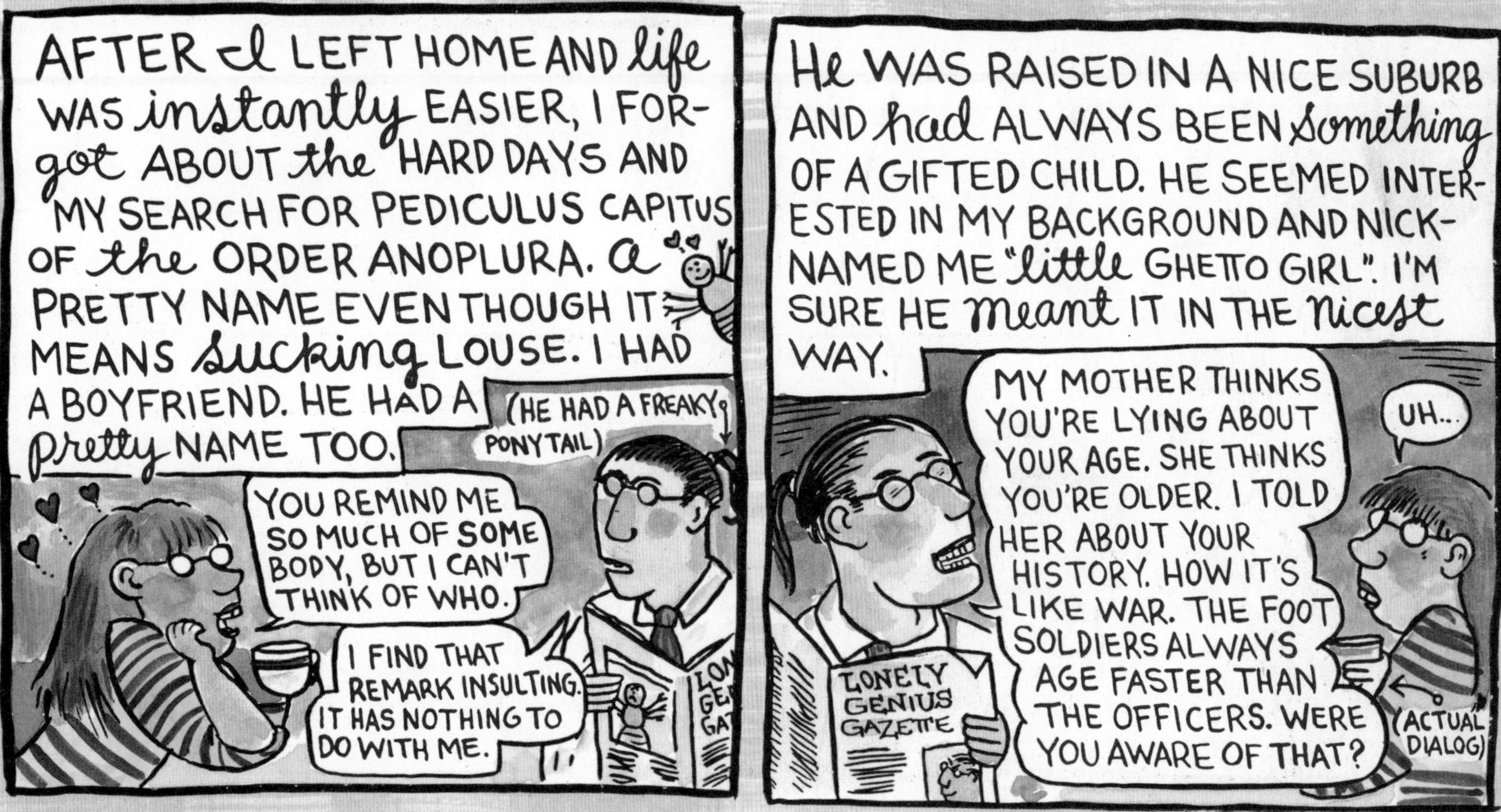
AFTER I LEFT HOME AND life WAS instantly EASIER, I FORgot ABOUT the HARD DAYS AND MY SEARCH FOR PEDICULUS CAPITUS OF the ORDER ANOPLURA. a PRETTY NAME EVEN THOUGH IT MEANS sucking LOUSE. I HAD A BOYFRIEND. HE HAD A pretty NAME TOO.
(HE HAD A FREAKY PONYTAIL)
YOU REMIND ME SO MUCH OF SOME BODY, BUT I CAN'T THINK OF WHO.
I FIND THAT REMARK INSULTING. IT HAS NOTHING TO DO WITH ME.
He WAS RAISED IN A NICE SUBURB AND had ALWAYS BEEN Something OF A GIFTED CHILD. HE SEEMED INTERESTED IN MY BACKGROUND AND NICKNAMED ME "little GHETTO GIRL". I'M SURE HE meant IT IN THE nicest WAY.
MY MOTHER THINKS YOU'RE LYING ABOUT YOUR AGE. SHE THINKS YOU'RE OLDER. I TOLD HER ABOUT YOUR HISTORY. HOW IT'S LIKE WAR. THE FOOT SOLDIERS ALWAYS AGE FASTER THAN THE OFFICERS. WERE YOU AWARE OF THAT?
UH...
(ACTUAL DIALOG)
LONELY GENIUS GAZETTE

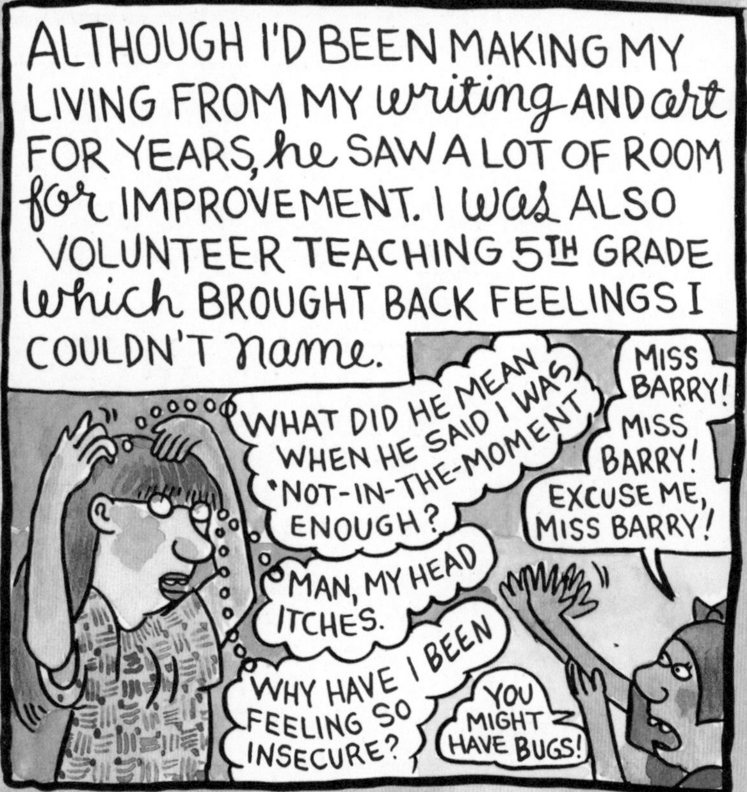
ALTHOUGH I'D BEEN MAKING MY LIVING FROM MY writing AND art FOR YEARS, he SAW A LOT OF ROOM for IMPROVEMENT. I was ALSO VOLUNTEER TEACHING 5TH GRADE which BROUGHT BACK FEELINGS I COULDN'T name.
WHAT DID HE MEAN WHEN HE SAID I WAS 'NOT-IN-THE-MOMENT ENOUGH?
MISS BARRY!
MISS BARRY!
EXCUSE ME, MISS BARRY!
MAN, MY HEAD ITCHES.
WHY HAVE I BEEN FEELING SO INSECURE?
YOU MIGHT HAVE BUGS!

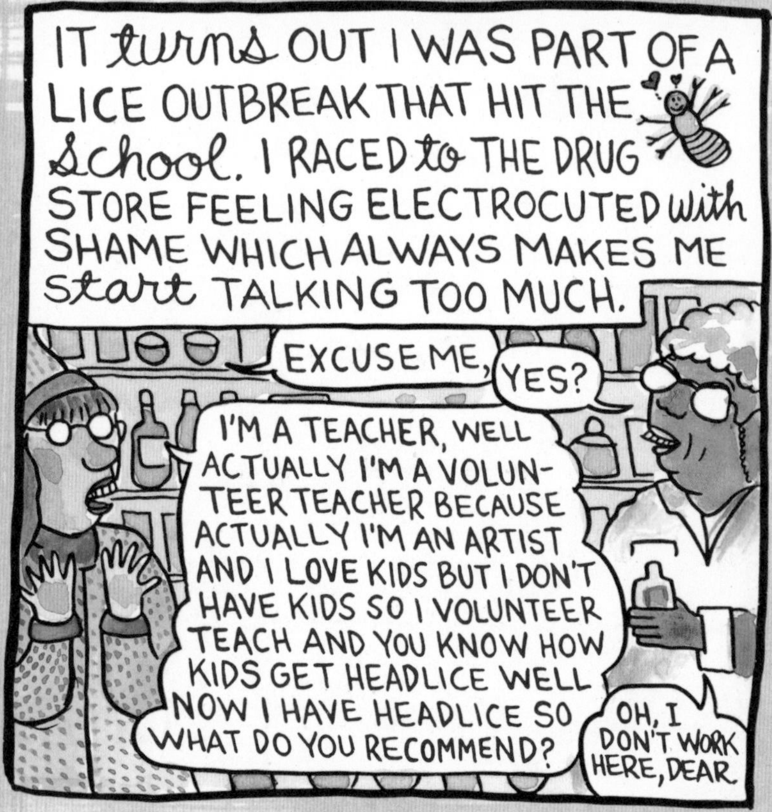
IT turns OUT I WAS PART OF A LICE OUTBREAK THAT HIT THE School. I RACED to THE DRUG STORE FEELING ELECTROCUTED with SHAME WHICH ALWAYS MAKES ME start TALKING TOO MUCH.
EXCUSE ME,
YES?
I'M A TEACHER, WELL ACTUALLY I'M A VOLUNTEER TEACHER BECAUSE ACTUALLY I'M AN ARTIST AND I LOVE KIDS BUT I DON'T HAVE KIDS SO I VOLUNTEER TEACH AND YOU KNOW HOW KIDS GET HEADLICE WELL NOW I HAVE HEADLICE SO WHAT DO YOU RECOMMEND?
OH, I DON'T WORK HERE, DEAR.

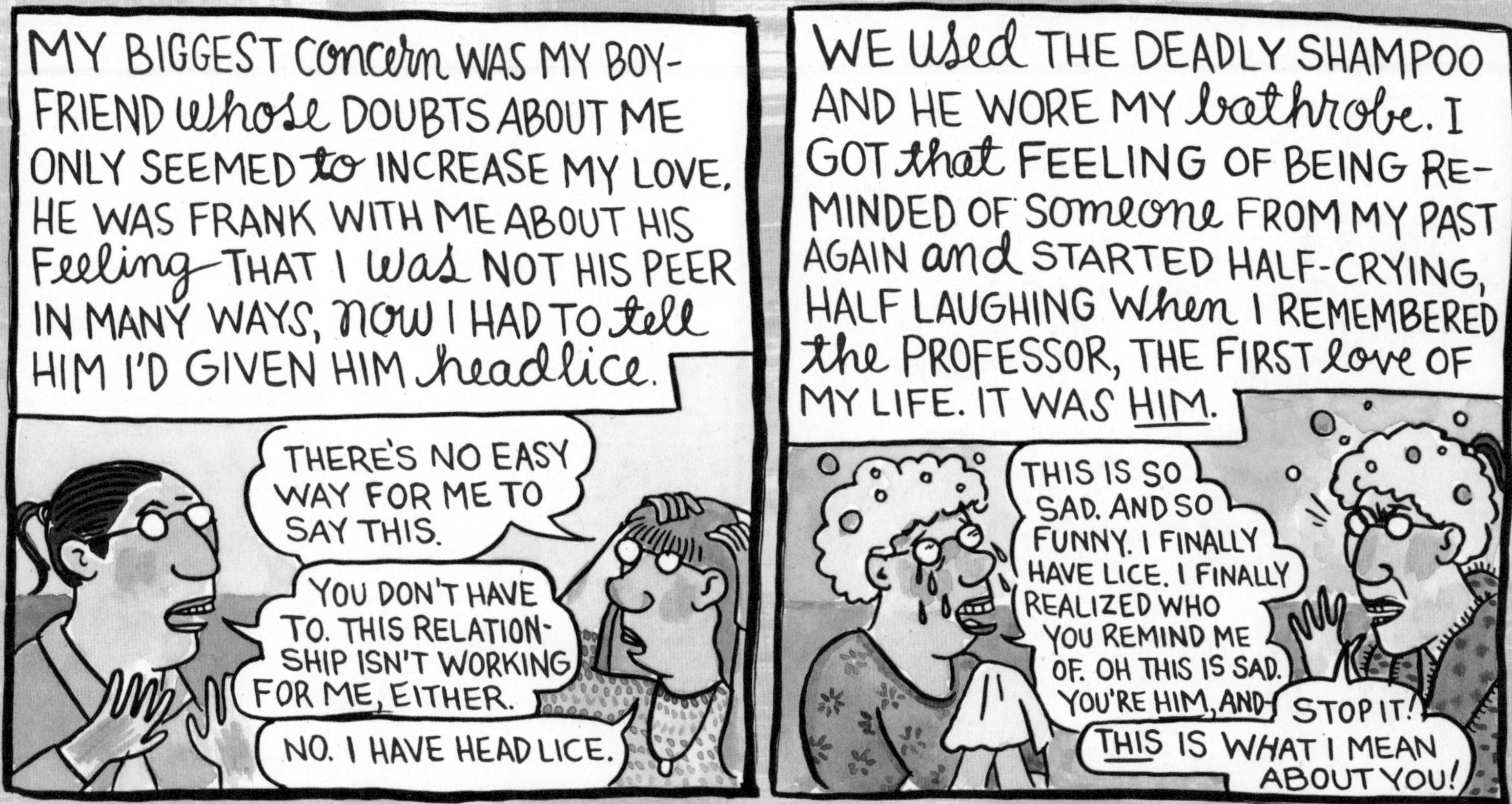
MY BIGGEST concern WAS MY BOY-FRIEND whose DOUBTS ABOUT ME ONLY SEEMED to INCREASE MY LOVE. HE WAS FRANK WITH ME ABOUT HIS Feeling THAT I was NOT HIS PEER IN MANY WAYS, now I HAD TO tell HIM I'D GIVEN HIM headlice.
THERE'S NO EASY WAY FOR ME TO SAY THIS.
YOU DON'T HAVE TO. THIS RELATIONSHIP ISN'T WORKING FOR ME, EITHER.
NO. I HAVE HEAD LICE.
WE used THE DEADLY SHAMPOO AND HE WORE MY bathrobe. I GOT that FEELING OF BEING REMINDED OF someone FROM MY PAST AGAIN and STARTED HALF-CRYING, HALF LAUGHING when I REMEMBERED the PROFESSOR, THE FIRST love OF MY LIFE. IT WAS HIM.
THIS IS SO SAD. AND SO FUNNY. I FINALLY HAVE LICE. I FINALLY REALIZED WHO YOU REMIND ME OF. OH THIS IS SAD. YOU'RE HIM, AND-
STOP IT! THIS IS WHAT I MEAN ABOUT YOU!

Cootie

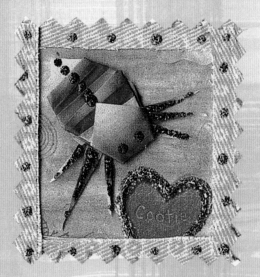

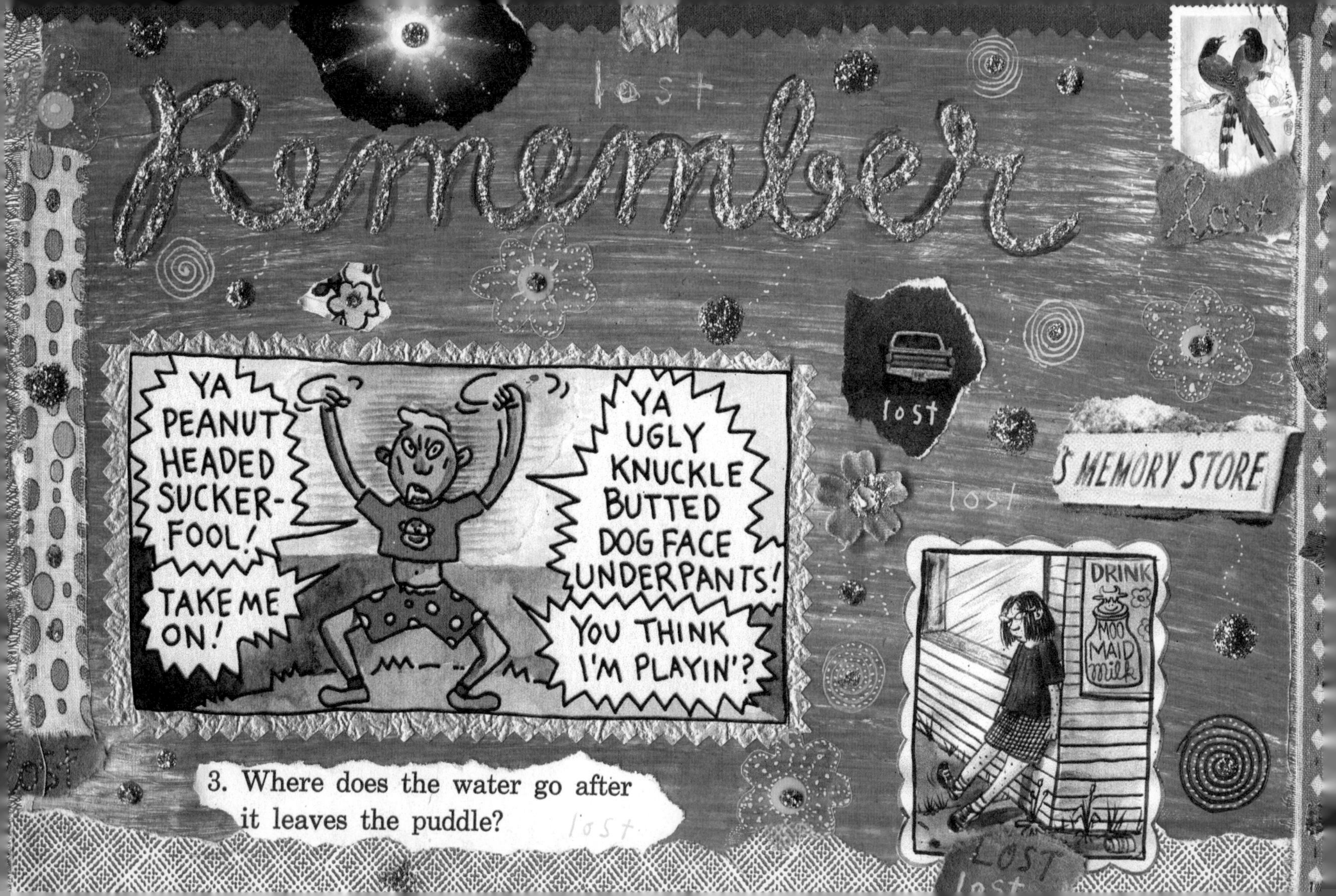
lost
Remember
lost
lost
'S MEMORY STORE
lost
YA PEANUT HEADED SUCKER-FOOL!
TAKE ME ON!
YA UGLY KNUCKLE BUTTED DOG FACE UNDERPANTS!
YOU THINK I'M PLAYIN'?
DRINK
MOO MAID milk
3. Where does the water go after it leaves the puddle?
lost
LOST
lost

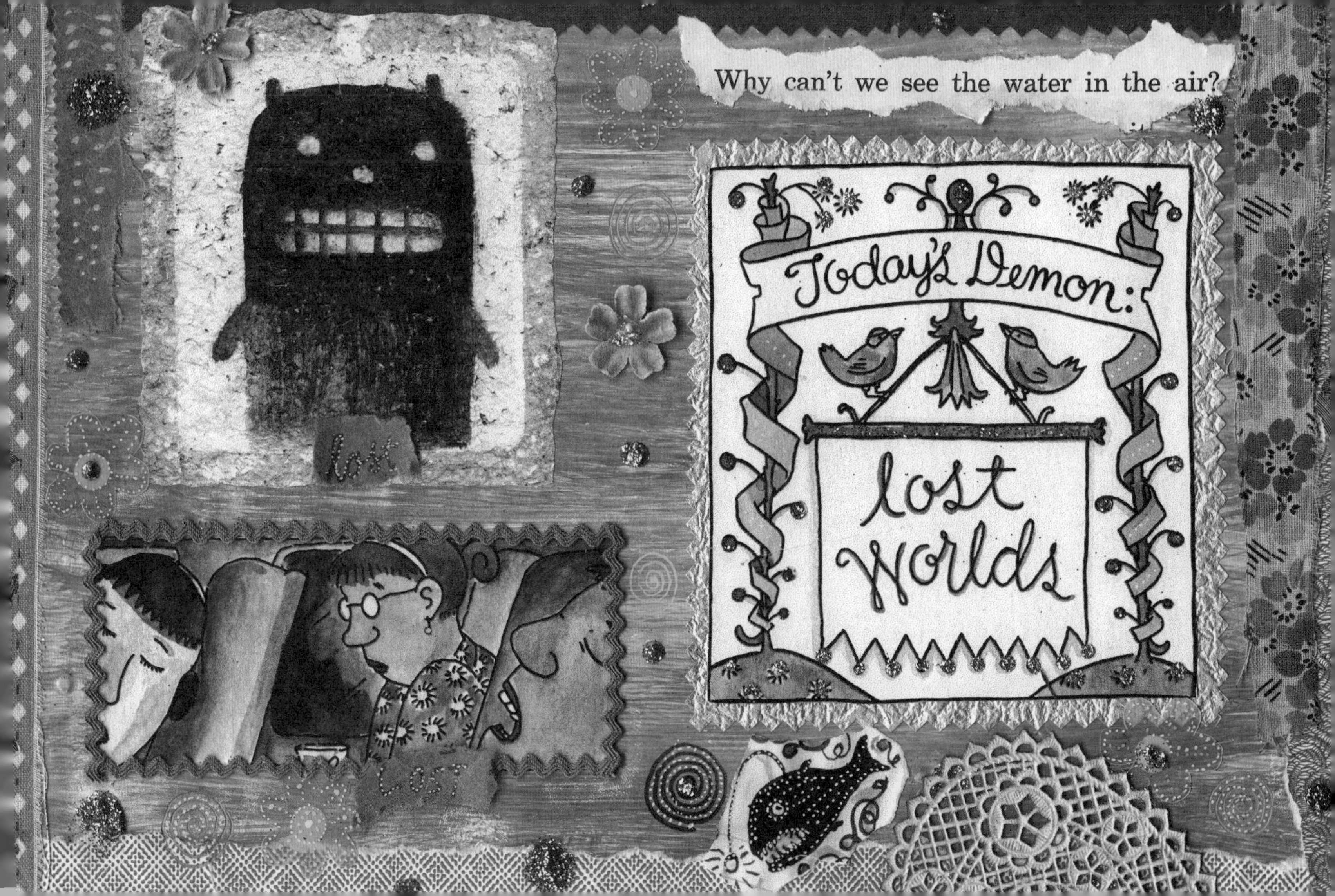
Why can't we see the water in the air?
lost
Today's Demon:
lost worlds
LOST

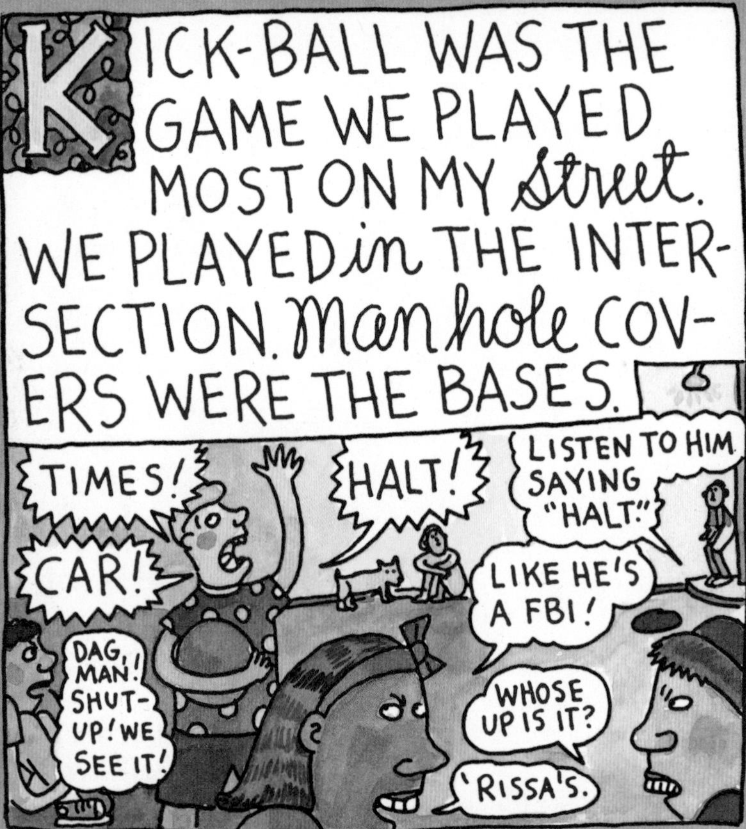
KICK-BALL WAS THE GAME WE PLAYED MOST ON MY street. WE PLAYED in THE INTER-SECTION. Manhole COVERS WERE THE BASES.
TIMES!
CAR!
HALT!
LISTEN TO HIM SAYING "HALT."
LIKE HE'S A FBI!
DAG, MAN! SHUT-UP! WE SEE IT!
WHOSE UP IS IT?
'RISSA'S.

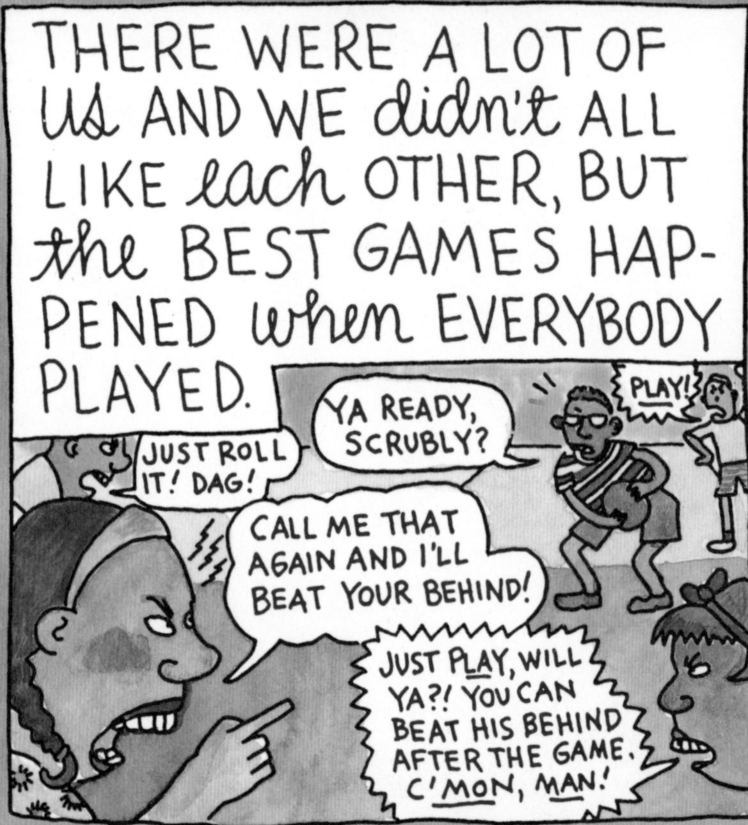
THERE WERE A LOT OF us AND WE didn't ALL LIKE each OTHER, BUT the BEST GAMES HAPPENED when EVERYBODY PLAYED.
YA READY, SCRUBLY?
PLAY!
JUST ROLL IT! DAG!
CALL ME THAT AGAIN AND I'LL BEAT YOUR BEHIND!
JUST PLAY, WILL YA?! YOU CAN BEAT HIS BEHIND AFTER THE GAME. C'MON, MAN!

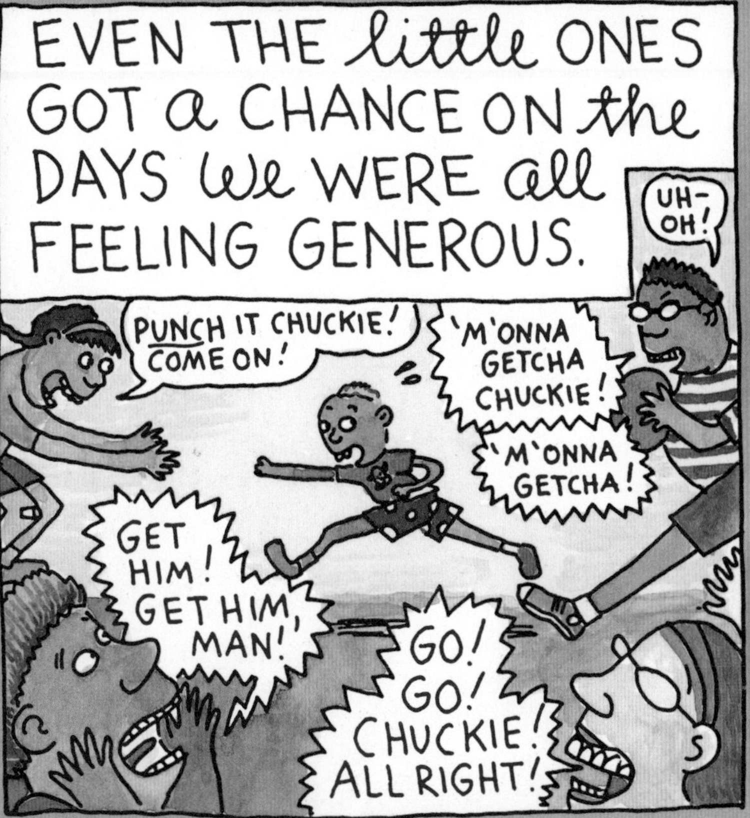
EVEN THE little ONES GOT a CHANCE ON the DAYS we WERE all FEELING GENEROUS.
UH-OH!
PUNCH IT CHUCKIE! COME ON!
'M'ONNA GETCHA CHUCKIE!
'M'ONNA GETCHA!
GET HIM! GET HIM, MAN!
GO! GO! CHUCKIE! ALL RIGHT!

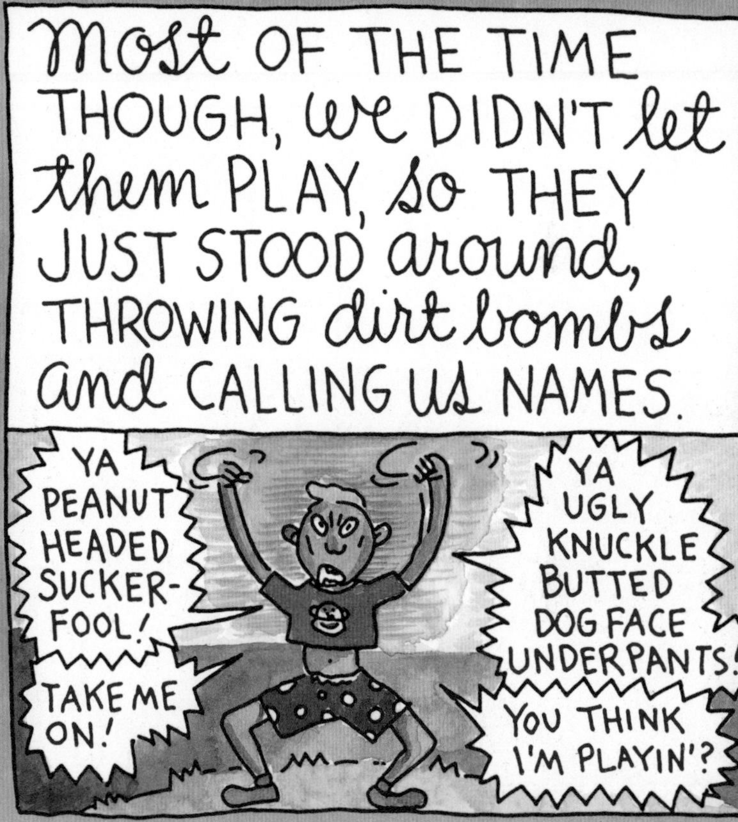
Most OF THE TIME THOUGH, we DIDN'T let them PLAY, so THEY JUST STOOD around, THROWING dirt bombs and CALLING us NAMES.
YA PEANUT HEADED SUCKER-FOOL!
TAKE ME ON!
YA UGLY KNUCKLE BUTTED DOG FACE UNDERPANTS!
YOU THINK I'M PLAYIN'?

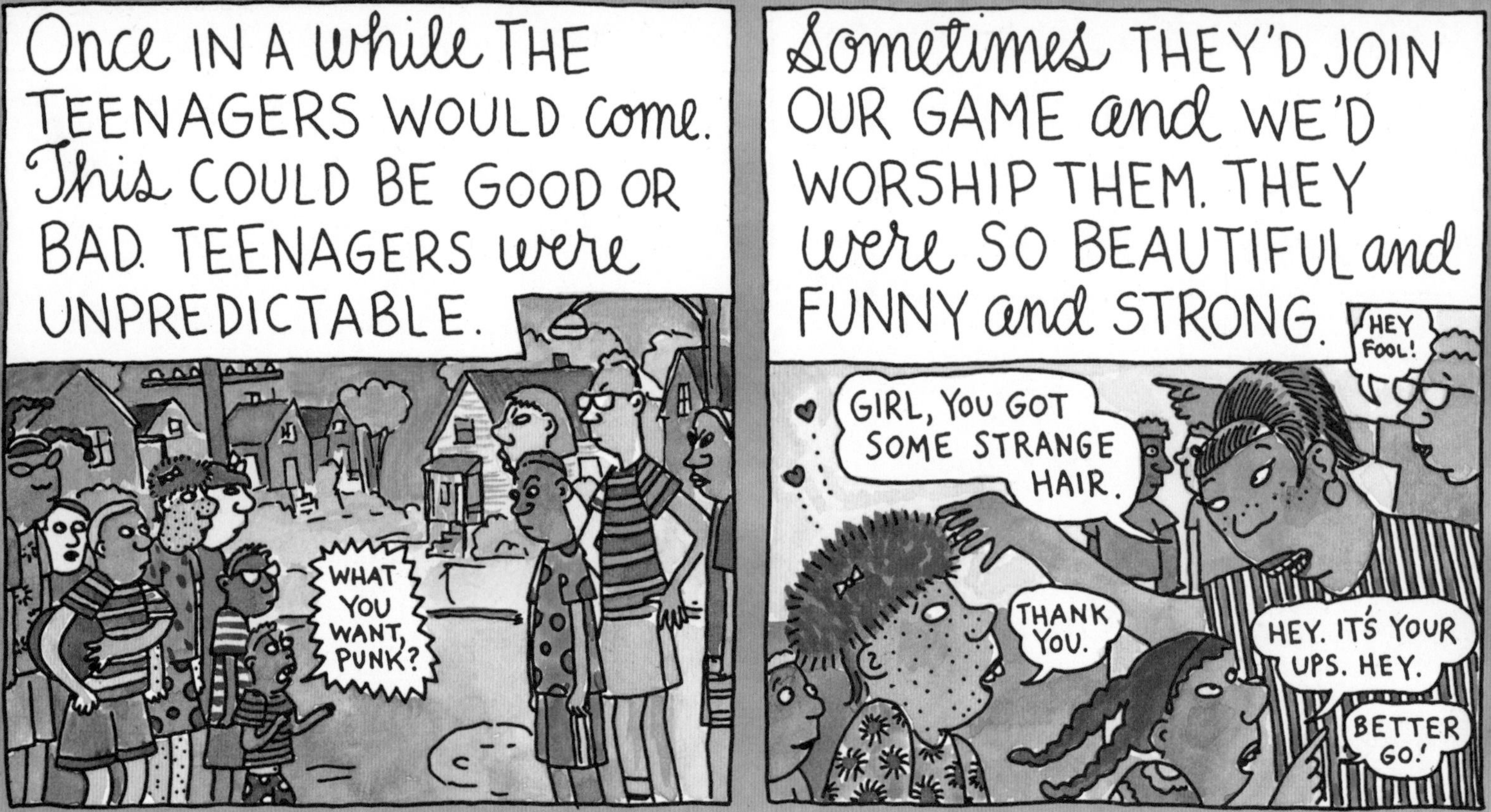
ONCE IN A WHILE THE TEENAGERS WOULD COME. THIS COULD BE GOOD OR BAD. TEENAGERS WERE UNPREDICTABLE.
WHAT YOU WANT, PUNK?
SOMETIMES THEY'D JOIN OUR GAME AND WE'D WORSHIP THEM. THEY WERE SO BEAUTIFUL AND FUNNY AND STRONG.
HEY FOOL!
GIRL, YOU GOT SOME STRANGE HAIR.
THANK YOU.
HEY. IT'S YOUR UPS. HEY.
BETTER GO!

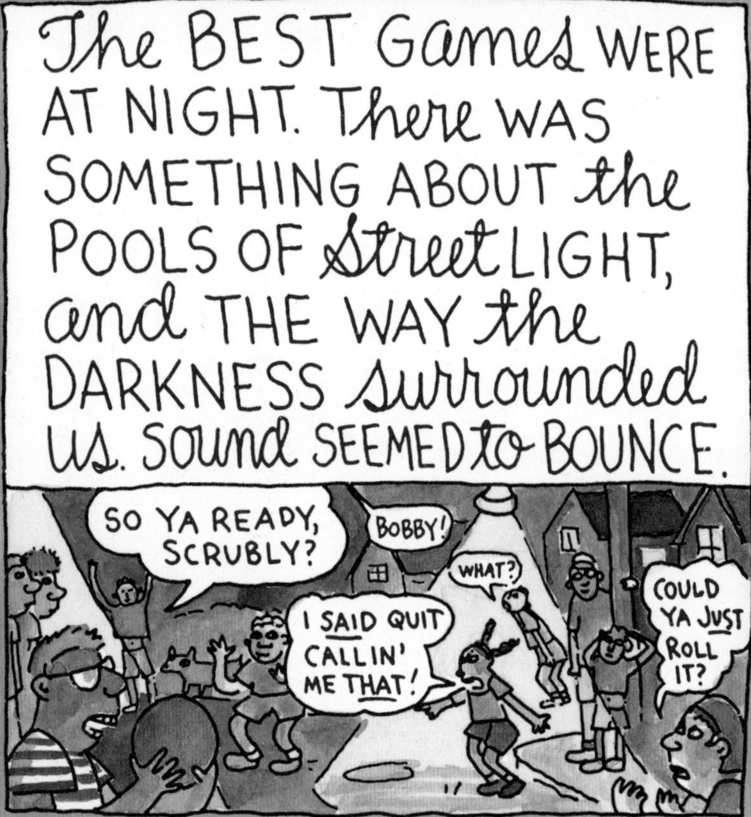
The BEST Games WERE AT NIGHT. There WAS SOMETHING ABOUT the POOLS OF Street LIGHT, and THE WAY the DARKNESS surrounded us. Sound SEEMED to BOUNCE.
SO YA READY, SCRUBLY?
BOBBY!
WHAT?
I SAID QUIT CALLIN' ME THAT!
COULD YA JUST ROLL IT?

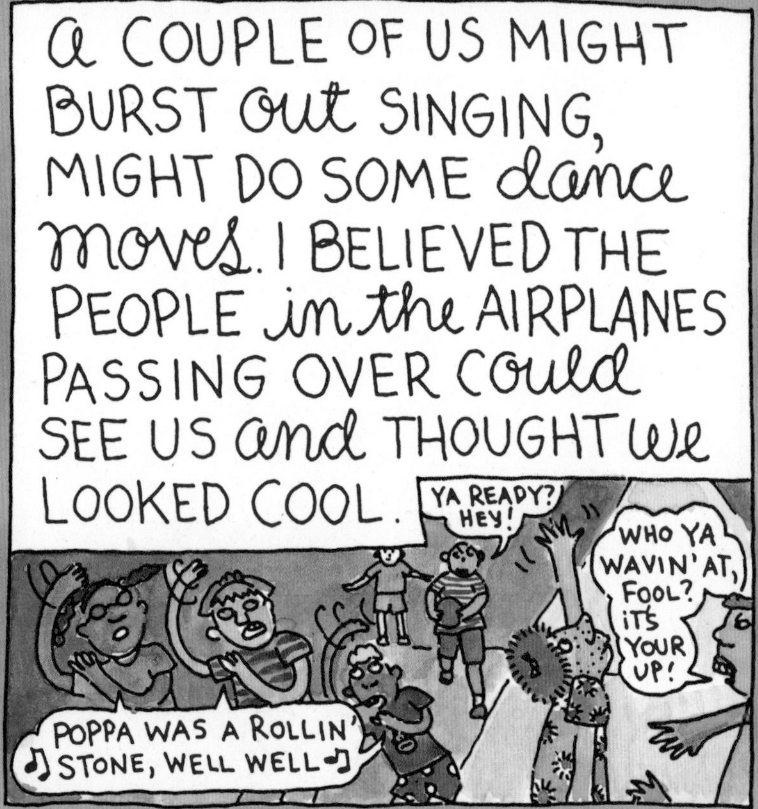
a COUPLE OF US MIGHT BURST out SINGING, MIGHT DO SOME dance moves. I BELIEVED THE PEOPLE in the AIRPLANES PASSING OVER could SEE US and THOUGHT we LOOKED COOL.
YA READY? HEY!
WHO YA WAVIN' AT, FOOL? IT'S YOUR UP!
♫ POPPA WAS A ROLLIN' STONE, WELL WELL ♫

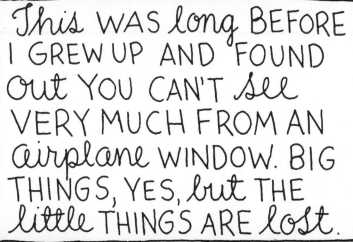

This WAS *long* BEFORE I GREW UP AND FOUND OUT YOU CAN'T *see* VERY MUCH FROM AN *airplane* WINDOW. BIG THINGS, YES, *but* THE *little* THINGS ARE *lost.*

The CITY IS *there* AND SO ARE *the* STREETS, BUT AT A CERTAIN *distance* PEOPLE DISAPPEAR. WHOLE NEIGHBORHOODS OF CHILDREN JUST VANISH.

MAN, FOR ONCE GIVE ME A DECENT ROLL, WILL YA?

YEAH, OK, YOUR MAJESTY OF IDIOTNESS.

JUST ROLL IT!

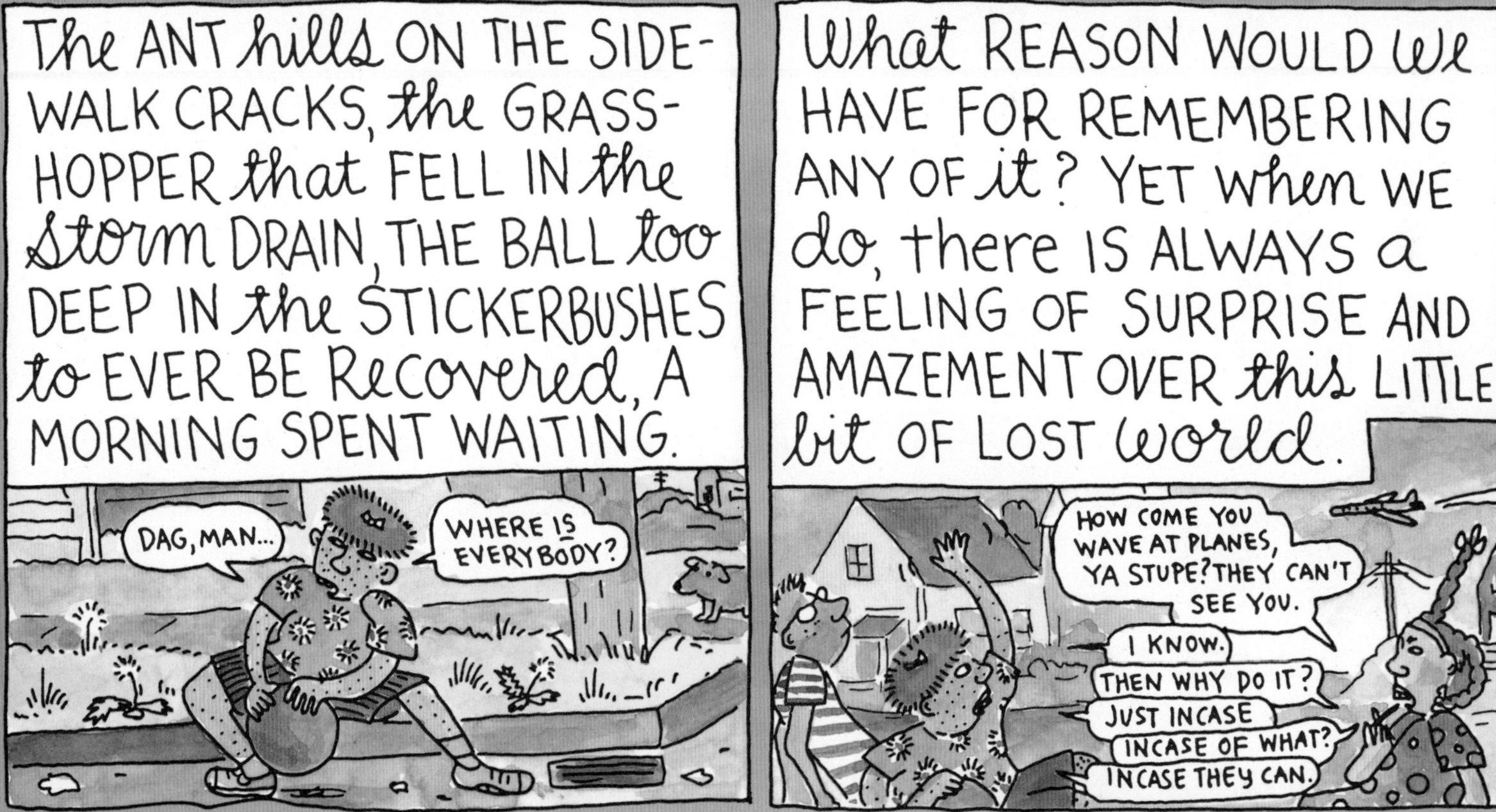
The ANT hills ON THE SIDEWALK CRACKS, the GRASSHOPPER that FELL IN the storm DRAIN, THE BALL too DEEP IN the STICKERBUSHES to EVER BE Recovered, A MORNING SPENT WAITING.
DAG, MAN...
WHERE IS EVERYBODY?
What REASON WOULD we HAVE FOR REMEMBERING ANY OF it? YET when WE do, there IS ALWAYS a FEELING OF SURPRISE AND AMAZEMENT OVER this LITTLE bit OF LOST world.
HOW COME YOU WAVE AT PLANES, YA STUPE? THEY CAN'T SEE YOU.
I KNOW.
THEN WHY DO IT?
JUST INCASE
INCASE OF WHAT?
INCASE THEY CAN.

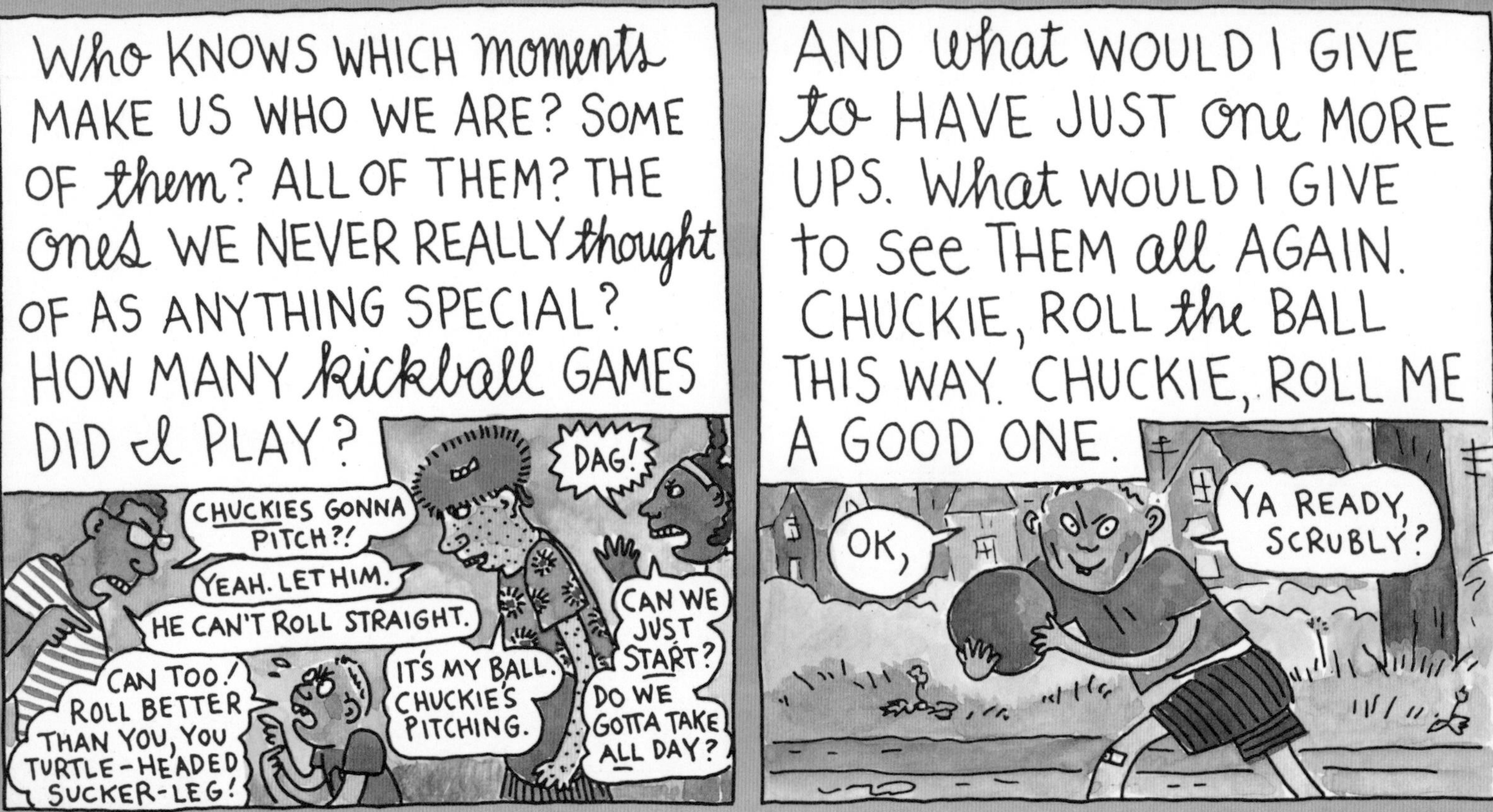
Who KNOWS WHICH moments MAKE US WHO WE ARE? SOME OF them? ALL OF THEM? THE ones WE NEVER REALLY thought OF AS ANYTHING SPECIAL? HOW MANY kickball GAMES DID I PLAY?
CHUCKIES GONNA PITCH?!
DAG!
YEAH. LET HIM.
HE CAN'T ROLL STRAIGHT.
CAN WE JUST START?
IT'S MY BALL. CHUCKIE'S PITCHING.
CAN TOO! ROLL BETTER THAN YOU, YOU TURTLE-HEADED SUCKER-LEG!
DO WE GOTTA TAKE ALL DAY?
AND what WOULD I GIVE to HAVE JUST one MORE UPS. What WOULD I GIVE to see THEM all AGAIN. CHUCKIE, ROLL the BALL THIS WAY. CHUCKIE, ROLL ME A GOOD ONE.
YA READY, SCRUBLY?
OK,

3. Where does the water go after it leaves the puddle?

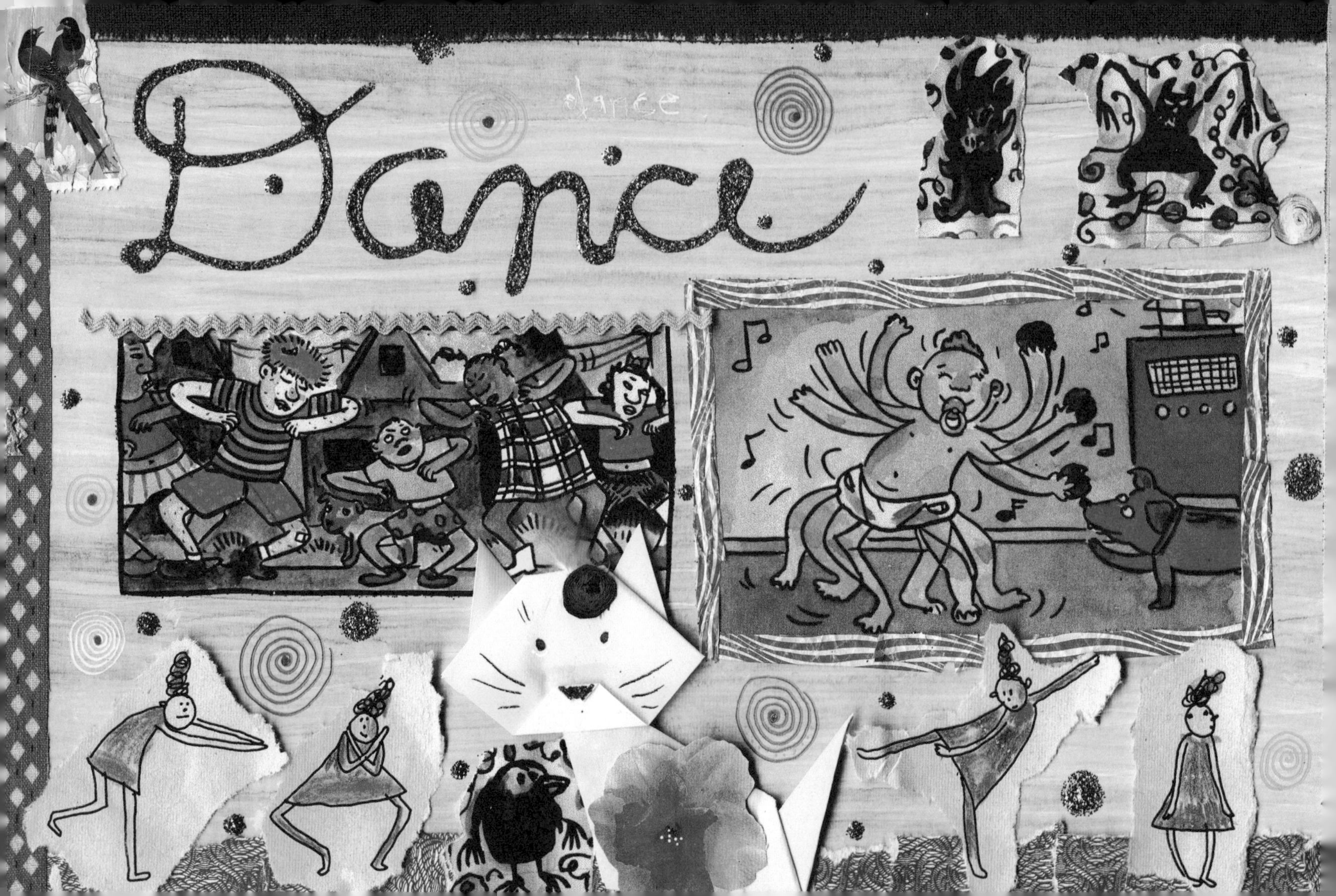
dance
Dance

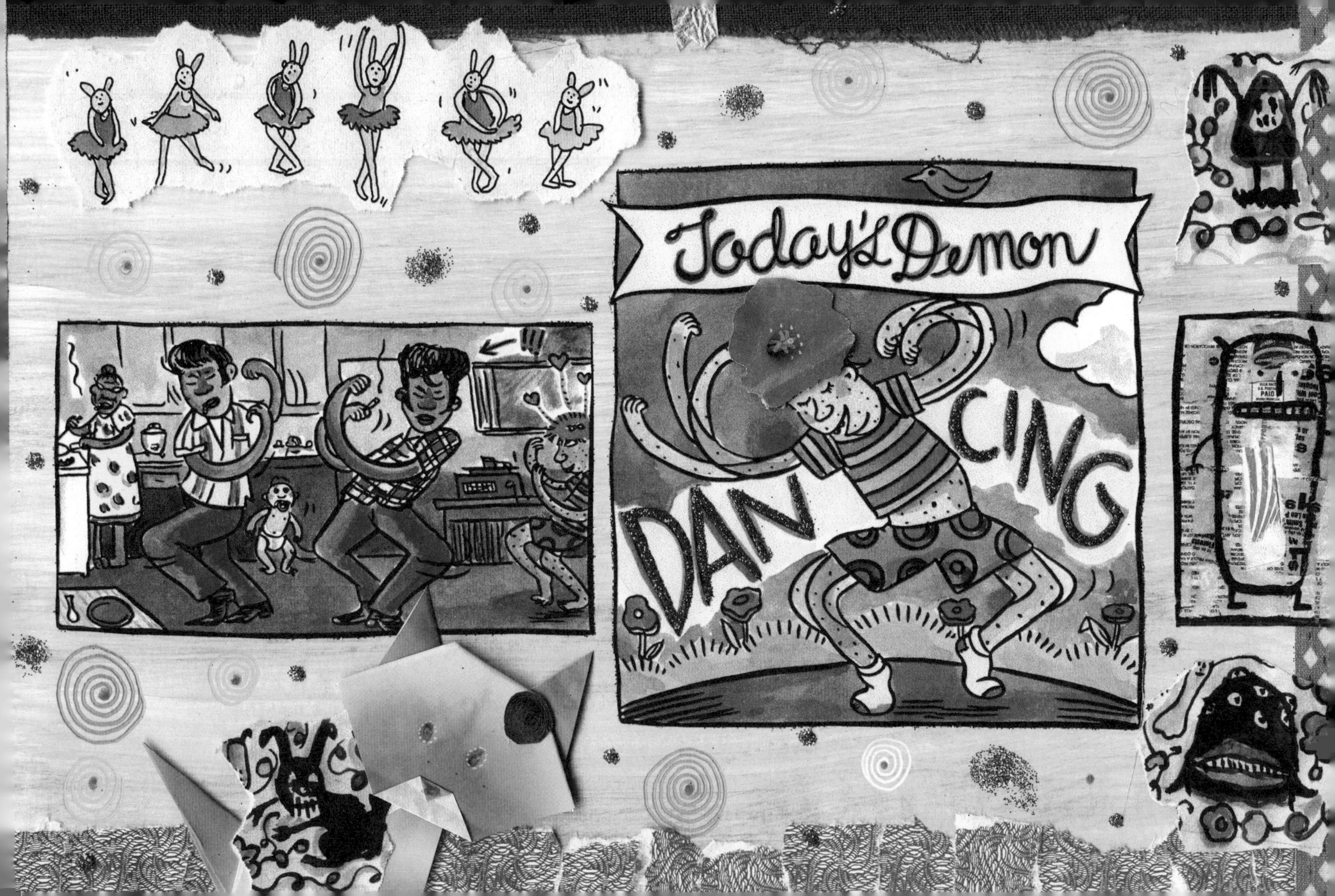
Today's Demon
DAN CING

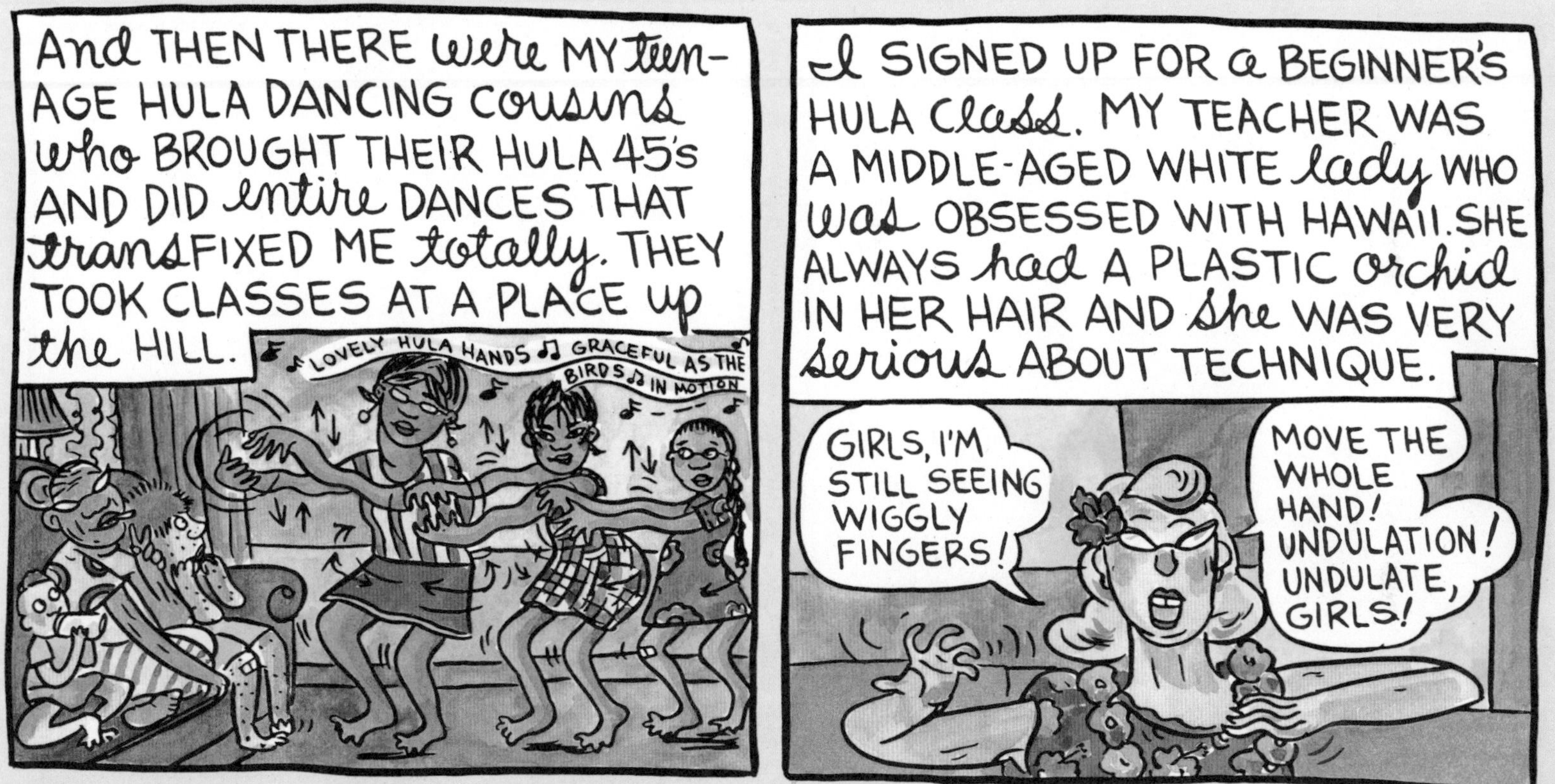
AND THEN THERE WERE MY TEEN-AGE HULA DANCING COUSINS WHO BROUGHT THEIR HULA 45's AND DID ENTIRE DANCES THAT TRANSFIXED ME TOTALLY. THEY TOOK CLASSES AT A PLACE UP THE HILL.
LOVELY HULA HANDS GRACEFUL AS THE BIRDS IN MOTION
I SIGNED UP FOR A BEGINNER'S HULA CLASS. MY TEACHER WAS A MIDDLE-AGED WHITE LADY WHO WAS OBSESSED WITH HAWAII. SHE ALWAYS HAD A PLASTIC ORCHID IN HER HAIR AND SHE WAS VERY SERIOUS ABOUT TECHNIQUE.
GIRLS, I'M STILL SEEING WIGGLY FINGERS!
MOVE THE WHOLE HAND! UNDULATION! UNDULATE, GIRLS!

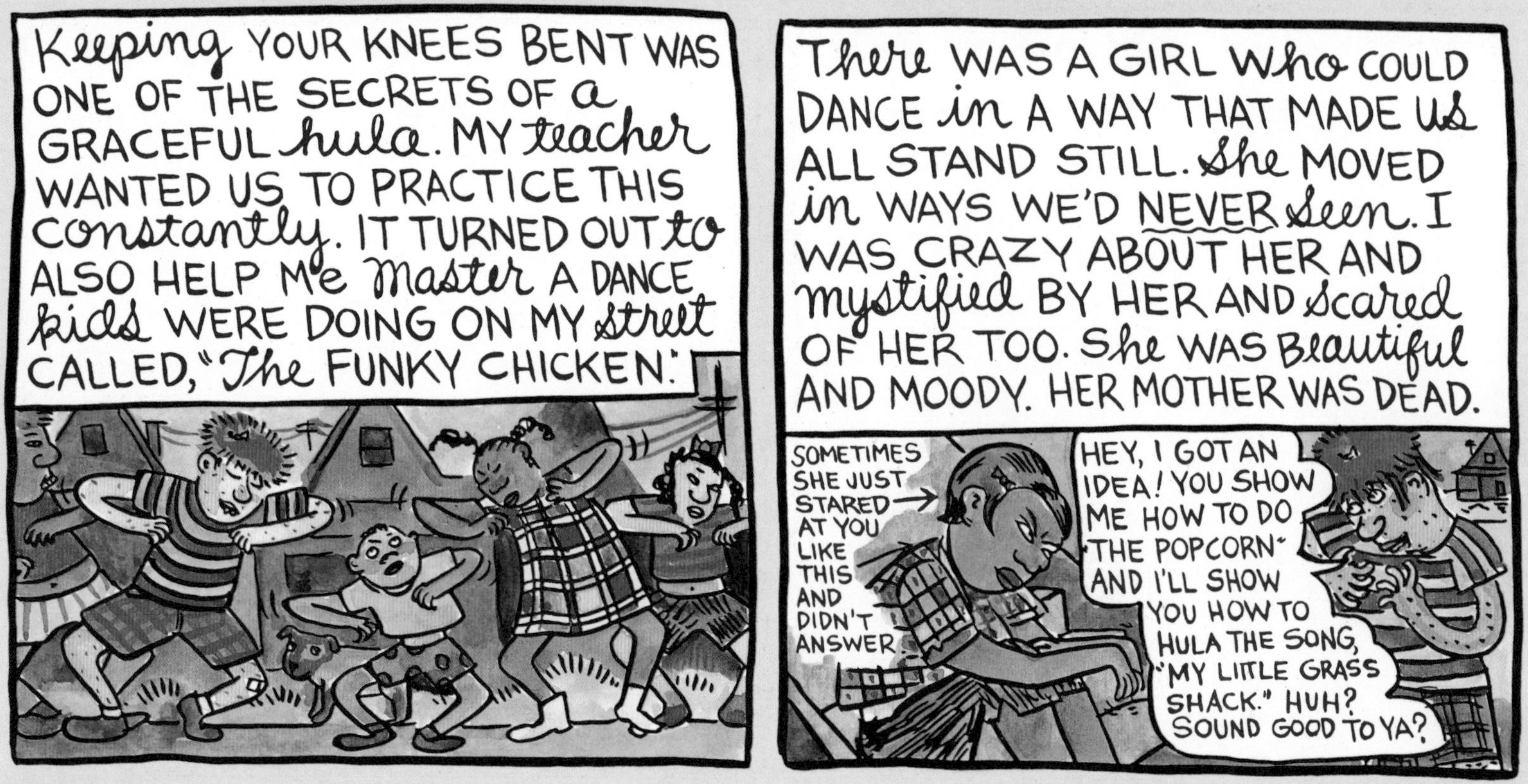
Keeping YOUR KNEES BENT WAS ONE OF THE SECRETS OF a GRACEFUL hula. MY teacher WANTED US TO PRACTICE THIS constantly. IT TURNED OUT to ALSO HELP Me master A DANCE kids WERE DOING ON MY street CALLED, "The FUNKY CHICKEN."
There WAS A GIRL Who COULD DANCE in A WAY THAT MADE US ALL STAND STILL. She MOVED in WAYS WE'D NEVER Seen. I WAS CRAZY ABOUT HER AND mystified BY HER AND Scared OF HER TOO. She WAS Beautiful AND MOODY. HER MOTHER WAS DEAD.
SOMETIMES SHE JUST STARED AT YOU LIKE THIS AND DIDN'T ANSWER.
HEY, I GOT AN IDEA! YOU SHOW ME HOW TO DO "THE POPCORN" AND I'LL SHOW YOU HOW TO HULA THE SONG, "MY LITTLE GRASS SHACK." HUH? SOUND GOOD TO YA?

43

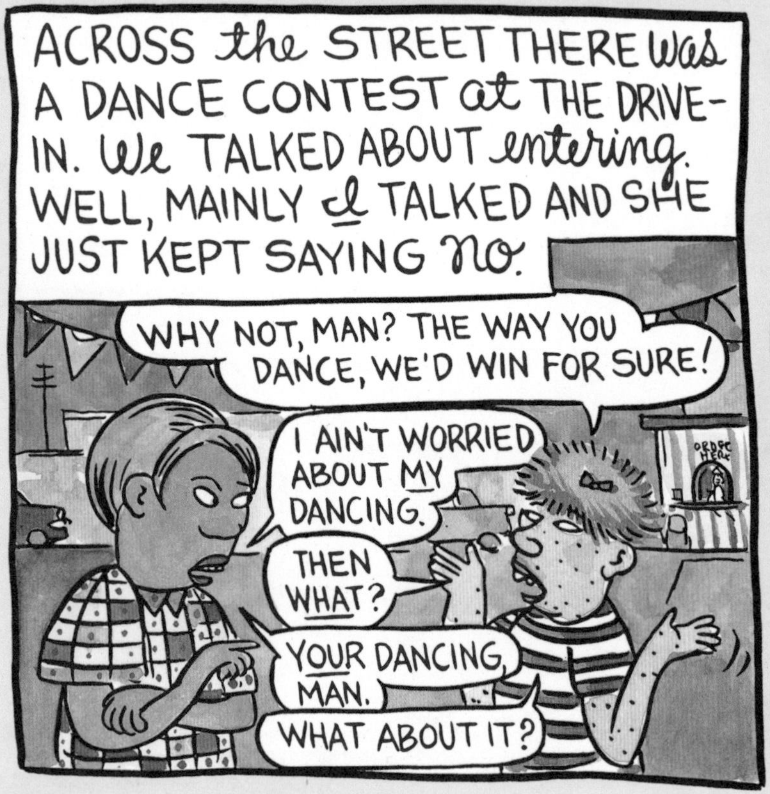
ACROSS the STREET THERE was A DANCE CONTEST at THE DRIVE-IN. We TALKED ABOUT entering. WELL, MAINLY I TALKED AND SHE JUST KEPT SAYING no.
WHY NOT, MAN? THE WAY YOU DANCE, WE'D WIN FOR SURE!
I AIN'T WORRIED ABOUT MY DANCING.
THEN WHAT?
YOUR DANCING, MAN.
WHAT ABOUT IT?

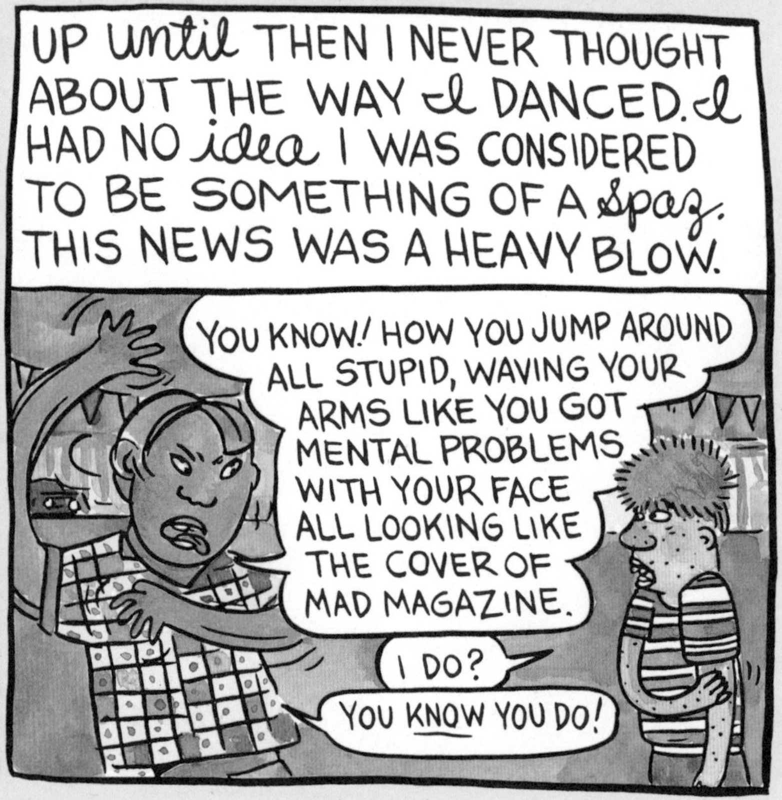
UP until THEN I NEVER THOUGHT ABOUT THE WAY I DANCED. I HAD NO idea I WAS CONSIDERED TO BE SOMETHING OF A spaz. THIS NEWS WAS A HEAVY BLOW.
YOU KNOW! HOW YOU JUMP AROUND ALL STUPID, WAVING YOUR ARMS LIKE YOU GOT MENTAL PROBLEMS WITH YOUR FACE ALL LOOKING LIKE THE COVER OF MAD MAGAZINE.
I DO?
YOU KNOW YOU DO!

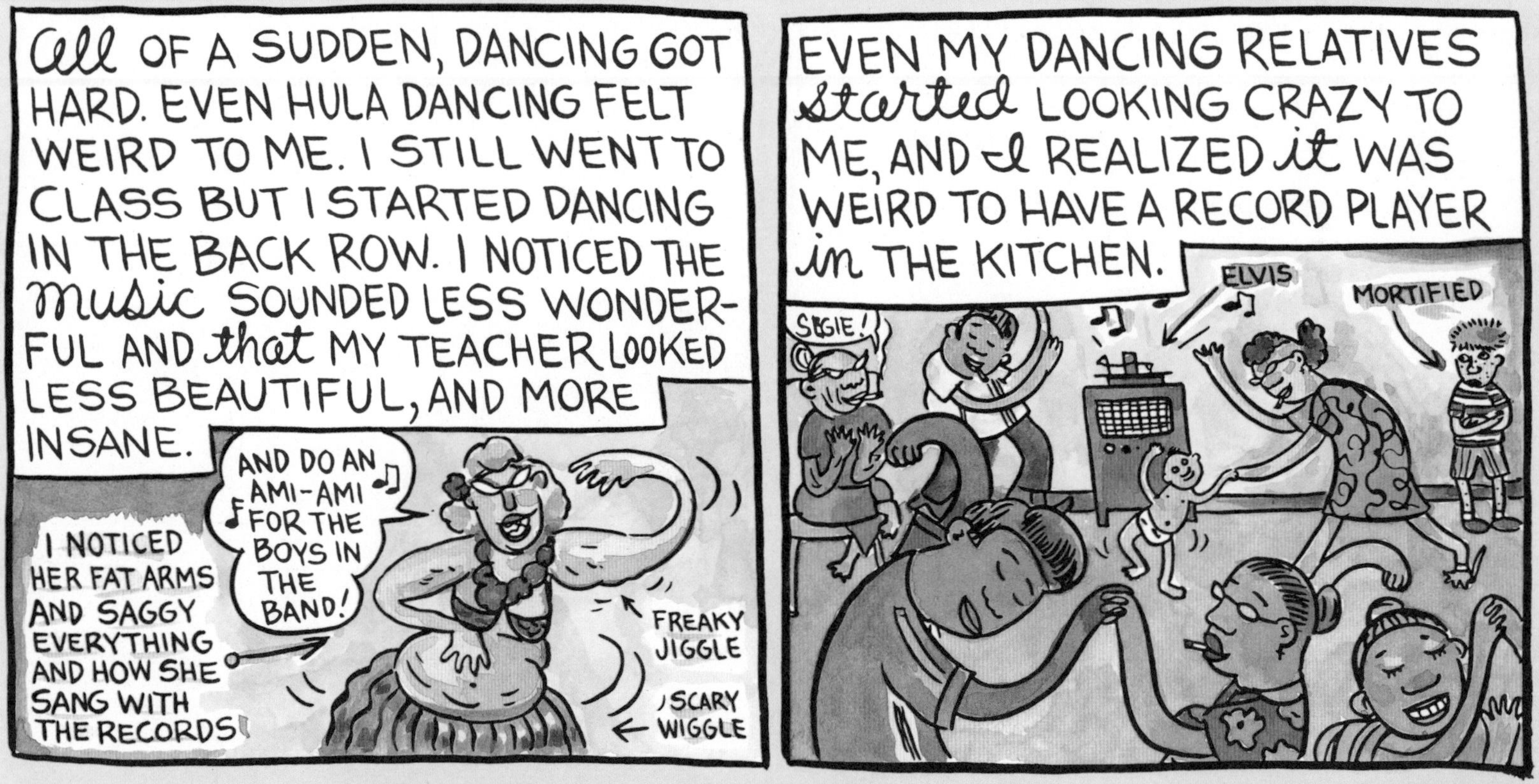

ALL OF A SUDDEN, DANCING GOT HARD. EVEN HULA DANCING FELT WEIRD TO ME. I STILL WENT TO CLASS BUT I STARTED DANCING IN THE BACK ROW. I NOTICED THE MUSIC SOUNDED LESS WONDERFUL AND THAT MY TEACHER LOOKED LESS BEAUTIFUL, AND MORE INSANE.
AND DO AN AMI-AMI FOR THE BOYS IN THE BAND!
I NOTICED HER FAT ARMS AND SAGGY EVERYTHING AND HOW SHE SANG WITH THE RECORDS!
FREAKY JIGGLE
SCARY WIGGLE
EVEN MY DANCING RELATIVES STARTED LOOKING CRAZY TO ME, AND I REALIZED IT WAS WEIRD TO HAVE A RECORD PLAYER IN THE KITCHEN.
SEGIE!
ELVIS
MORTIFIED

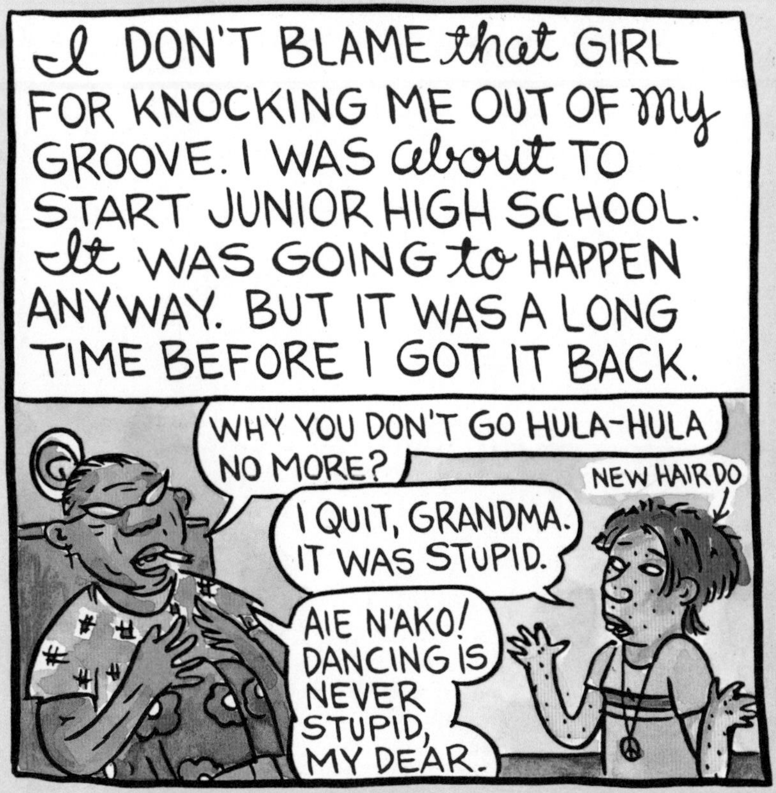
I DON'T BLAME that GIRL FOR KNOCKING ME OUT OF my GROOVE. I WAS about TO START JUNIOR HIGH SCHOOL. It WAS GOING to HAPPEN ANYWAY. BUT IT WAS A LONG TIME BEFORE I GOT IT BACK.
WHY YOU DON'T GO HULA-HULA NO MORE?
NEW HAIRDO
I QUIT, GRANDMA. IT WAS STUPID.
AIE N'AKO! DANCING IS NEVER STUPID, MY DEAR.

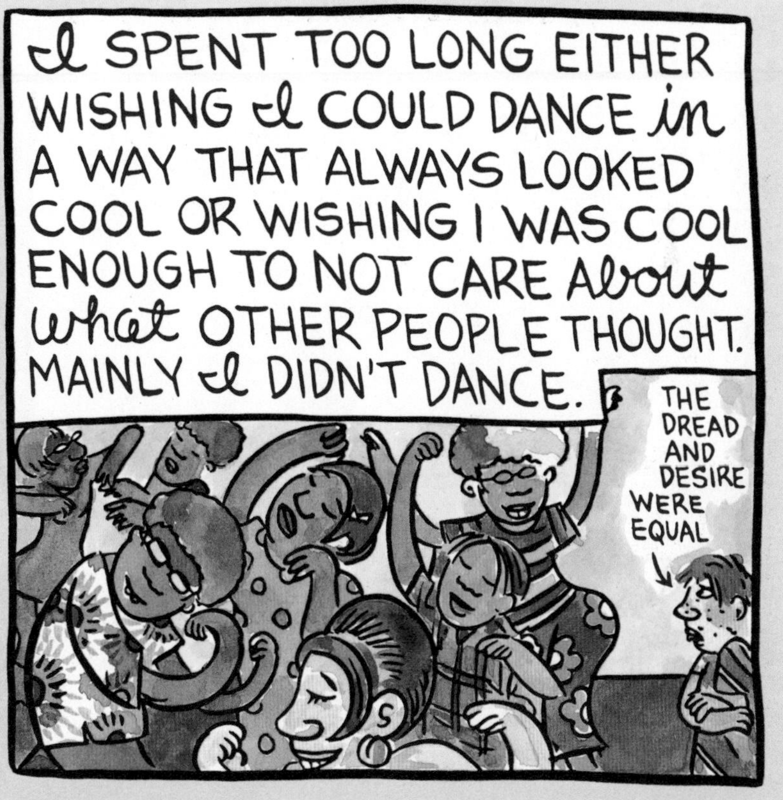
I SPENT TOO LONG EITHER WISHING I COULD DANCE in A WAY THAT ALWAYS LOOKED COOL OR WISHING I WAS COOL ENOUGH TO NOT CARE About what OTHER PEOPLE THOUGHT. MAINLY I DIDN'T DANCE.
THE DREAD AND DESIRE WERE EQUAL

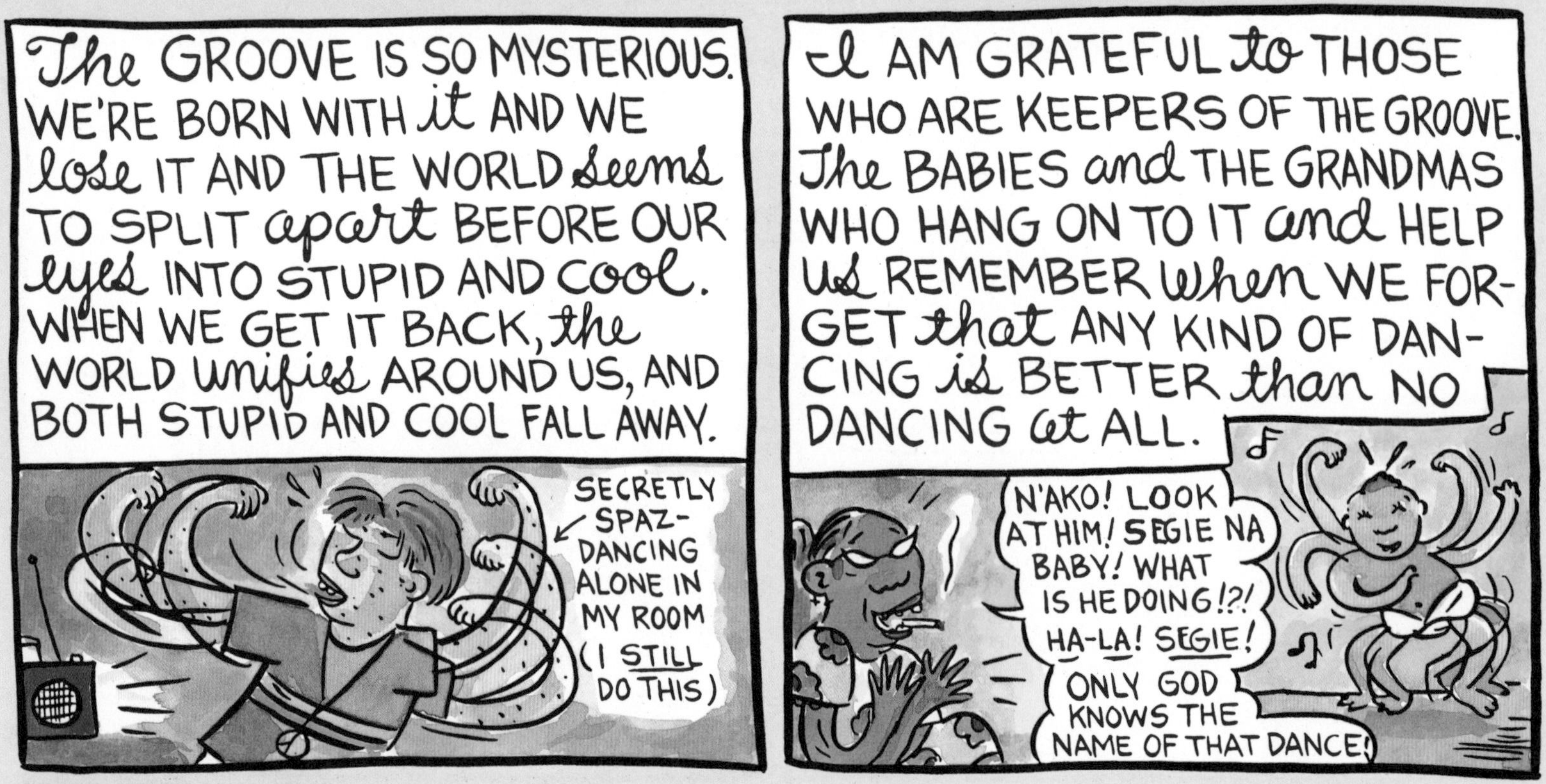
The GROOVE IS SO MYSTERIOUS. WE'RE BORN WITH it AND WE lose IT AND THE WORLD seems TO SPLIT apart BEFORE OUR eyes INTO STUPID AND cool. WHEN WE GET IT BACK, the WORLD unifies AROUND US, AND BOTH STUPID AND COOL FALL AWAY.
SECRETLY SPAZ-DANCING ALONE IN MY ROOM (I STILL DO THIS)
I AM GRATEFUL to THOSE WHO ARE KEEPERS OF THE GROOVE. The BABIES and THE GRANDMAS WHO HANG ON TO IT and HELP us REMEMBER when WE FORGET that ANY KIND OF DANCING is BETTER than NO DANCING at ALL.
N'AKO! LOOK AT HIM! SEGIE NA BABY! WHAT IS HE DOING!?!
HA-LA! SEGIE!
ONLY GOD KNOWS THE NAME OF THAT DANCE!

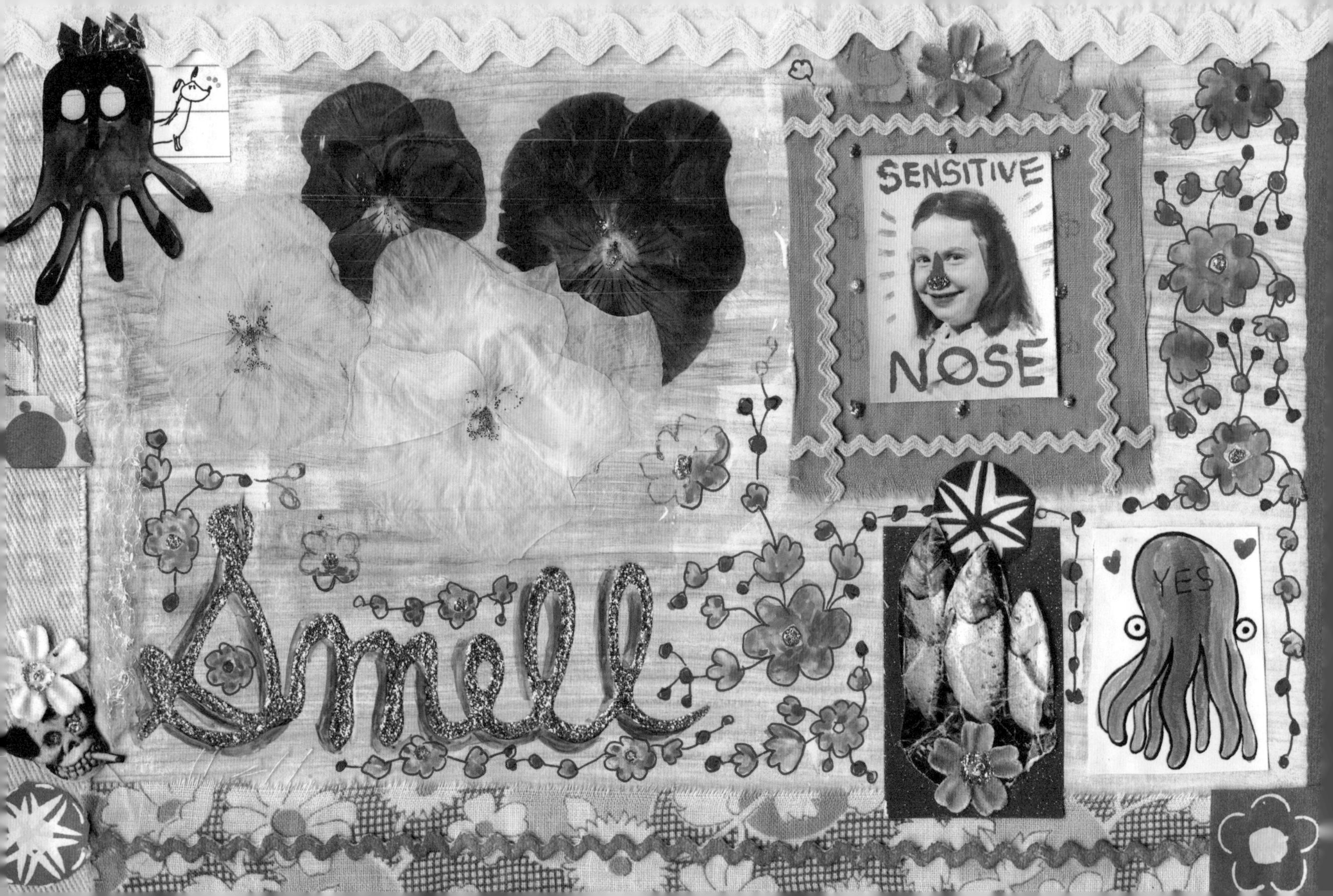
SENSITIVE
NOSE
Smell
YES

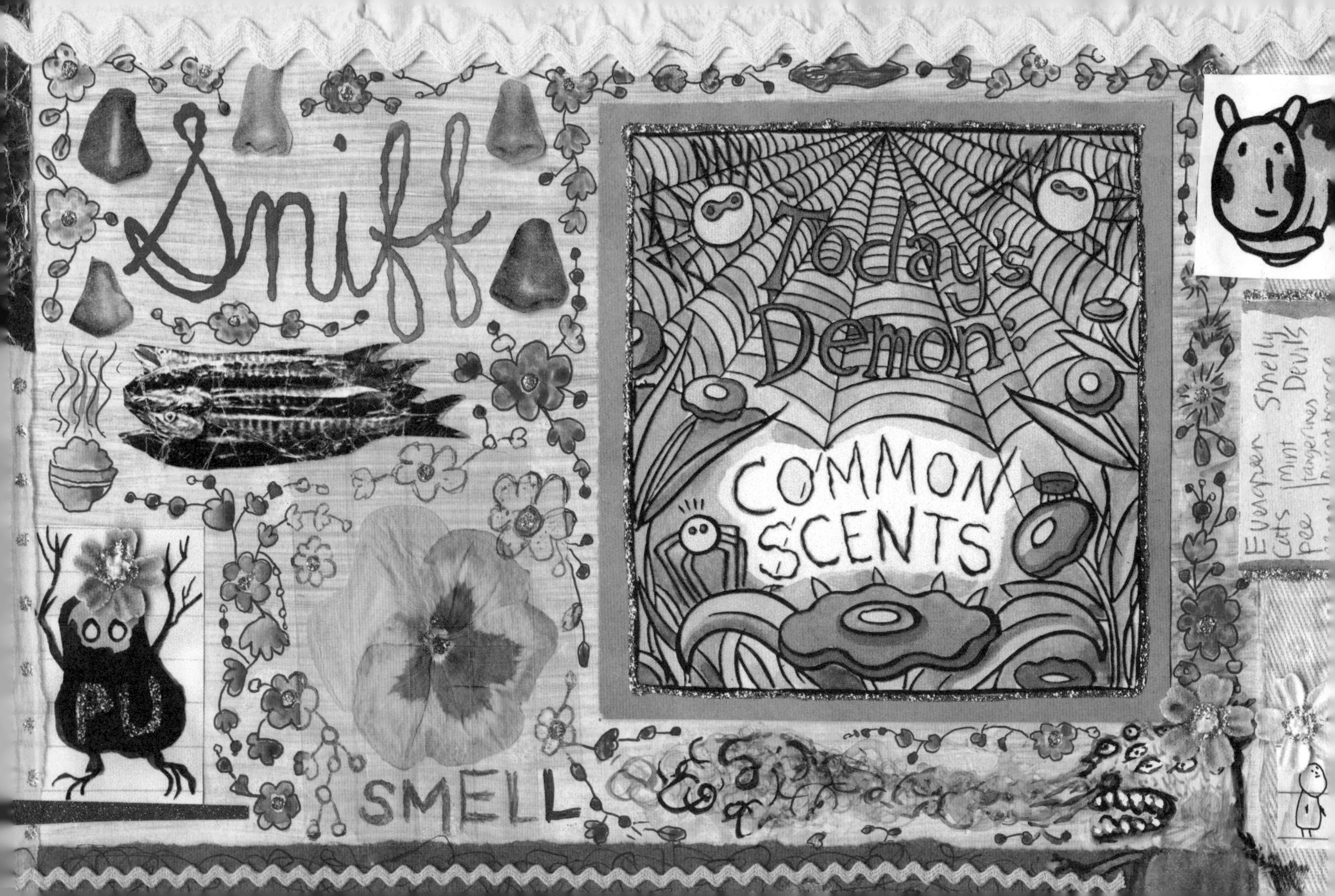
Sniff
Today's Demon:
COMMON SCENTS
PU
SMELL
Evergreen Smelly
Cats | Mint
pee | tangerines Devils

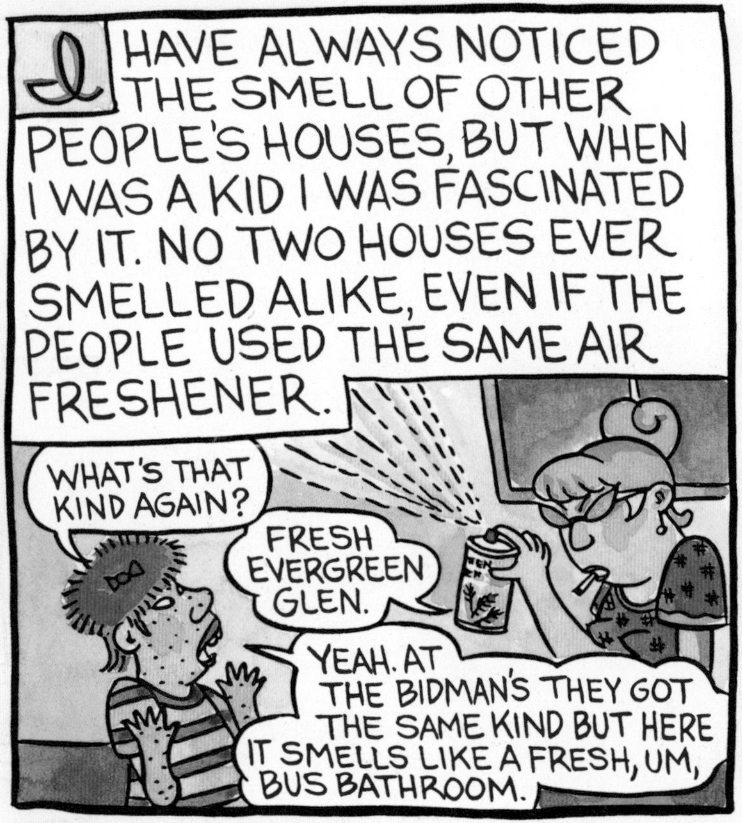
I HAVE ALWAYS NOTICED THE SMELL OF OTHER PEOPLE'S HOUSES, BUT WHEN I WAS A KID I WAS FASCINATED BY IT. NO TWO HOUSES EVER SMELLED ALIKE, EVEN IF THE PEOPLE USED THE SAME AIR FRESHENER.
WHAT'S THAT KIND AGAIN?
FRESH EVERGREEN GLEN.
YEAH. AT THE BIDMAN'S THEY GOT THE SAME KIND BUT HERE IT SMELLS LIKE A FRESH, UM, BUS BATHROOM.

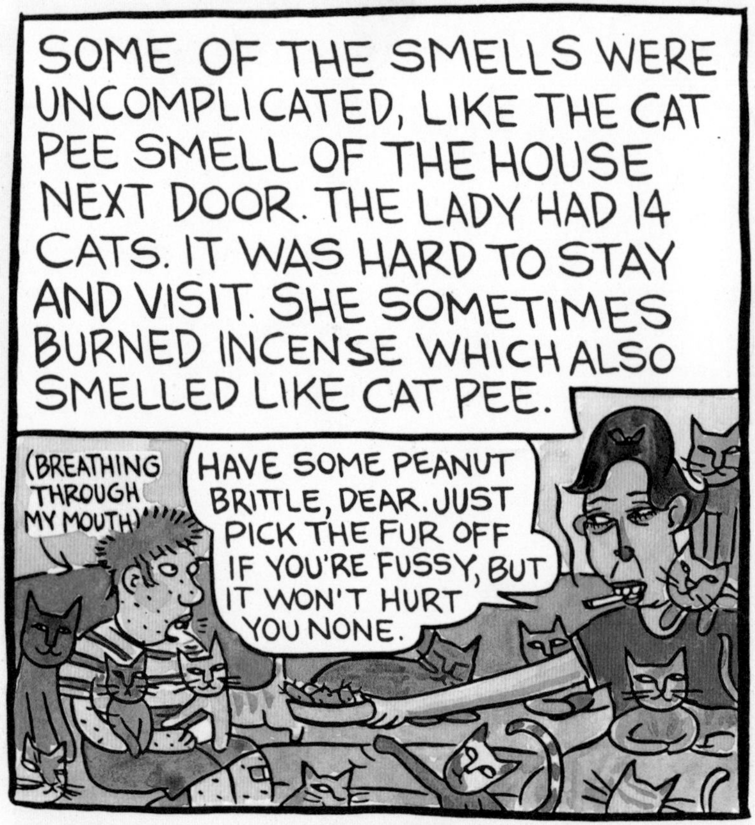
SOME OF THE SMELLS WERE UNCOMPLICATED, LIKE THE CAT PEE SMELL OF THE HOUSE NEXT DOOR. THE LADY HAD 14 CATS. IT WAS HARD TO STAY AND VISIT. SHE SOMETIMES BURNED INCENSE WHICH ALSO SMELLED LIKE CAT PEE.
(BREATHING THROUGH MY MOUTH)
HAVE SOME PEANUT BRITTLE, DEAR. JUST PICK THE FUR OFF IF YOU'RE FUSSY, BUT IT WON'T HURT YOU NONE.

54

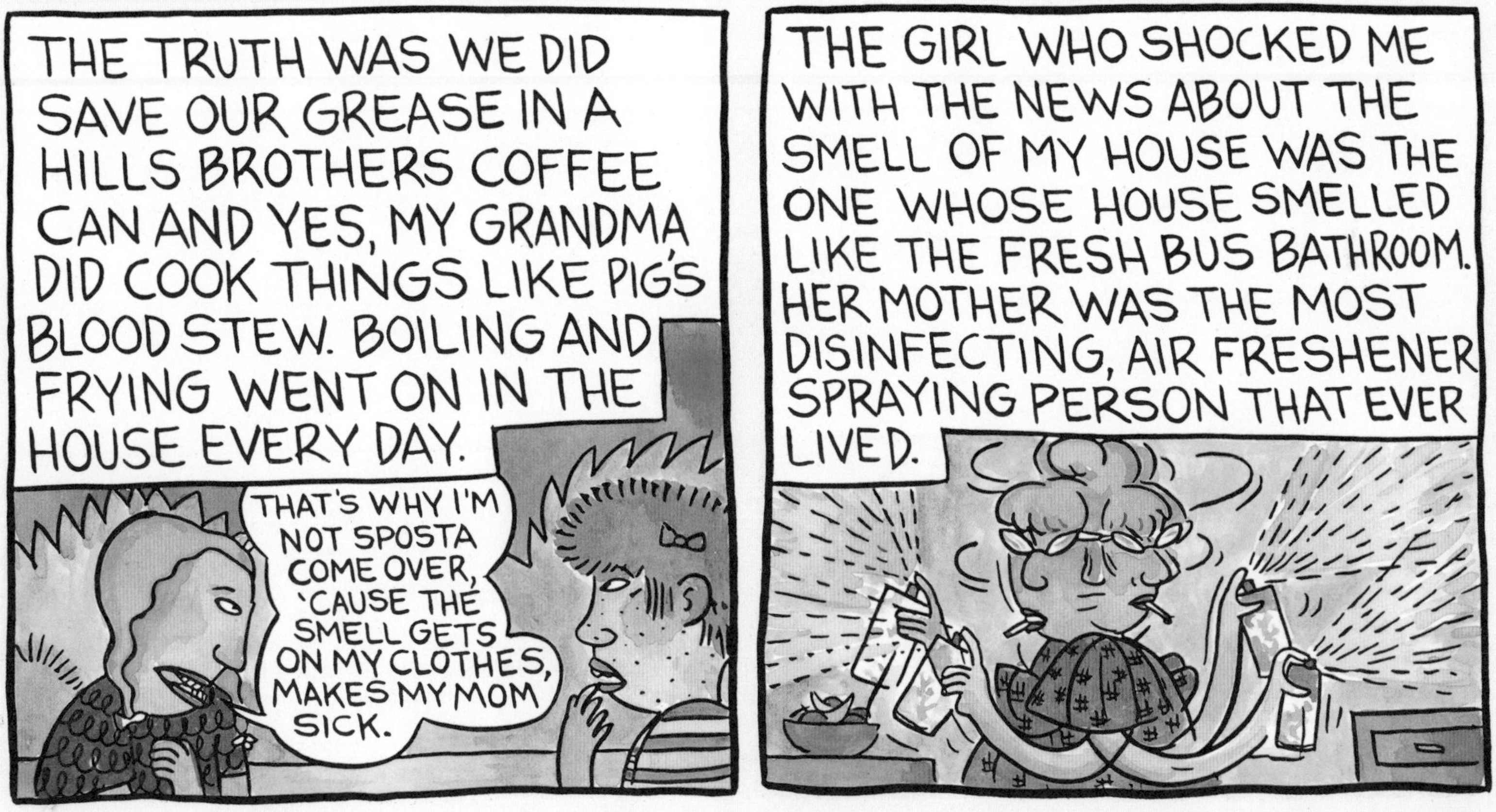
THE TRUTH WAS WE DID SAVE OUR GREASE IN A HILLS BROTHERS COFFEE CAN AND YES, MY GRANDMA DID COOK THINGS LIKE PIG'S BLOOD STEW. BOILING AND FRYING WENT ON IN THE HOUSE EVERY DAY.
THAT'S WHY I'M NOT SPOSTA COME OVER, 'CAUSE THE SMELL GETS ON MY CLOTHES, MAKES MY MOM SICK.
THE GIRL WHO SHOCKED ME WITH THE NEWS ABOUT THE SMELL OF MY HOUSE WAS THE ONE WHOSE HOUSE SMELLED LIKE THE FRESH BUS BATHROOM. HER MOTHER WAS THE MOST DISINFECTING, AIR FRESHENER SPRAYING PERSON THAT EVER LIVED.

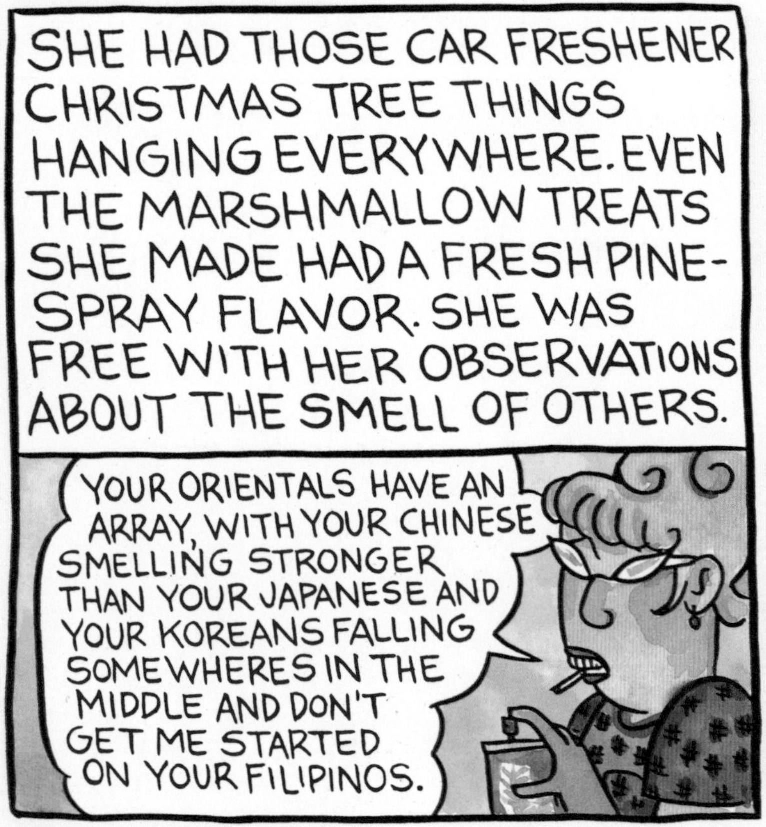

SHE HAD THOSE CAR FRESHENER CHRISTMAS TREE THINGS HANGING EVERYWHERE. EVEN THE MARSHMALLOW TREATS SHE MADE HAD A FRESH PINE-SPRAY FLAVOR. SHE WAS FREE WITH HER OBSERVATIONS ABOUT THE SMELL OF OTHERS.
YOUR ORIENTALS HAVE AN ARRAY, WITH YOUR CHINESE SMELLING STRONGER THAN YOUR JAPANESE AND YOUR KOREANS FALLING SOMEWHERES IN THE MIDDLE AND DON'T GET ME STARTED ON YOUR FILIPINOS.

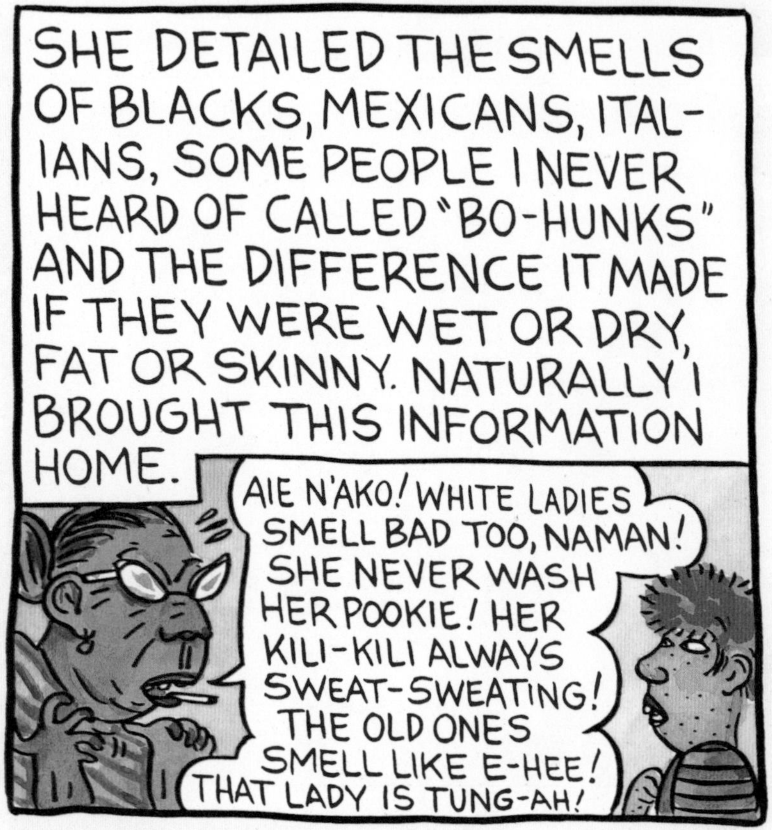

SHE DETAILED THE SMELLS OF BLACKS, MEXICANS, ITALIANS, SOME PEOPLE I NEVER HEARD OF CALLED "BO-HUNKS" AND THE DIFFERENCE IT MADE IF THEY WERE WET OR DRY, FAT OR SKINNY. NATURALLY I BROUGHT THIS INFORMATION HOME.
AIE N'AKO! WHITE LADIES SMELL BAD TOO, NAMAN! SHE NEVER WASH HER POOKIE! HER KILI-KILI ALWAYS SWEAT-SWEATING! THE OLD ONES SMELL LIKE E-HEE! THAT LADY IS TUNG-AH!

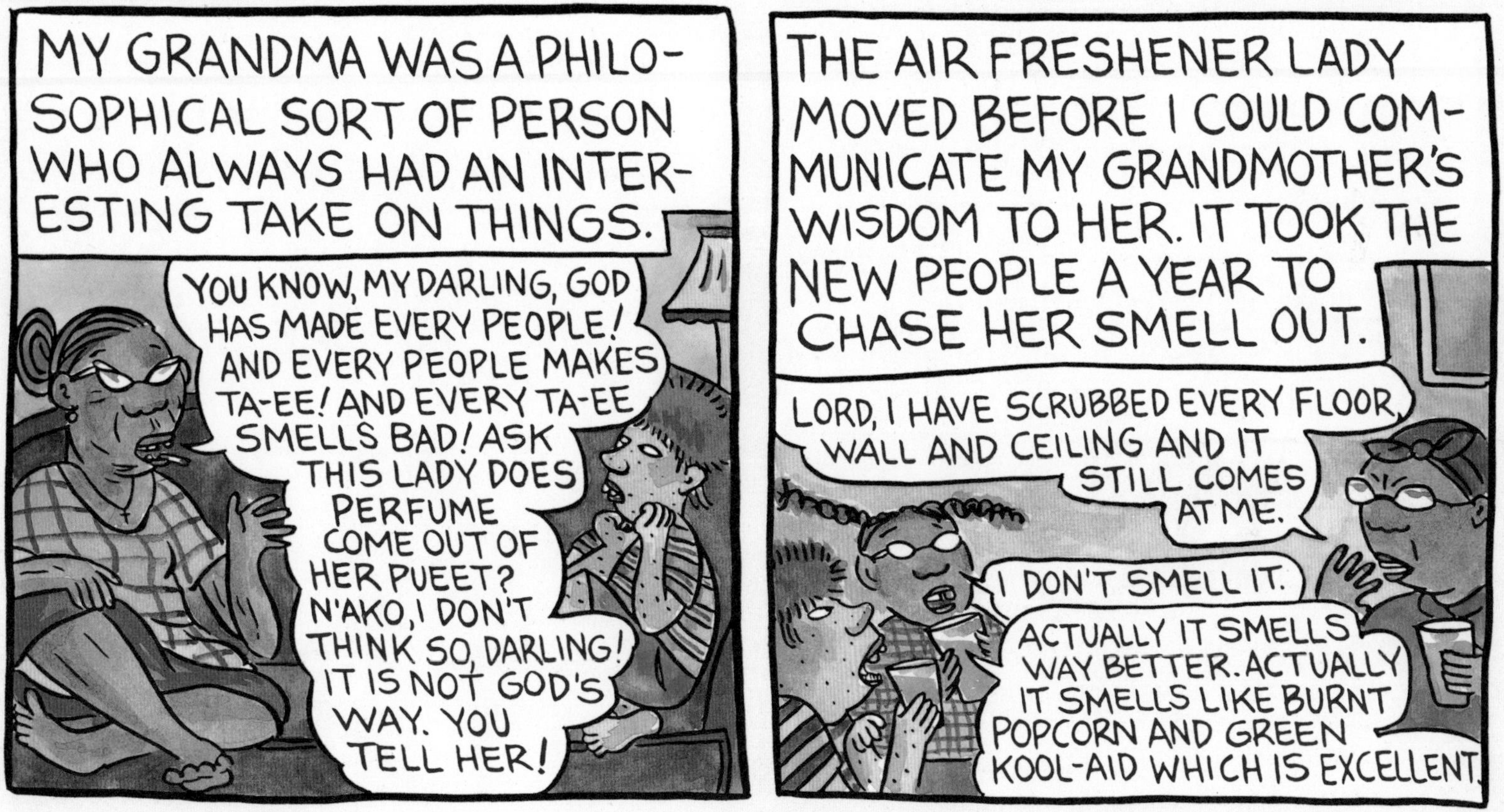
MY GRANDMA WAS A PHILOSOPHICAL SORT OF PERSON WHO ALWAYS HAD AN INTERESTING TAKE ON THINGS.
YOU KNOW, MY DARLING, GOD HAS MADE EVERY PEOPLE! AND EVERY PEOPLE MAKES TA-EE! AND EVERY TA-EE SMELLS BAD! ASK THIS LADY DOES PERFUME COME OUT OF HER PUEET? N'AKO, I DON'T THINK SO, DARLING! IT IS NOT GOD'S WAY. YOU TELL HER!
THE AIR FRESHENER LADY MOVED BEFORE I COULD COMMUNICATE MY GRANDMOTHER'S WISDOM TO HER. IT TOOK THE NEW PEOPLE A YEAR TO CHASE HER SMELL OUT.
LORD, I HAVE SCRUBBED EVERY FLOOR, WALL AND CEILING AND IT STILL COMES AT ME.
I DON'T SMELL IT.
ACTUALLY IT SMELLS WAY BETTER. ACTUALLY IT SMELLS LIKE BURNT POPCORN AND GREEN KOOL-AID WHICH IS EXCELLENT.

58

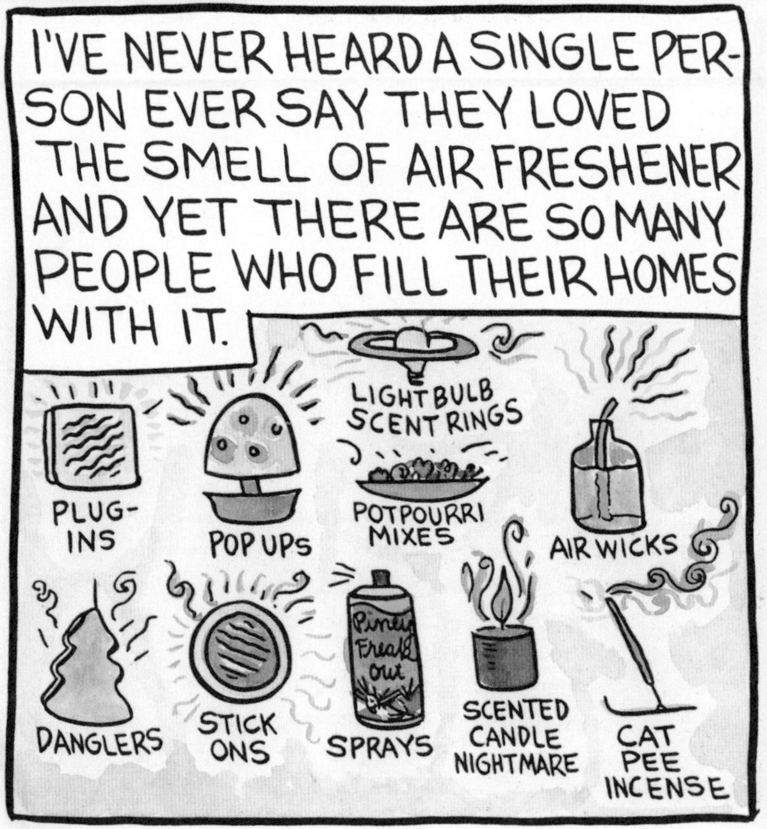
I'VE NEVER HEARD A SINGLE PERSON EVER SAY THEY LOVED THE SMELL OF AIR FRESHENER AND YET THERE ARE SO MANY PEOPLE WHO FILL THEIR HOMES WITH IT.
PLUG-INS
POP UPS
LIGHT BULB SCENT RINGS
POTPOURRI MIXES
AIR WICKS
DANGLERS
STICK ONS
Piney Freak out
SPRAYS
SCENTED CANDLE NIGHTMARE
CAT PEE INCENSE
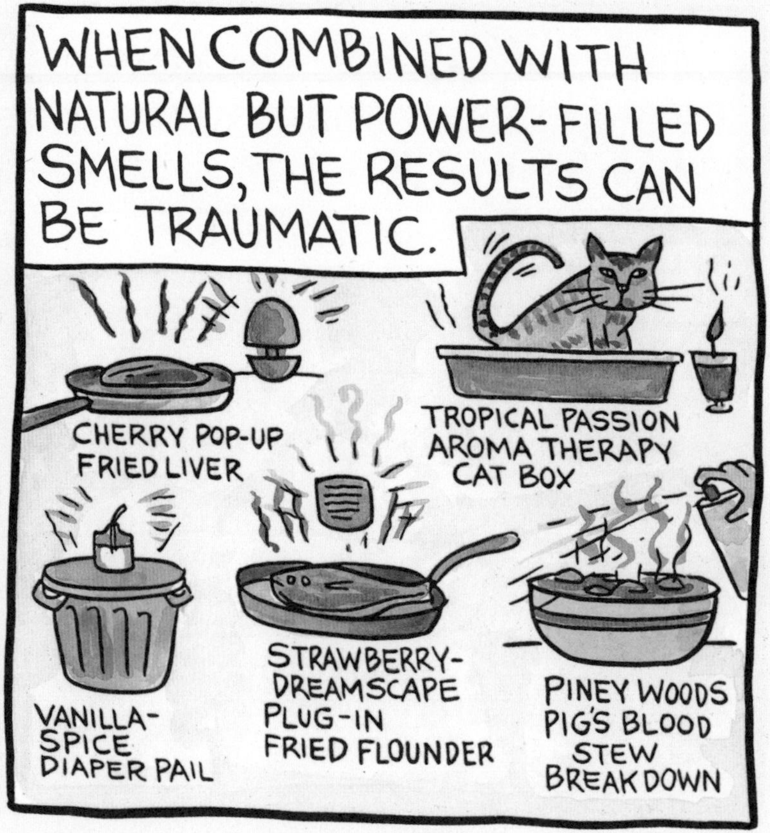
WHEN COMBINED WITH NATURAL BUT POWER-FILLED SMELLS, THE RESULTS CAN BE TRAUMATIC.
CHERRY POP-UP FRIED LIVER
TROPICAL PASSION AROMA THERAPY CAT BOX
VANILLA-SPICE DIAPER PAIL
STRAWBERRY-DREAMSCAPE PLUG-IN FRIED FLOUNDER
PINEY WOODS PIG'S BLOOD STEW BREAK DOWN

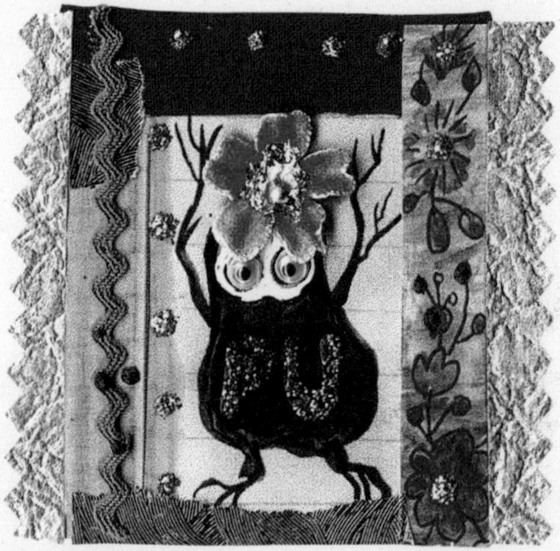
FU

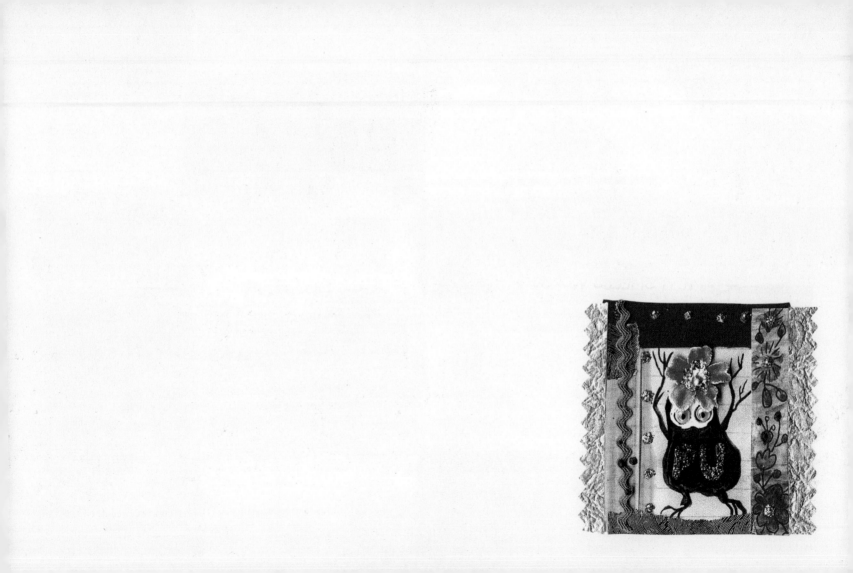

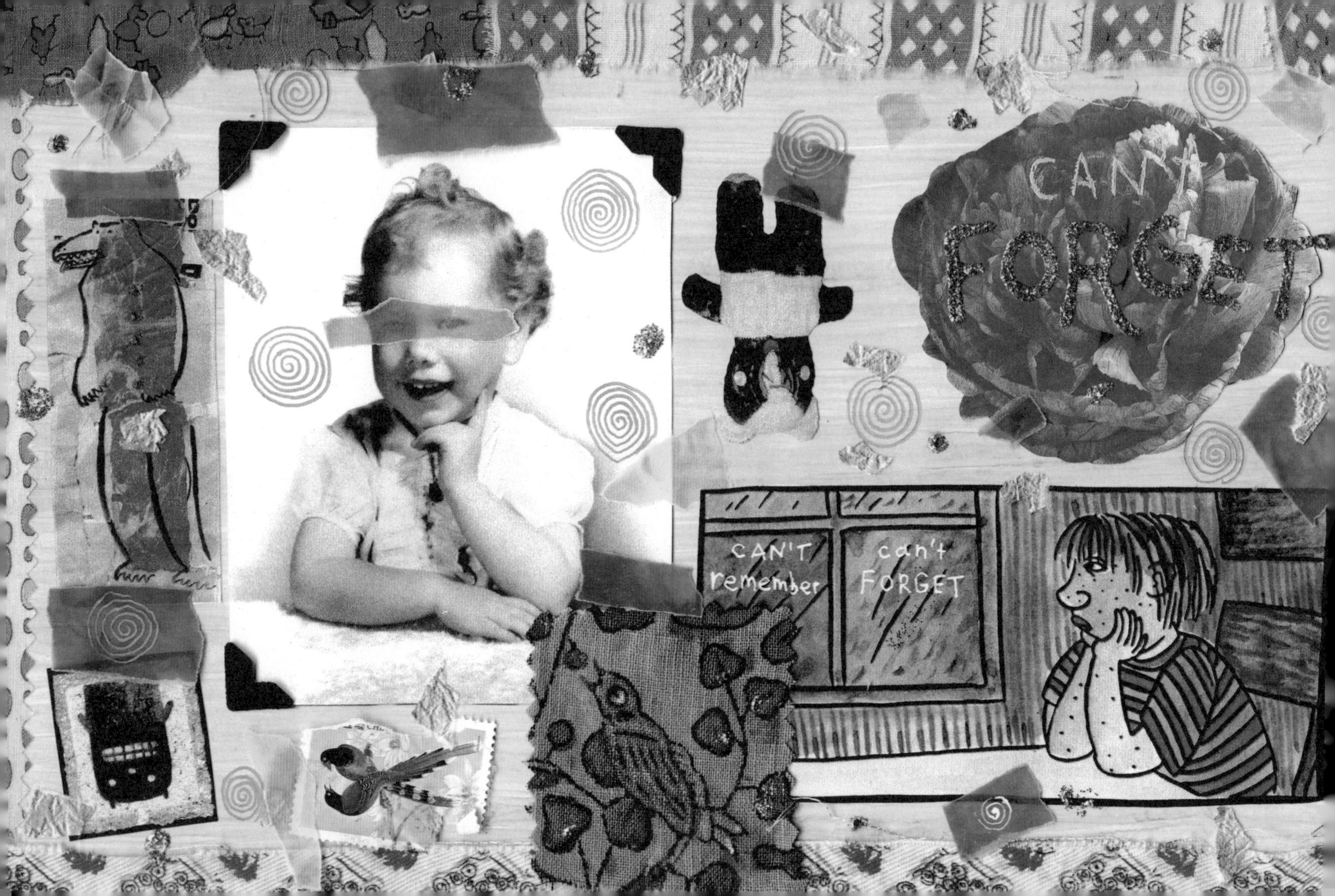
CAN'T
FORGET
CAN'T
remember
can't
FORGET

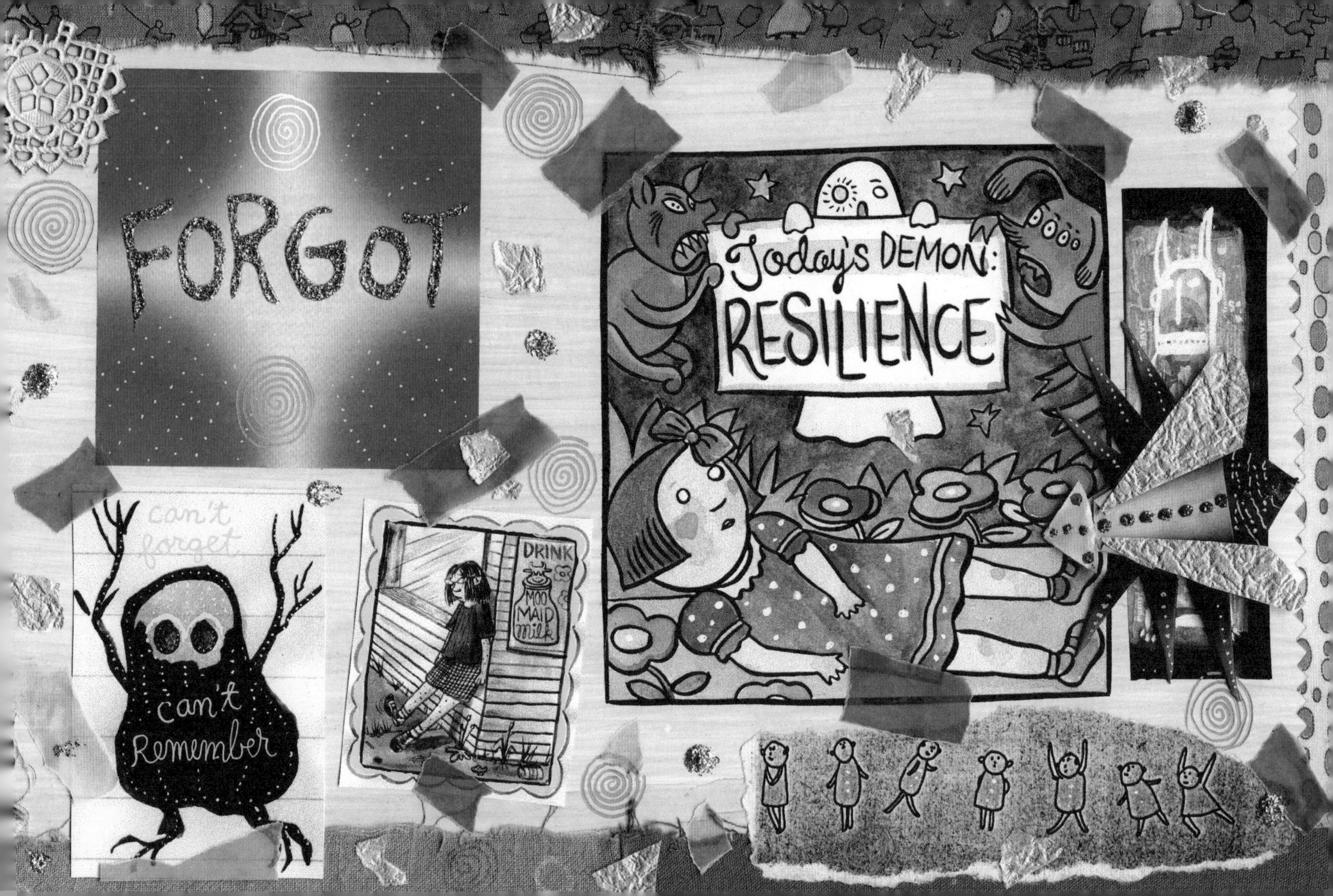
FORGOT
can't forget.
can't Remember
DRINK
MOO MAID milk
Today's DEMON:
RESILIENCE

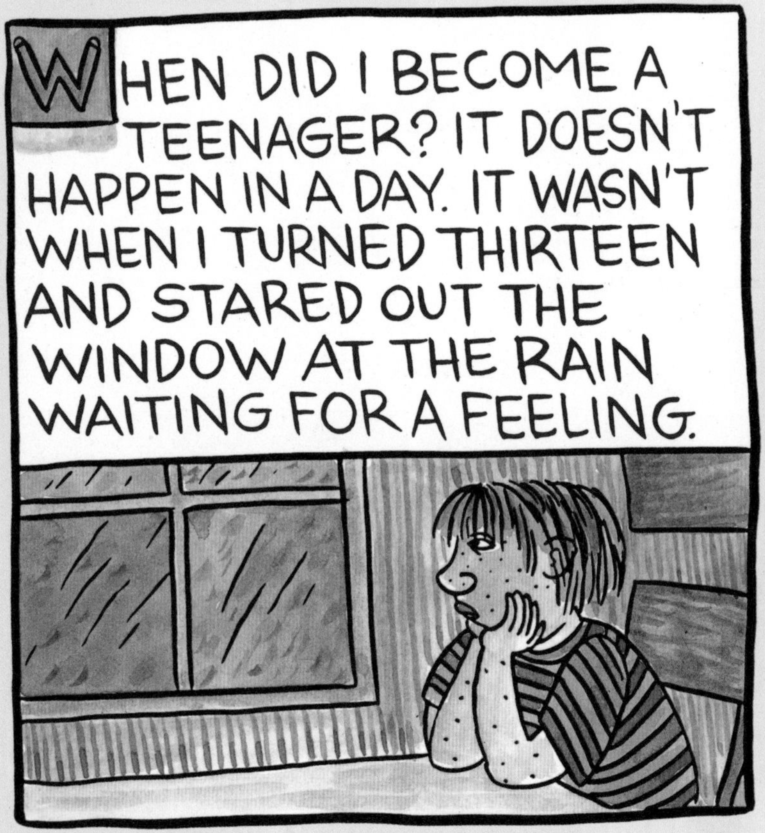
WHEN DID I BECOME A TEENAGER? IT DOESN'T HAPPEN IN A DAY. IT WASN'T WHEN I TURNED THIRTEEN AND STARED OUT THE WINDOW AT THE RAIN WAITING FOR A FEELING.

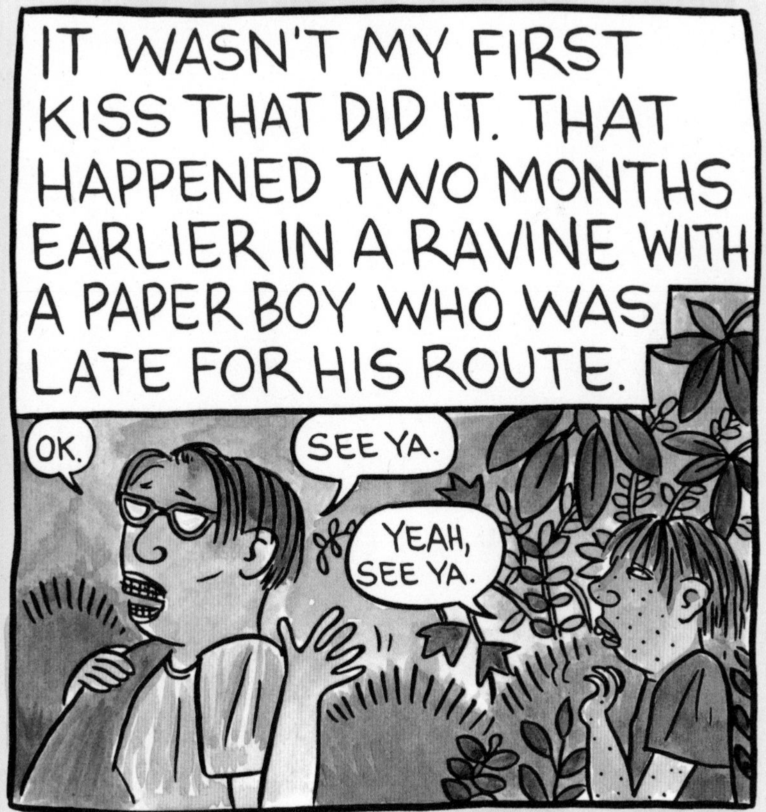
IT WASN'T MY FIRST KISS THAT DID IT. THAT HAPPENED TWO MONTHS EARLIER IN A RAVINE WITH A PAPER BOY WHO WAS LATE FOR HIS ROUTE.
OK.
SEE YA.
YEAH, SEE YA.

65

I WASN'T ALONE IN MY KNOW-LEDGE. NEARLY EVERY KID IN MY NEIGHBORHOOD KNEW TOO MUCH TOO SOON. SOME PEO-PLE CALL IT "GROWING UP TOO FAST" BUT ACTUALLY IT MADE SOME OF US UNABLE TO GROW UP AT ALL.

HE WANTS TO GET TOGETHER TOMORROW.

HE SAYS HE KNOWS A BETTER PLACE.

MORE "COMFORTABLE"

WHAT AM I GOING TO DO?

I CRINGE WHEN PEOPLE TALK ABOUT THE RESILIENCY OF CHILDREN. IT'S A HOPE ADULTS HAVE ABOUT THE NATURE OF A CHILD'S INNER LIFE, THAT IT'S SIMPLE, THAT WHAT CAN BE FORGOTTEN CAN NO LONGER AFFECT US. BUT WHAT IS FOR-GETTING?

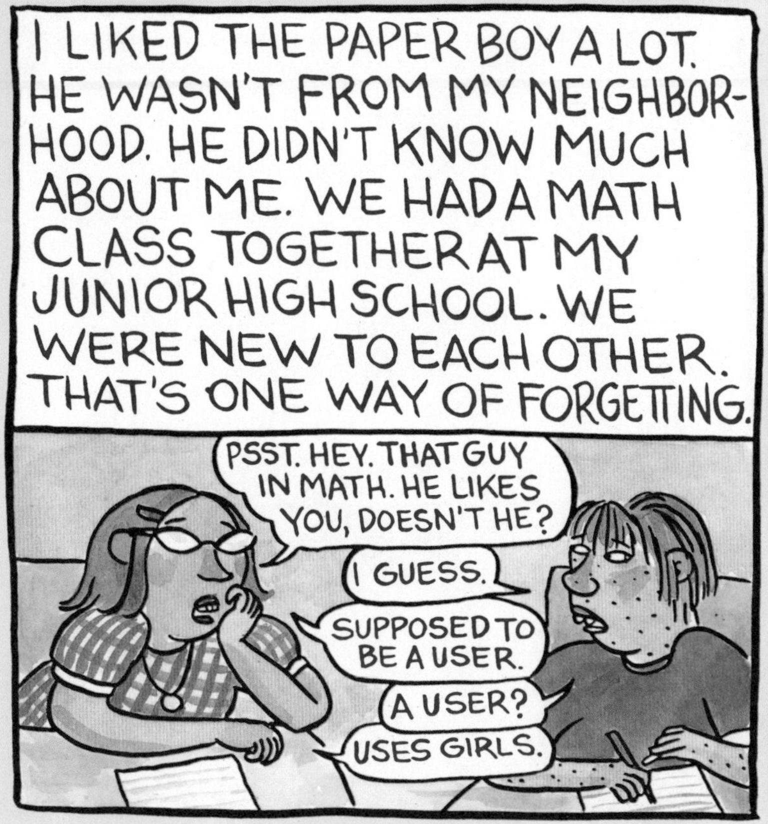
I LIKED THE PAPER BOY A LOT. HE WASN'T FROM MY NEIGHBORHOOD. HE DIDN'T KNOW MUCH ABOUT ME. WE HAD A MATH CLASS TOGETHER AT MY JUNIOR HIGH SCHOOL. WE WERE NEW TO EACH OTHER. THAT'S ONE WAY OF FORGETTING.
PSST. HEY. THAT GUY IN MATH. HE LIKES YOU, DOESN'T HE?
I GUESS.
SUPPOSED TO BE A USER.
A USER?
USES GIRLS.

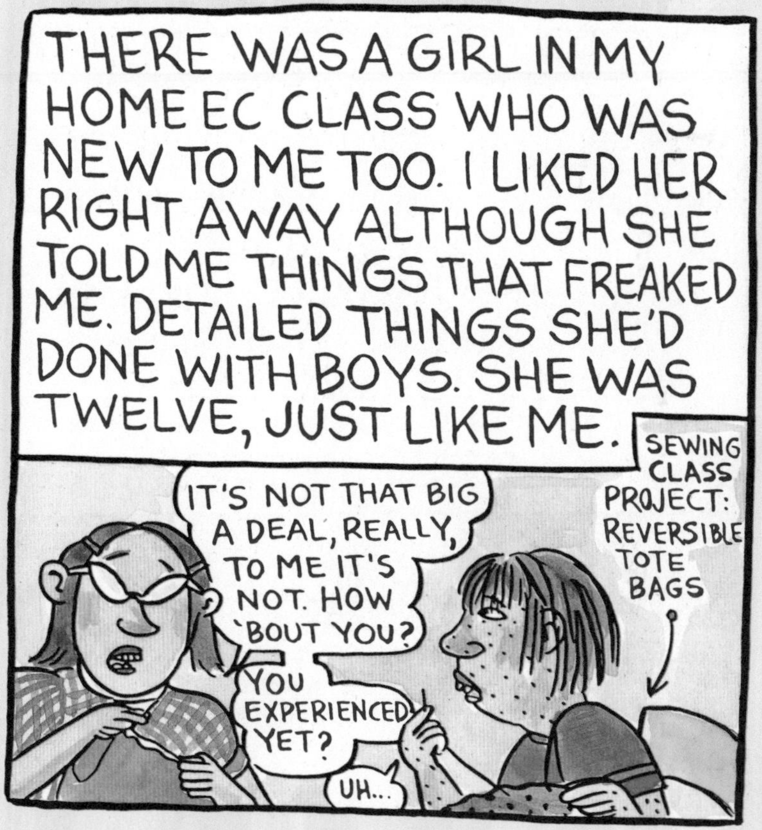
THERE WAS A GIRL IN MY HOME EC CLASS WHO WAS NEW TO ME TOO. I LIKED HER RIGHT AWAY ALTHOUGH SHE TOLD ME THINGS THAT FREAKED ME. DETAILED THINGS SHE'D DONE WITH BOYS. SHE WAS TWELVE, JUST LIKE ME.
SEWING CLASS PROJECT: REVERSIBLE TOTE BAGS
IT'S NOT THAT BIG A DEAL, REALLY, TO ME IT'S NOT. HOW 'BOUT YOU?
YOU EXPERIENCED YET?
UH...

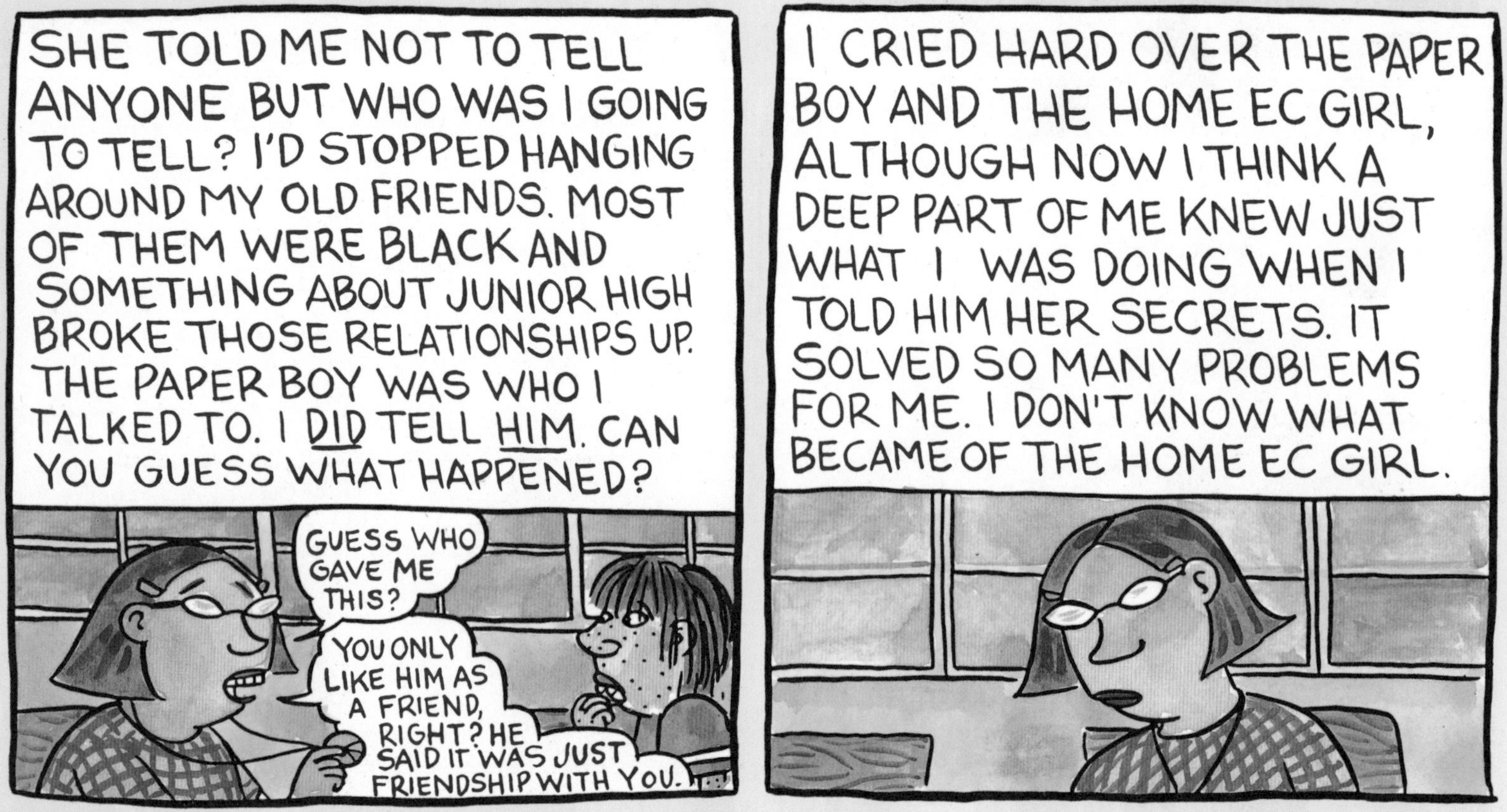
SHE TOLD ME NOT TO TELL ANYONE BUT WHO WAS I GOING TO TELL? I'D STOPPED HANGING AROUND MY OLD FRIENDS. MOST OF THEM WERE BLACK AND SOMETHING ABOUT JUNIOR HIGH BROKE THOSE RELATIONSHIPS UP. THE PAPER BOY WAS WHO I TALKED TO. I DID TELL HIM. CAN YOU GUESS WHAT HAPPENED?
GUESS WHO GAVE ME THIS?
YOU ONLY LIKE HIM AS A FRIEND, RIGHT? HE SAID IT WAS JUST FRIENDSHIP WITH YOU.
I CRIED HARD OVER THE PAPER BOY AND THE HOME EC GIRL, ALTHOUGH NOW I THINK A DEEP PART OF ME KNEW JUST WHAT I WAS DOING WHEN I TOLD HIM HER SECRETS. IT SOLVED SO MANY PROBLEMS FOR ME. I DON'T KNOW WHAT BECAME OF THE HOME EC GIRL.

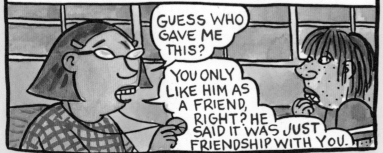

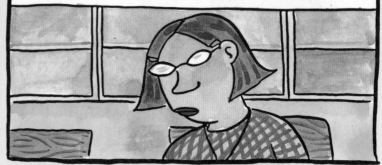

70

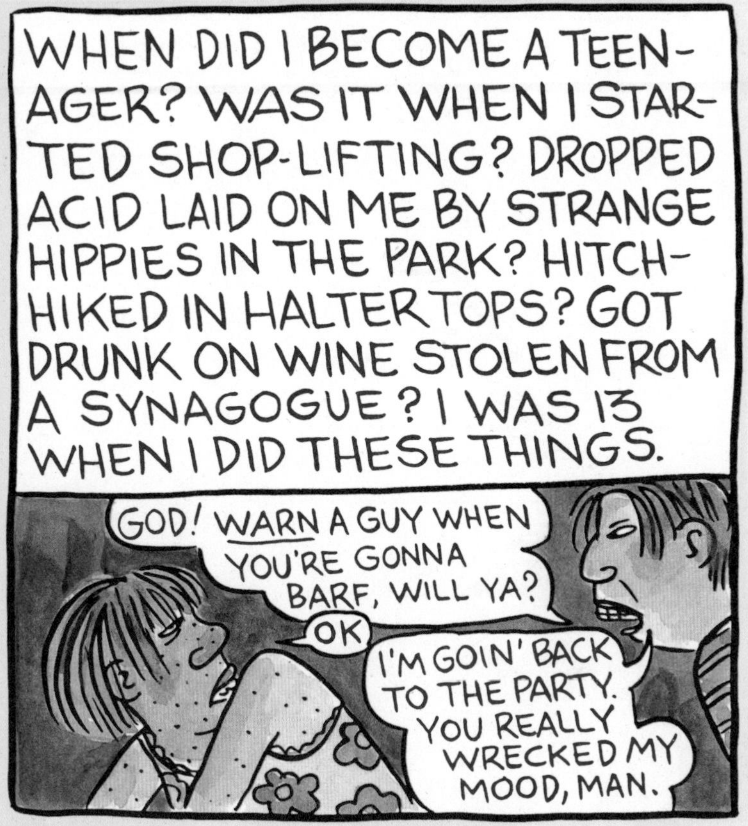
WHEN DID I BECOME A TEEN-AGER? WAS IT WHEN I STARTED SHOP-LIFTING? DROPPED ACID LAID ON ME BY STRANGE HIPPIES IN THE PARK? HITCH-HIKED IN HALTER TOPS? GOT DRUNK ON WINE STOLEN FROM A SYNAGOGUE? I WAS 13 WHEN I DID THESE THINGS.
GOD! WARN A GUY WHEN YOU'RE GONNA BARF, WILL YA?
OK
I'M GOIN' BACK TO THE PARTY. YOU REALLY WRECKED MY MOOD, MAN.

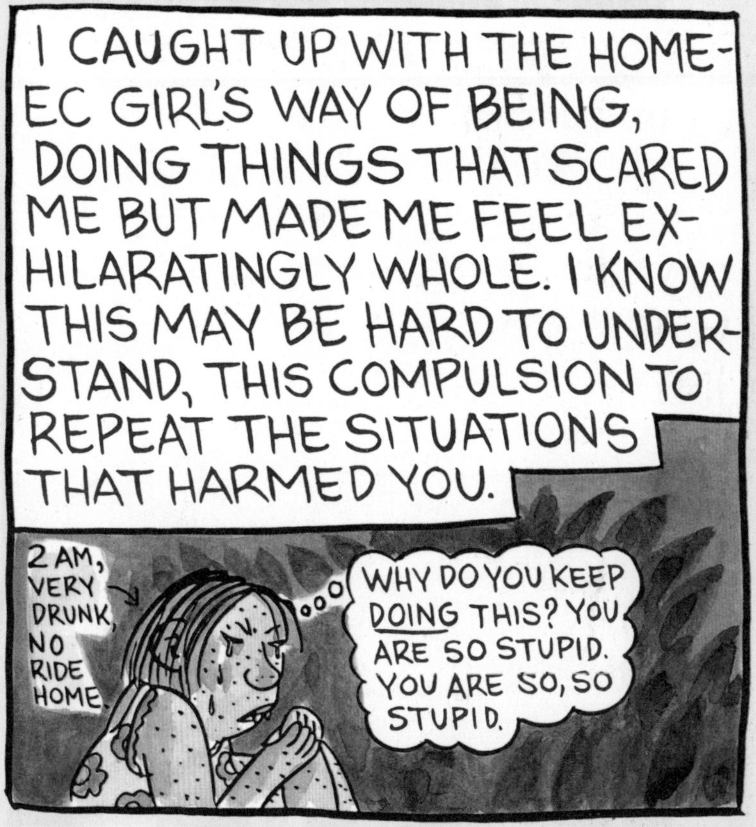
I CAUGHT UP WITH THE HOME-EC GIRL'S WAY OF BEING, DOING THINGS THAT SCARED ME BUT MADE ME FEEL EX-HILARATINGLY WHOLE. I KNOW THIS MAY BE HARD TO UNDER-STAND, THIS COMPULSION TO REPEAT THE SITUATIONS THAT HARMED YOU.
2 AM, VERY DRUNK, NO RIDE HOME
WHY DO YOU KEEP DOING THIS? YOU ARE SO STUPID. YOU ARE SO, SO STUPID.

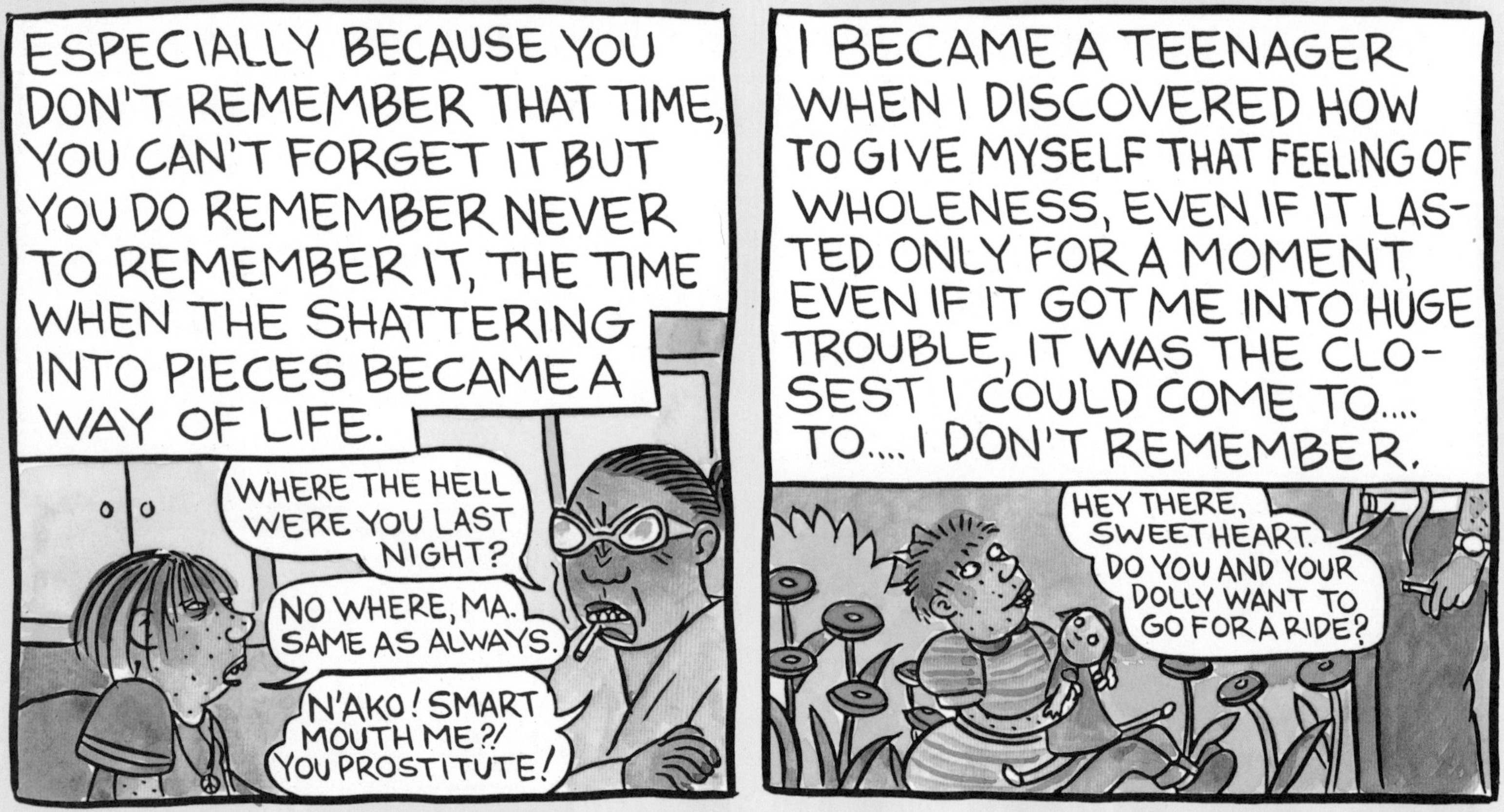
ESPECIALLY BECAUSE YOU DON'T REMEMBER THAT TIME, YOU CAN'T FORGET IT BUT YOU DO REMEMBER NEVER TO REMEMBER IT, THE TIME WHEN THE SHATTERING INTO PIECES BECAME A WAY OF LIFE.
WHERE THE HELL WERE YOU LAST NIGHT?
NO WHERE, MA. SAME AS ALWAYS.
N'AKO! SMART MOUTH ME?! YOU PROSTITUTE!
I BECAME A TEENAGER WHEN I DISCOVERED HOW TO GIVE MYSELF THAT FEELING OF WHOLENESS, EVEN IF IT LASTED ONLY FOR A MOMENT, EVEN IF IT GOT ME INTO HUGE TROUBLE, IT WAS THE CLOSEST I COULD COME TO.... TO.... I DON'T REMEMBER.
HEY THERE, SWEETHEART. DO YOU AND YOUR DOLLY WANT TO GO FOR A RIDE?

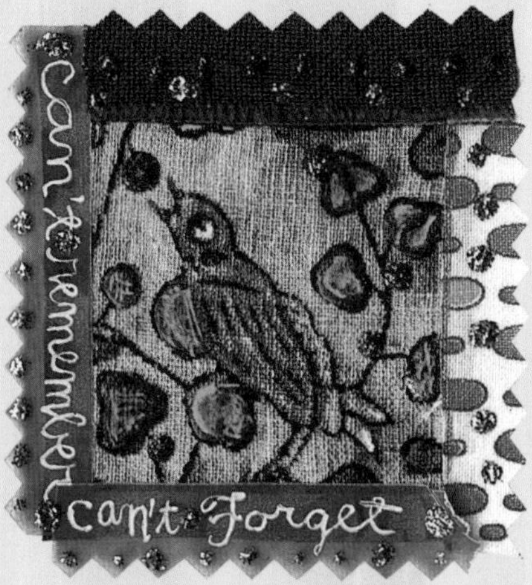

can't remember
can't forget

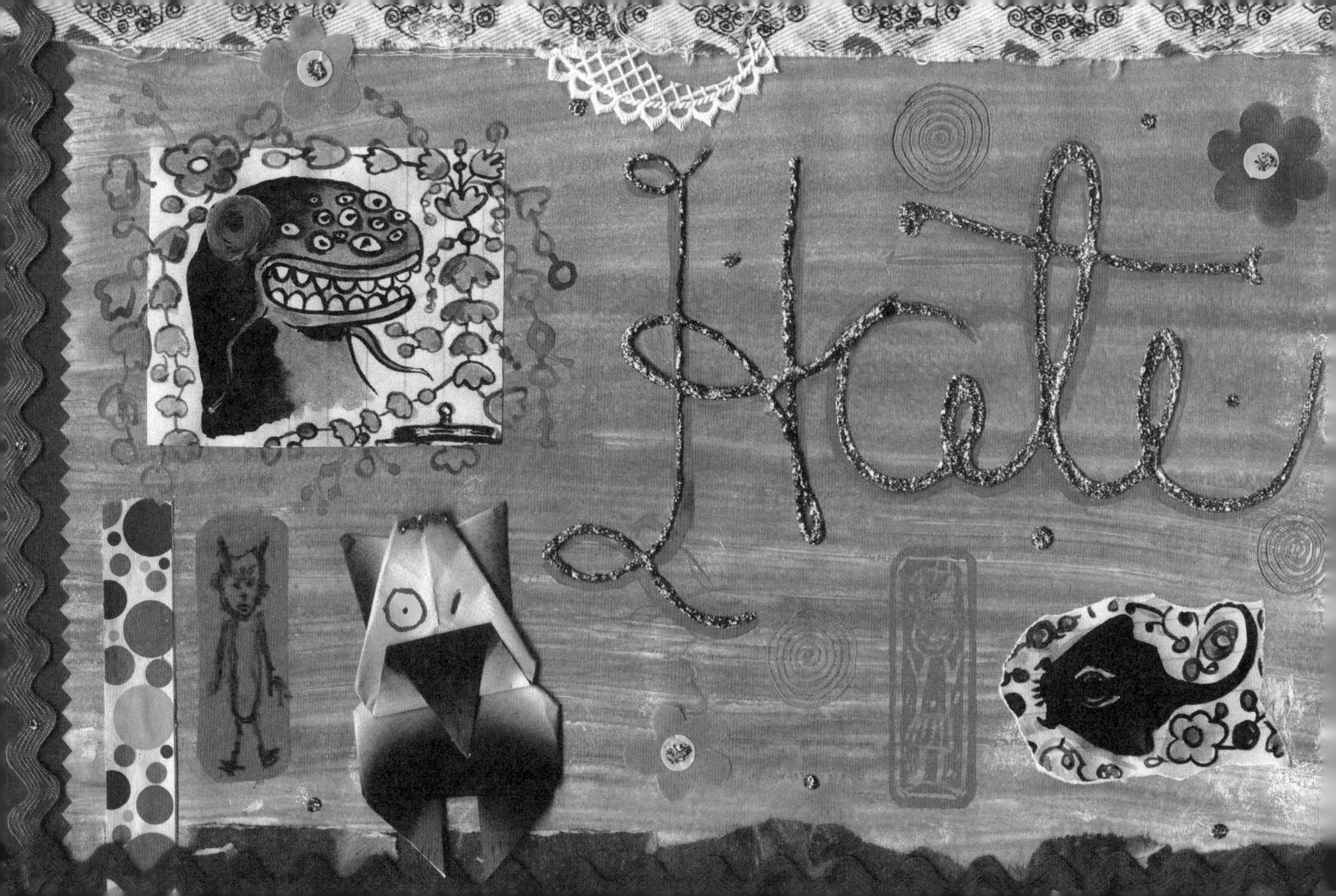
Hate

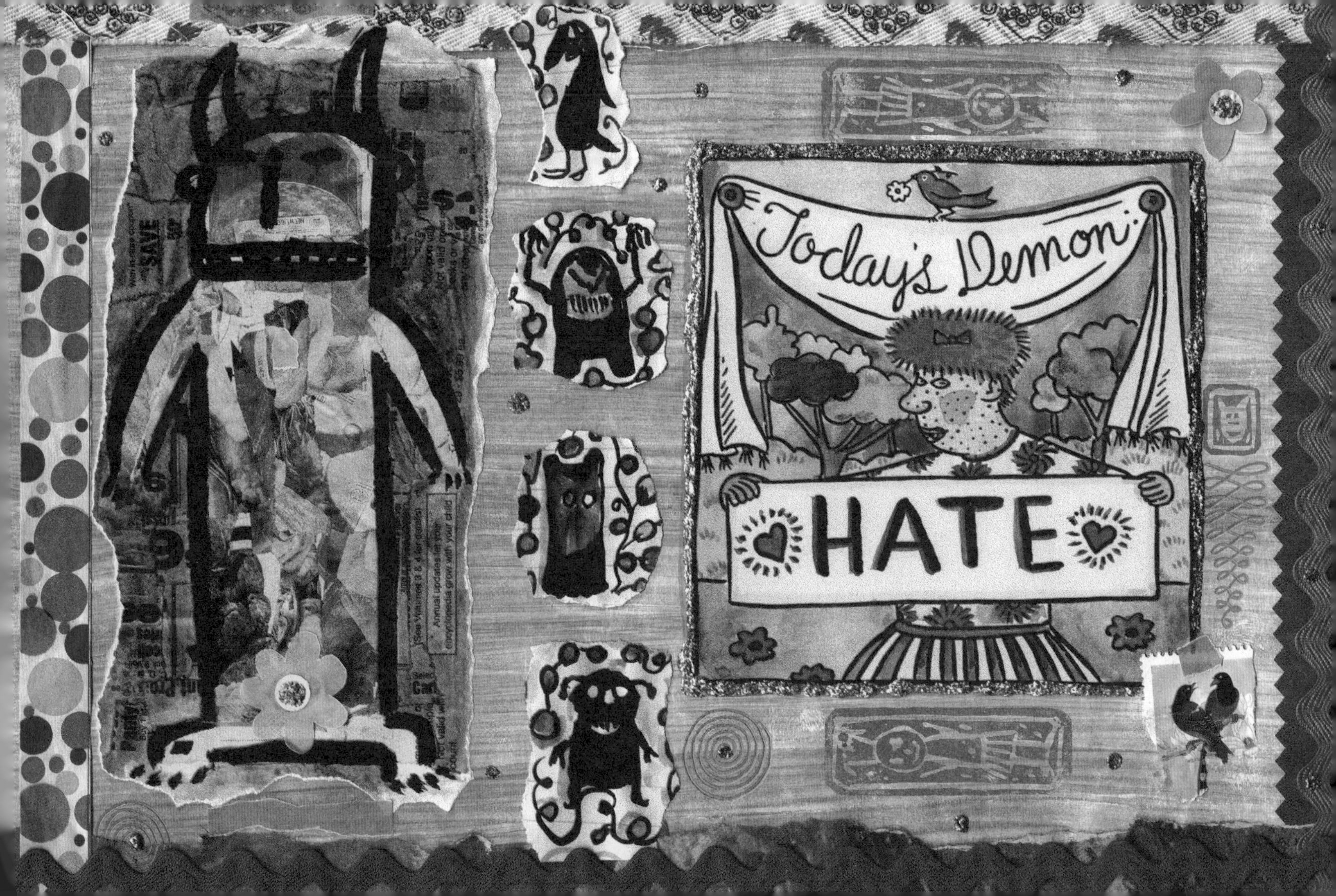
Today's Demon:
HATE

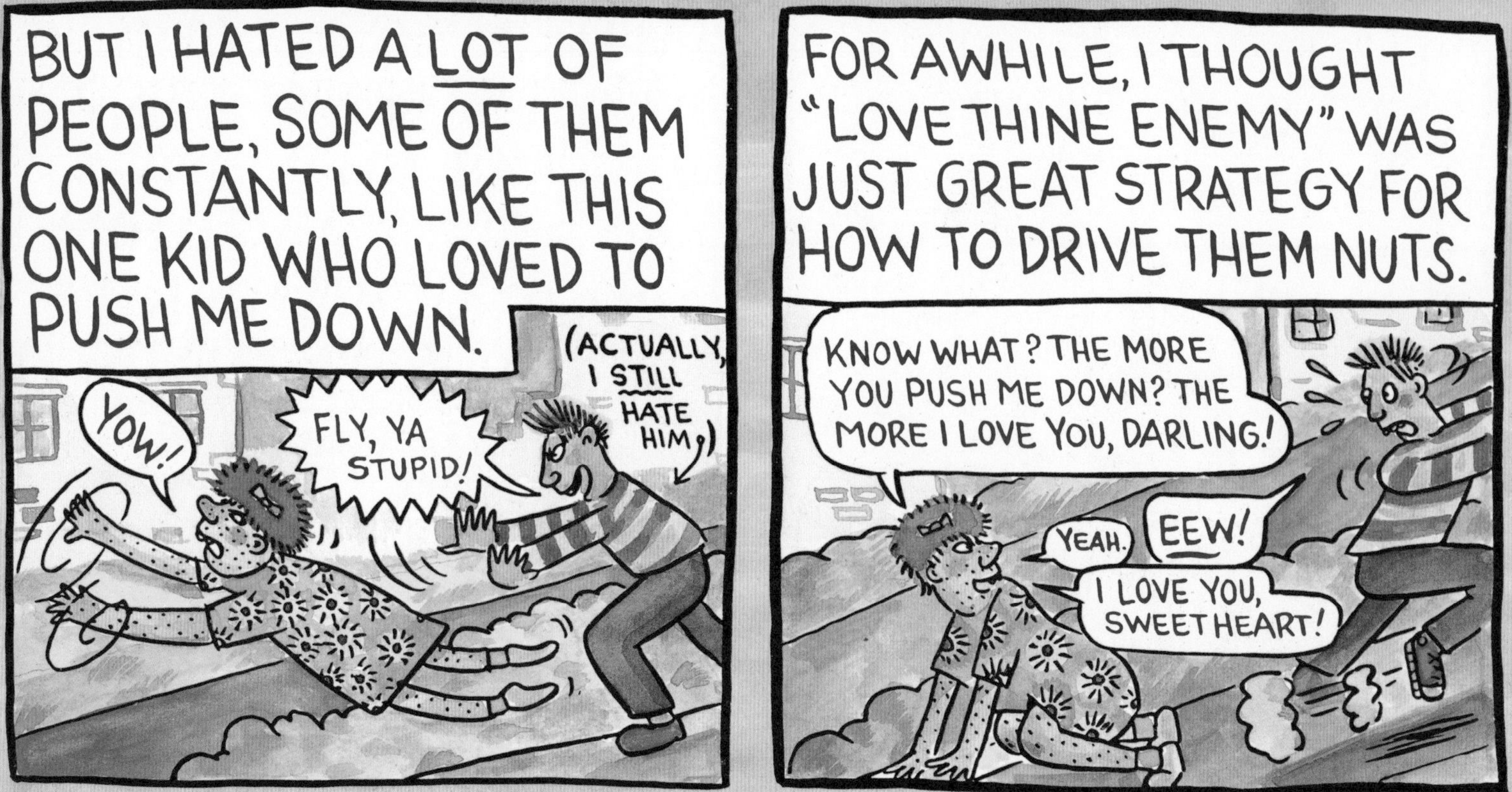
BUT I HATED A LOT OF PEOPLE, SOME OF THEM CONSTANTLY, LIKE THIS ONE KID WHO LOVED TO PUSH ME DOWN.
YOW!
FLY, YA STUPID!
(ACTUALLY, I STILL HATE HIM.)
FOR AWHILE, I THOUGHT "LOVE THINE ENEMY" WAS JUST GREAT STRATEGY FOR HOW TO DRIVE THEM NUTS.
KNOW WHAT? THE MORE YOU PUSH ME DOWN? THE MORE I LOVE YOU, DARLING!
YEAH.
EEW!
I LOVE YOU, SWEETHEART!

79

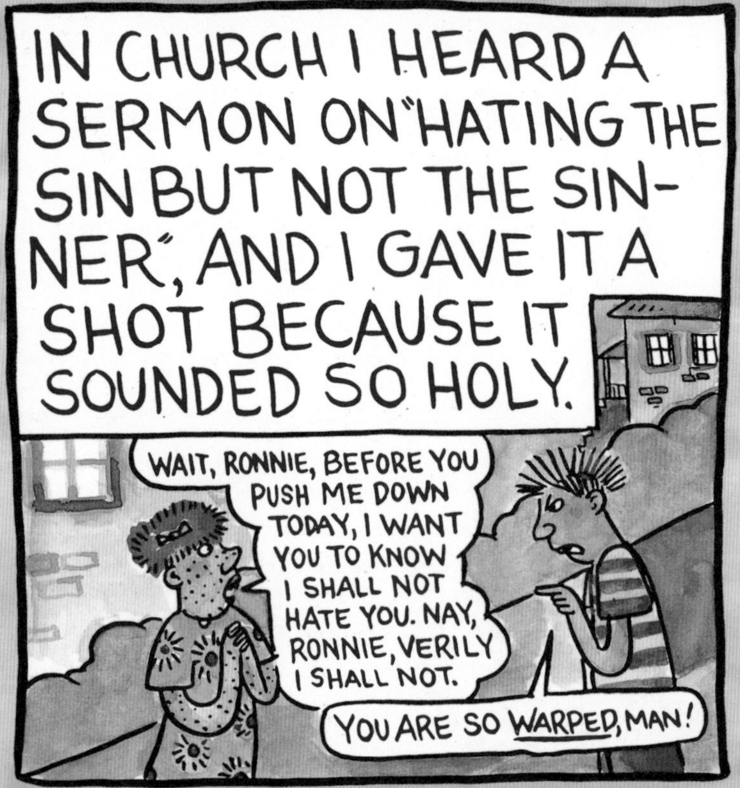
IN CHURCH I HEARD A SERMON ON "HATING THE SIN BUT NOT THE SINNER", AND I GAVE IT A SHOT BECAUSE IT SOUNDED SO HOLY.
WAIT, RONNIE, BEFORE YOU PUSH ME DOWN TODAY, I WANT YOU TO KNOW I SHALL NOT HATE YOU. NAY, RONNIE, VERILY I SHALL NOT.
YOU ARE SO WARPED, MAN!

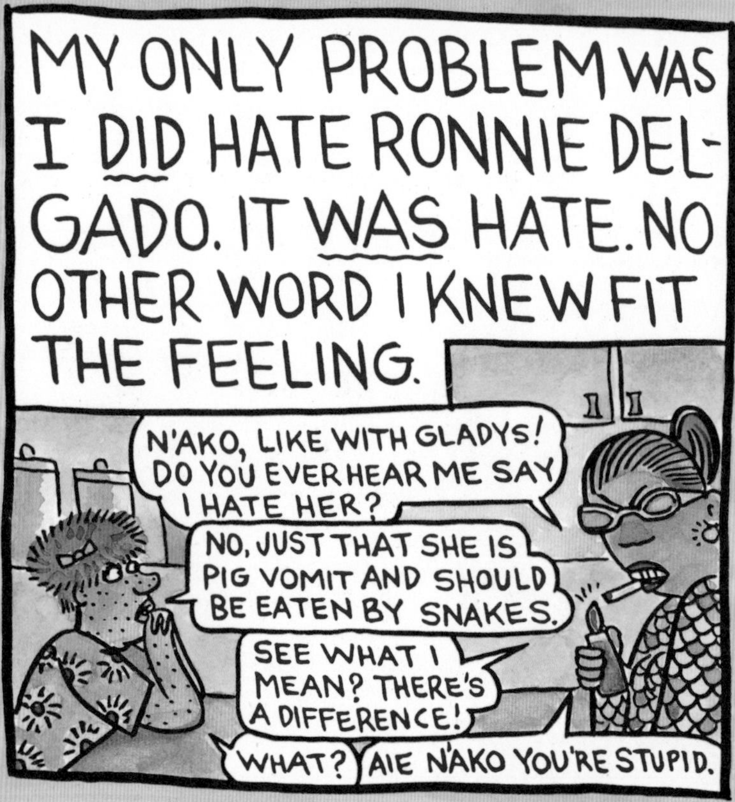
MY ONLY PROBLEM WAS I DID HATE RONNIE DELGADO. IT WAS HATE. NO OTHER WORD I KNEW FIT THE FEELING.
N'AKO, LIKE WITH GLADYS! DO YOU EVER HEAR ME SAY I HATE HER?
NO, JUST THAT SHE IS PIG VOMIT AND SHOULD BE EATEN BY SNAKES.
SEE WHAT I MEAN? THERE'S A DIFFERENCE!
WHAT?
AIE N'AKO YOU'RE STUPID.

81

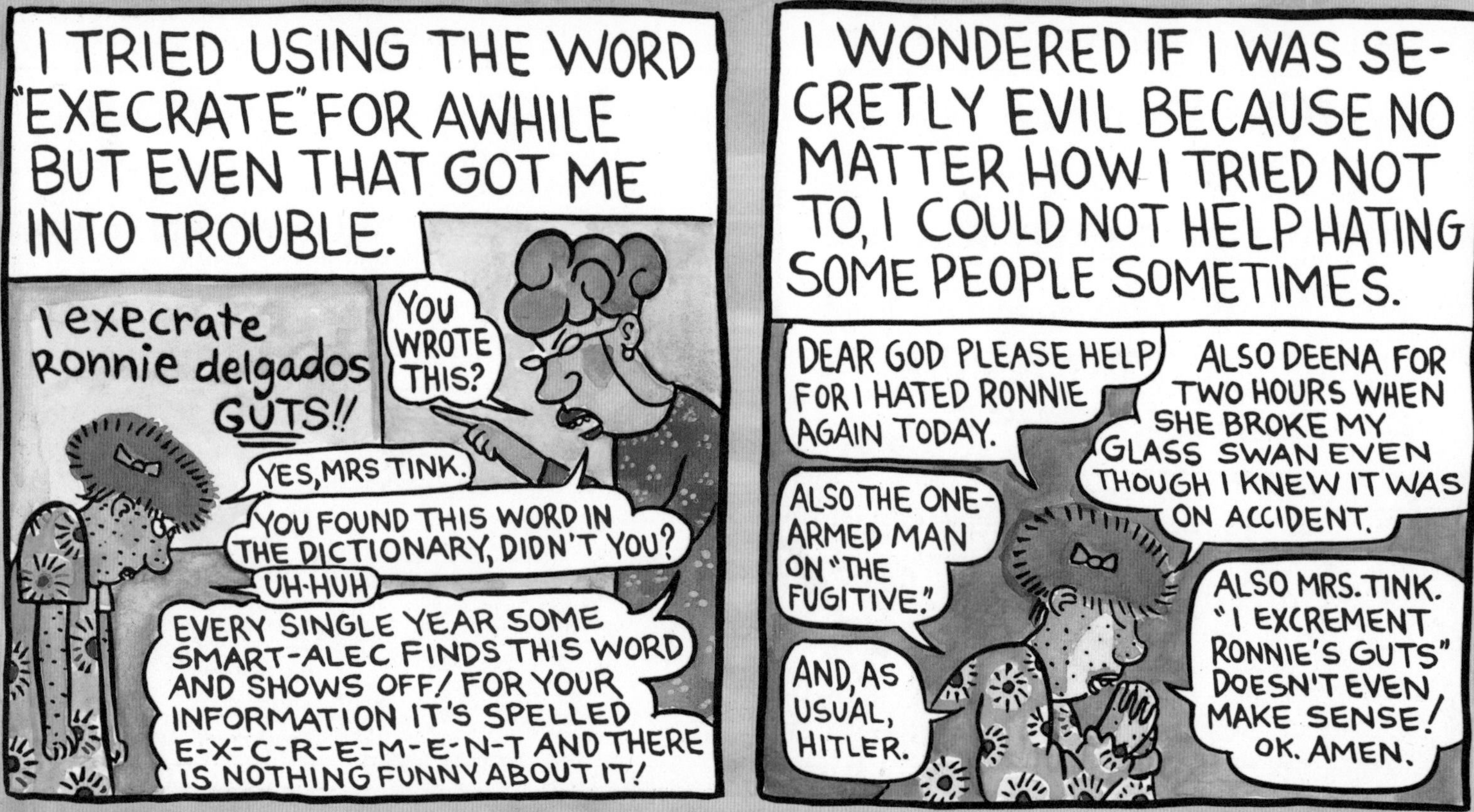
I TRIED USING THE WORD "EXECRATE" FOR AWHILE BUT EVEN THAT GOT ME INTO TROUBLE.
I execrate ronnie delgados GUTS!!
YOU WROTE THIS?
YES, MRS TINK.
YOU FOUND THIS WORD IN THE DICTIONARY, DIDN'T YOU?
UH-HUH
EVERY SINGLE YEAR SOME SMART-ALEC FINDS THIS WORD AND SHOWS OFF! FOR YOUR INFORMATION IT'S SPELLED E-X-C-R-E-M-E-N-T AND THERE IS NOTHING FUNNY ABOUT IT!
I WONDERED IF I WAS SE-CRETLY EVIL BECAUSE NO MATTER HOW I TRIED NOT TO, I COULD NOT HELP HATING SOME PEOPLE SOMETIMES.
DEAR GOD PLEASE HELP FOR I HATED RONNIE AGAIN TODAY.
ALSO DEENA FOR TWO HOURS WHEN SHE BROKE MY GLASS SWAN EVEN THOUGH I KNEW IT WAS ON ACCIDENT.
ALSO THE ONE-ARMED MAN ON "THE FUGITIVE."
ALSO MRS. TINK. "I EXCREMENT RONNIE'S GUTS" DOESN'T EVEN MAKE SENSE! OK. AMEN.
AND, AS USUAL, HITLER.

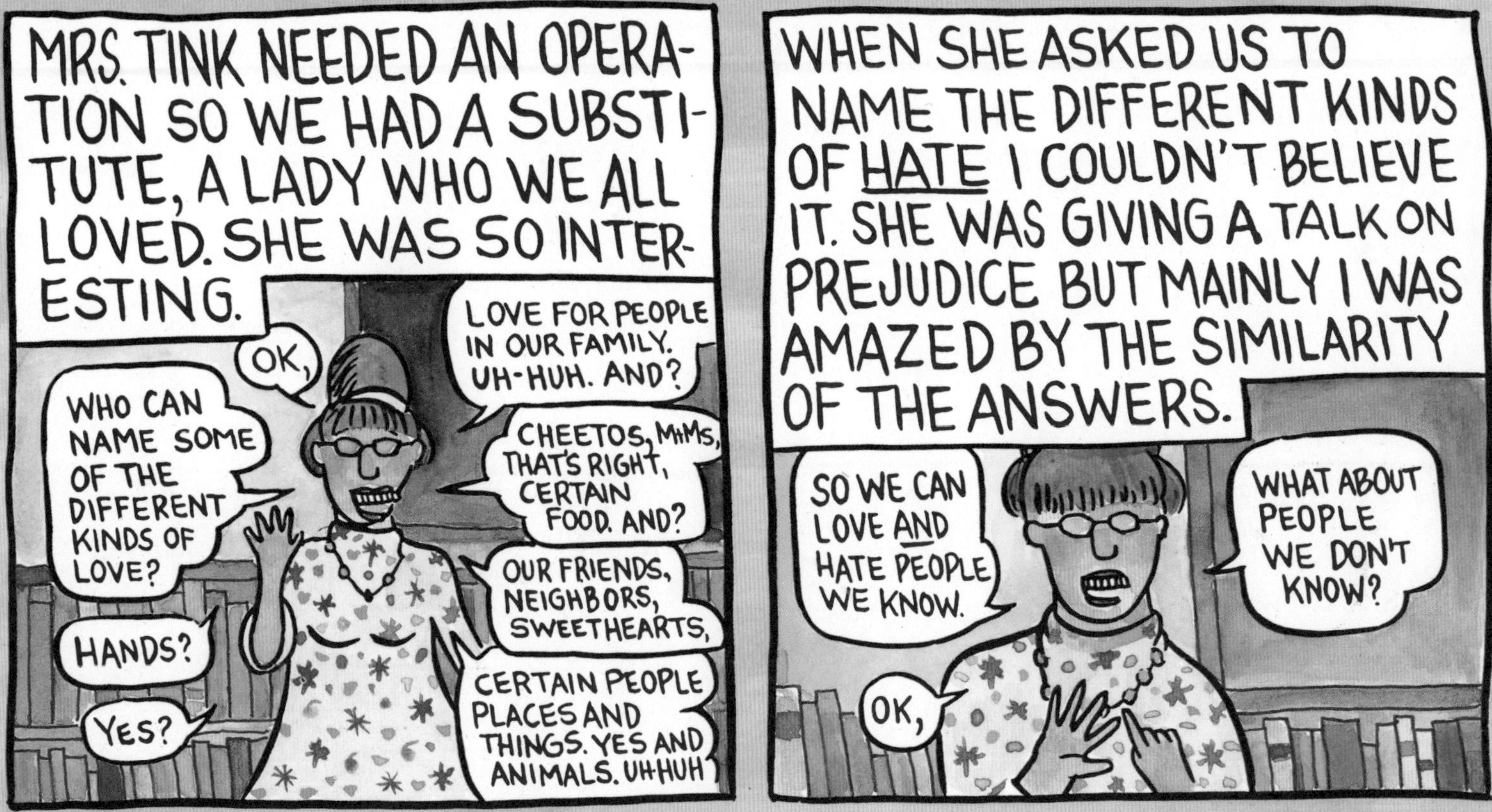
MRS. TINK NEEDED AN OPERATION SO WE HAD A SUBSTITUTE, A LADY WHO WE ALL LOVED. SHE WAS SO INTERESTING.
WHO CAN NAME SOME OF THE DIFFERENT KINDS OF LOVE?
HANDS?
YES?
OK,
LOVE FOR PEOPLE IN OUR FAMILY. UH-HUH. AND?
CHEETOS, M&MS, THAT'S RIGHT, CERTAIN FOOD. AND?
OUR FRIENDS, NEIGHBORS, SWEETHEARTS,
CERTAIN PEOPLE PLACES AND THINGS. YES AND ANIMALS. UH-HUH
WHEN SHE ASKED US TO NAME THE DIFFERENT KINDS OF HATE I COULDN'T BELIEVE IT. SHE WAS GIVING A TALK ON PREJUDICE BUT MAINLY I WAS AMAZED BY THE SIMILARITY OF THE ANSWERS.
SO WE CAN LOVE AND HATE PEOPLE WE KNOW.
OK,
WHAT ABOUT PEOPLE WE DON'T KNOW?

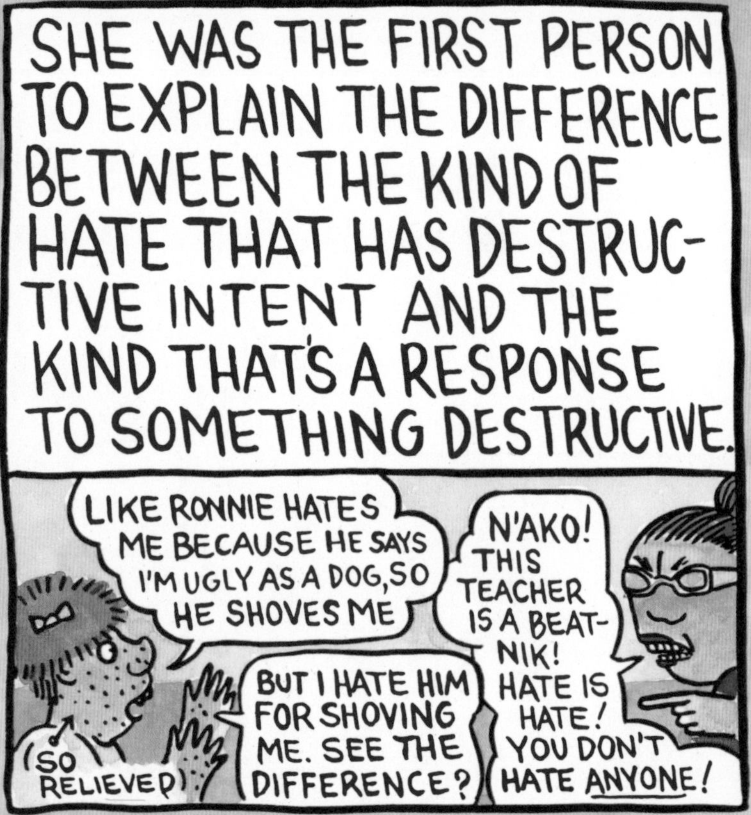
SHE WAS THE FIRST PERSON TO EXPLAIN THE DIFFERENCE BETWEEN THE KIND OF HATE THAT HAS DESTRUCTIVE INTENT AND THE KIND THAT'S A RESPONSE TO SOMETHING DESTRUCTIVE.
LIKE RONNIE HATES ME BECAUSE HE SAYS I'M UGLY AS A DOG, SO HE SHOVES ME
(SO RELIEVED)
BUT I HATE HIM FOR SHOVING ME. SEE THE DIFFERENCE?
N'AKO! THIS TEACHER IS A BEATNIK! HATE IS HATE! YOU DON'T HATE ANYONE!

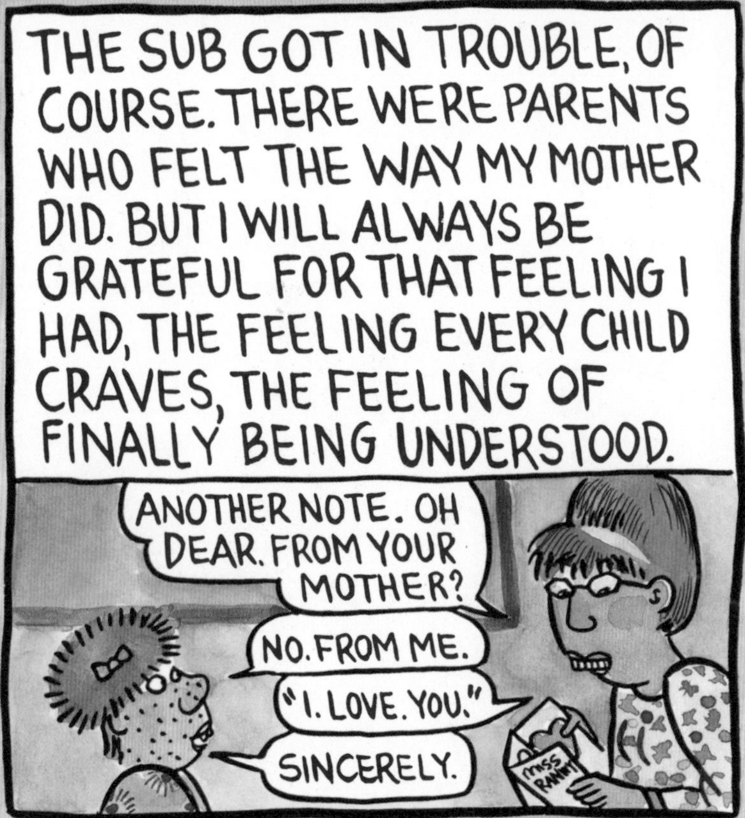
THE SUB GOT IN TROUBLE, OF COURSE. THERE WERE PARENTS WHO FELT THE WAY MY MOTHER DID. BUT I WILL ALWAYS BE GRATEFUL FOR THAT FEELING I HAD, THE FEELING EVERY CHILD CRAVES, THE FEELING OF FINALLY BEING UNDERSTOOD.
ANOTHER NOTE. OH DEAR. FROM YOUR MOTHER?
NO. FROM ME.
"I. LOVE. YOU."
SINCERELY.

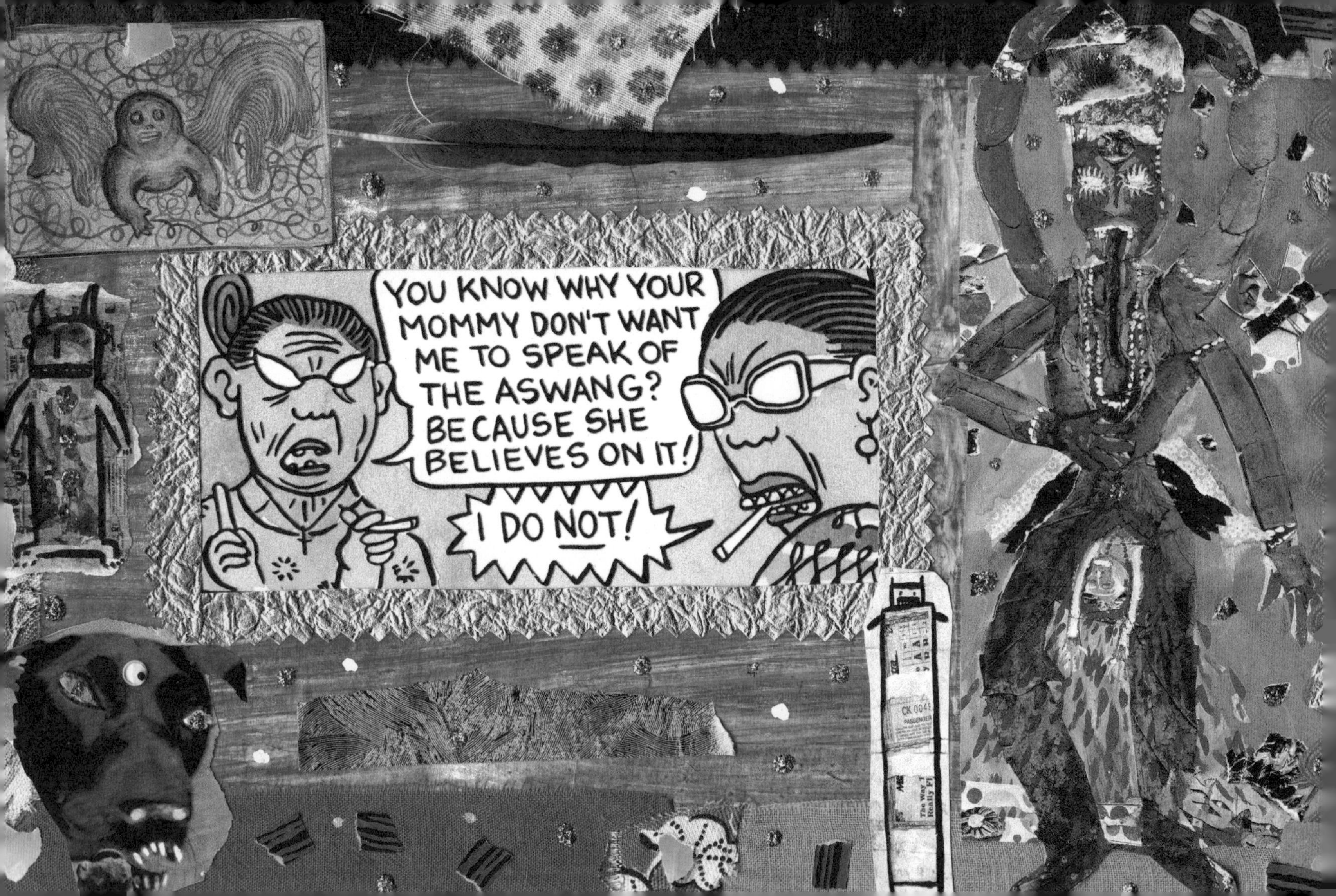
YOU KNOW WHY YOUR MOMMY DON'T WANT ME TO SPEAK OF THE ASWANG? BECAUSE SHE BELIEVES ON IT!
I DO NOT!

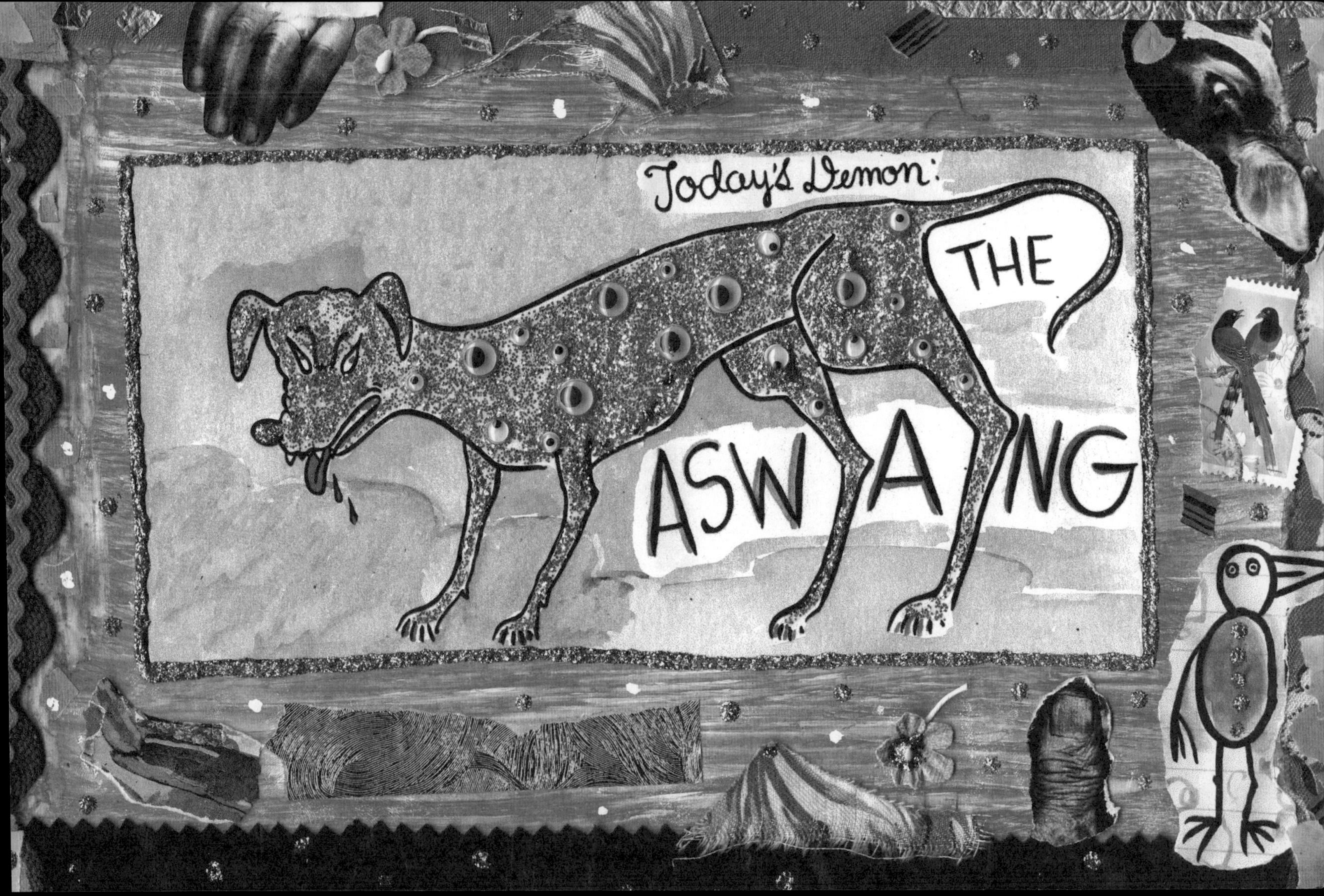
Today's Demon:
THE
ASWANG

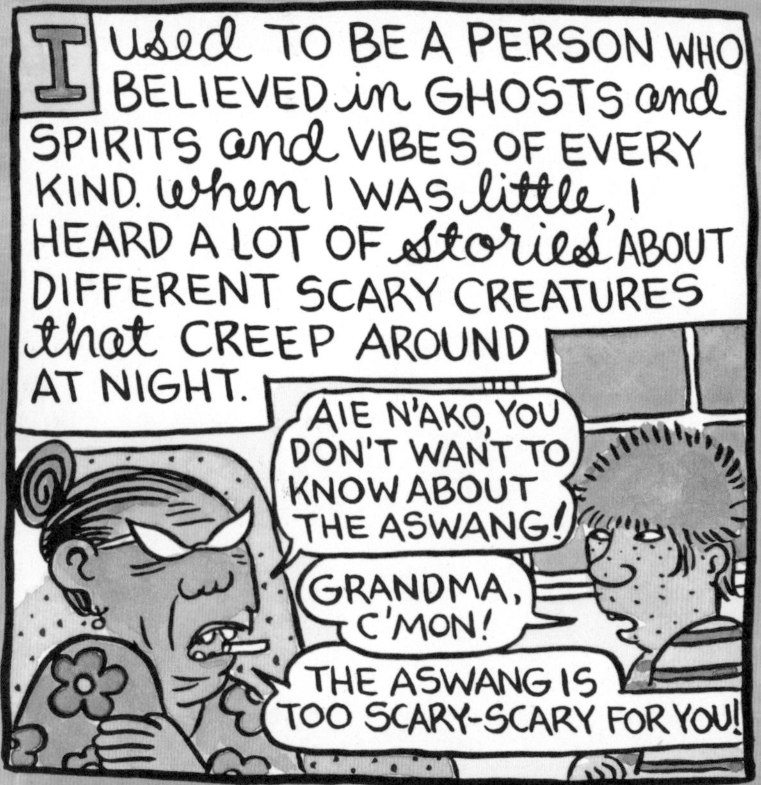
I used TO BE A PERSON WHO BELIEVED in GHOSTS and SPIRITS and VIBES OF EVERY KIND. When I WAS little, I HEARD A LOT OF stories ABOUT DIFFERENT SCARY CREATURES that CREEP AROUND AT NIGHT.
AIE N'AKO, YOU DON'T WANT TO KNOW ABOUT THE ASWANG!
GRANDMA, C'MON!
THE ASWANG IS TOO SCARY-SCARY FOR YOU!

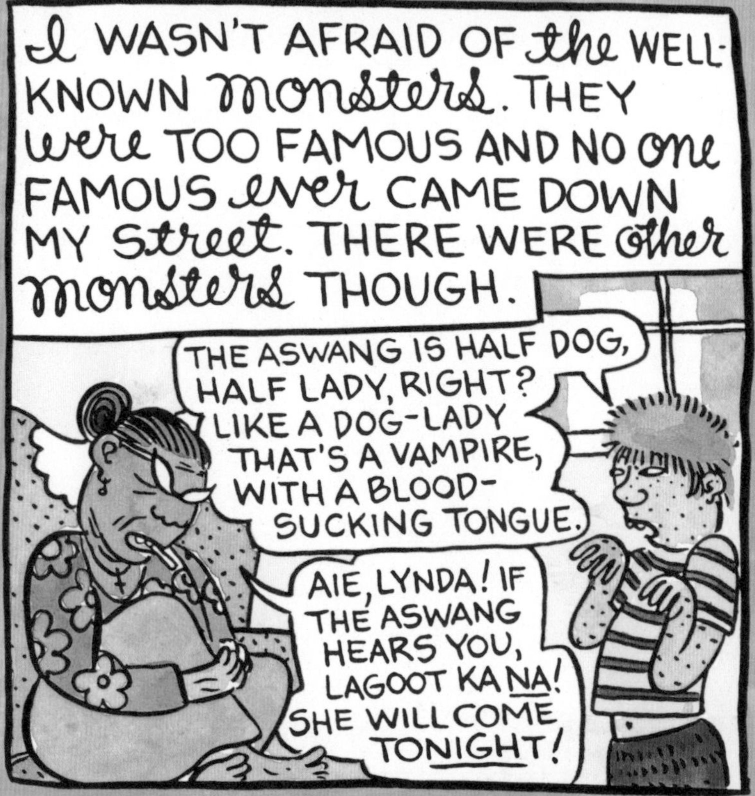
I WASN'T AFRAID OF the WELL-KNOWN monsters. THEY were TOO FAMOUS AND NO one FAMOUS ever CAME DOWN MY street. THERE WERE other monsters THOUGH.
THE ASWANG IS HALF DOG, HALF LADY, RIGHT? LIKE A DOG-LADY THAT'S A VAMPIRE, WITH A BLOOD-SUCKING TONGUE.
AIE, LYNDA! IF THE ASWANG HEARS YOU, LAGOOT KA NA! SHE WILL COME TONIGHT!

90

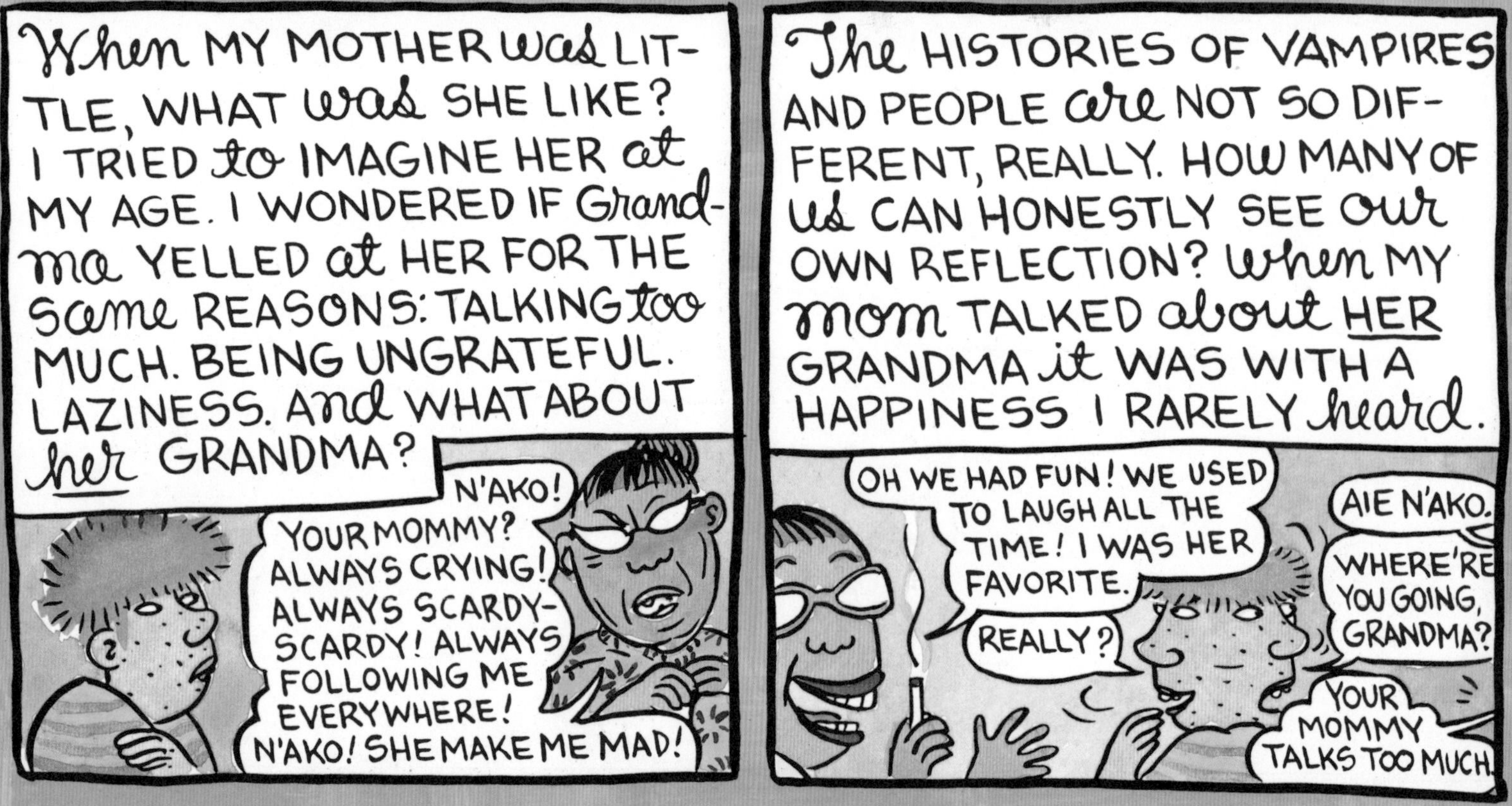
When MY MOTHER was LITTLE, WHAT was SHE LIKE? I TRIED to IMAGINE HER at MY AGE. I WONDERED IF Grandma YELLED at HER FOR THE same REASONS: TALKING too MUCH. BEING UNGRATEFUL. LAZINESS. And WHAT ABOUT her GRANDMA?
N'AKO!
YOUR MOMMY? ALWAYS CRYING! ALWAYS SCARDY-SCARDY! ALWAYS FOLLOWING ME EVERYWHERE!
N'AKO! SHE MAKE ME MAD!
The HISTORIES OF VAMPIRES AND PEOPLE are NOT SO DIFFERENT, REALLY. HOW MANY OF us CAN HONESTLY SEE our OWN REFLECTION? When MY mom TALKED about HER GRANDMA it WAS WITH A HAPPINESS I RARELY heard.
OH WE HAD FUN! WE USED TO LAUGH ALL THE TIME! I WAS HER FAVORITE.
REALLY?
AIE N'AKO.
WHERE'RE YOU GOING, GRANDMA?
YOUR MOMMY TALKS TOO MUCH.

In THE EXPOSING LIGHT OF DAY, HOW MANY OF *our* DARK TRUTHS WOULD CAUSE US TO FEEL *an* AGONY WE *could not* ENDURE? EVEN THE MOST INEXPERIENCED VAMPIRES KNOW THEY *must* AVOID *the* SUN AT ALL COSTS.

GRANDMA. WHAT'S WRONG?

NOTHING.

IS IT 'CAUSE WE WERE TALKING ABOUT YOUR MOM?

AIE N'AKO. GO <u>AWAY</u> FROM ME!

Mom USED TO *Scream* THAT SHE COULDN'T WAIT UNTIL *I had* CHILDREN SO *I* WOULD KNOW *what* HELL WAS LIKE. MY GRANDMA *would* PUT HER *arm* AROUND ME AND LAUGH. I LOVED *them* BOTH. IT *was in* MY BLOOD *to* LOVE *them*.

YOU WAIT! YOU'LL SEE! YOU'LL BE SO SORRY YOU EVER HAD KIDS! CHILDREN ARE A PUNISHMENT! YOU JUST WAIT!

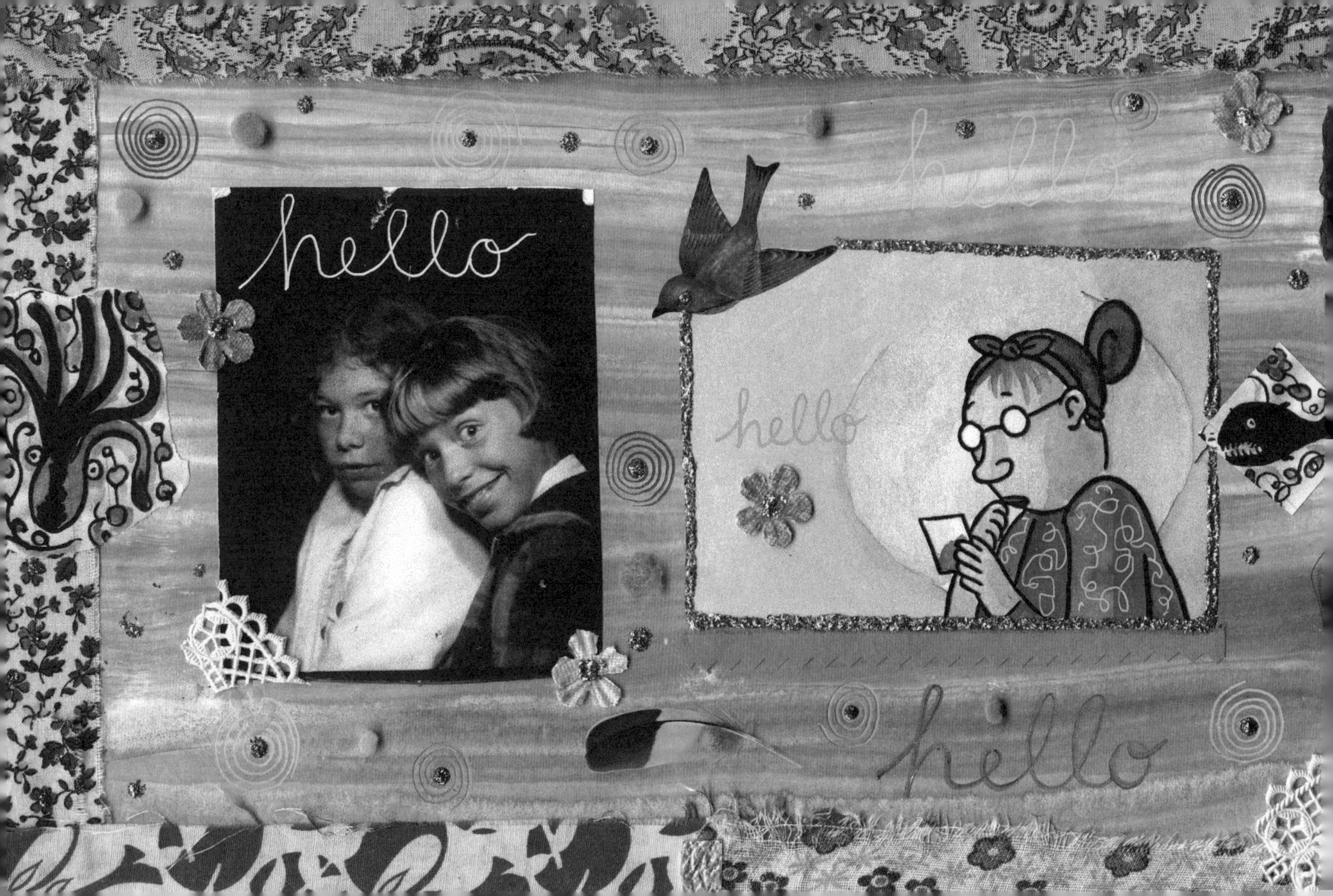
hello
hello
hello
hello

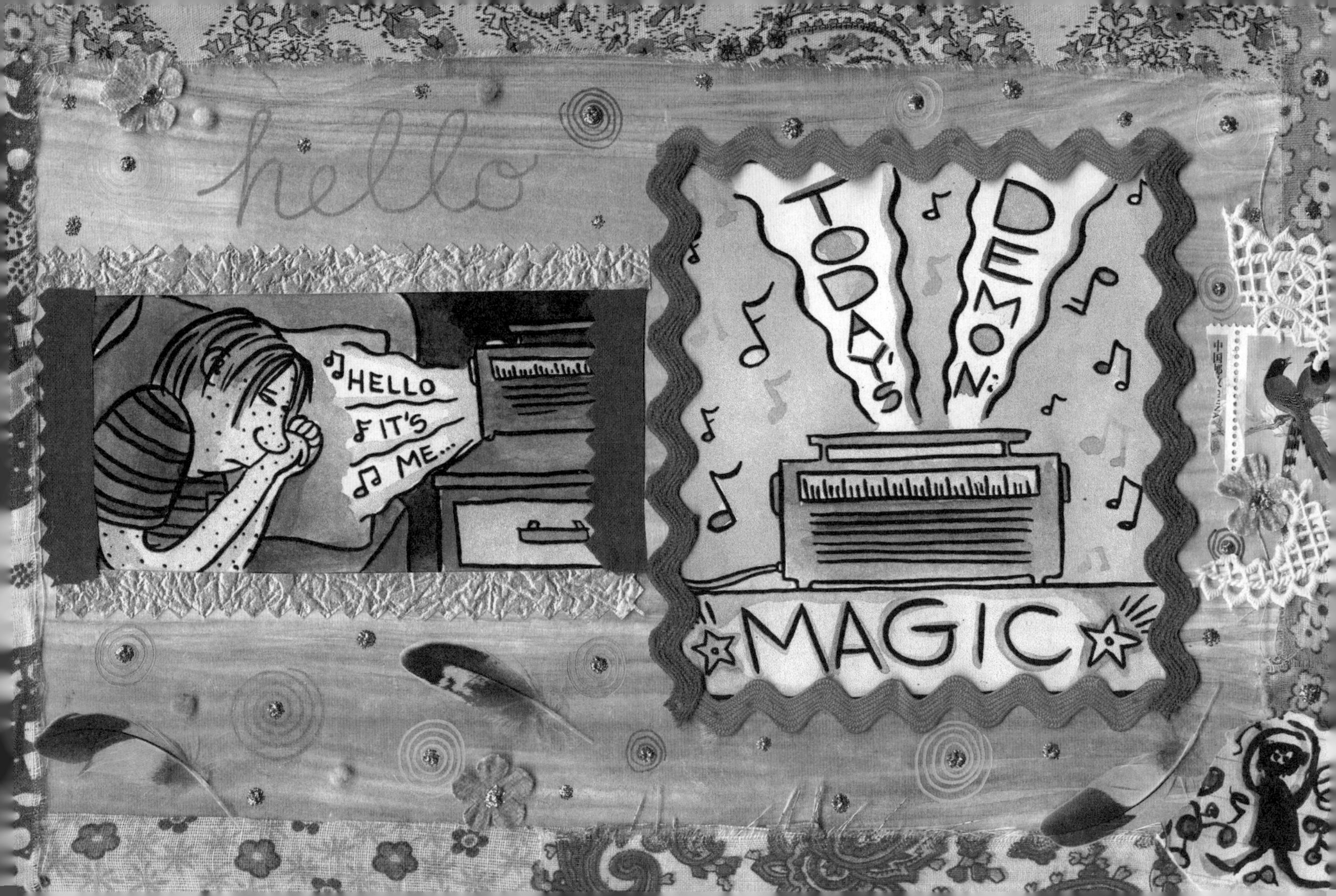

hello
HELLO
IT'S
ME...
TODAY'S
DEMON:
MAGIC

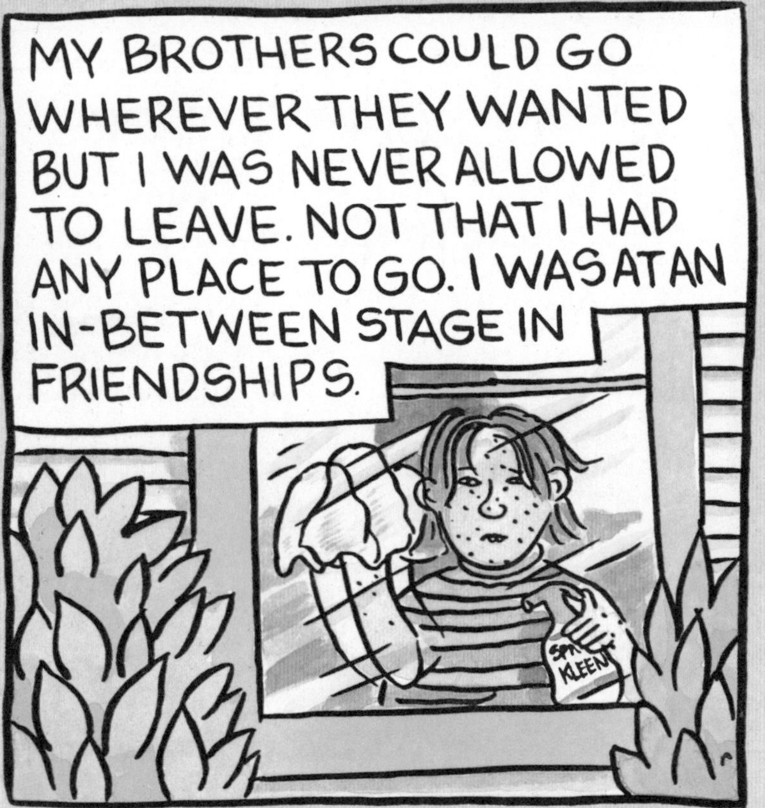
MY BROTHERS COULD GO WHEREVER THEY WANTED BUT I WAS NEVER ALLOWED TO LEAVE. NOT THAT I HAD ANY PLACE TO GO. I WAS AT AN IN-BETWEEN STAGE IN FRIENDSHIPS.
SPRA KLEEN

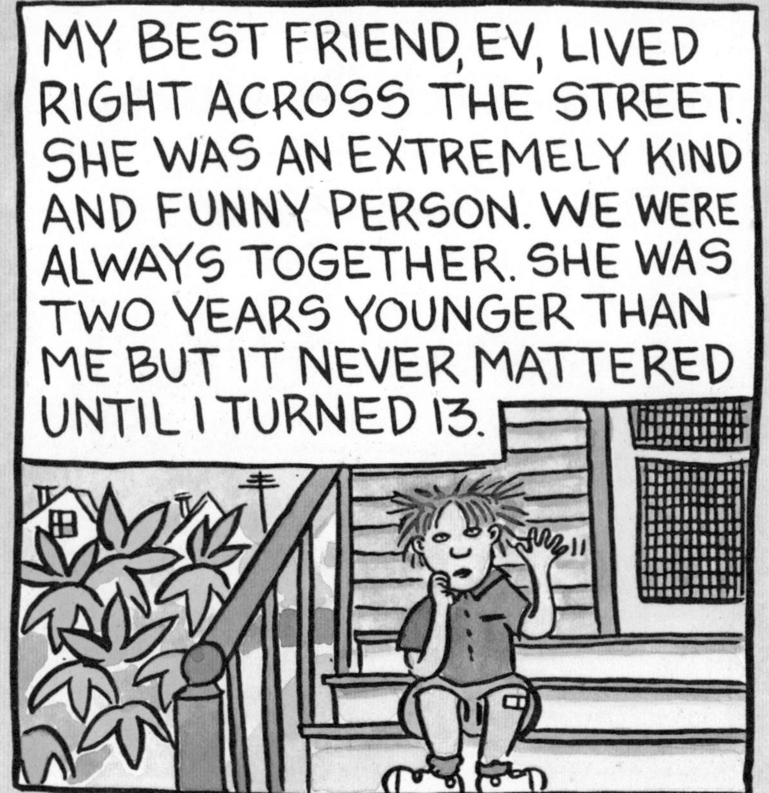
MY BEST FRIEND, EV, LIVED RIGHT ACROSS THE STREET. SHE WAS AN EXTREMELY KIND AND FUNNY PERSON. WE WERE ALWAYS TOGETHER. SHE WAS TWO YEARS YOUNGER THAN ME BUT IT NEVER MATTERED UNTIL I TURNED 13.

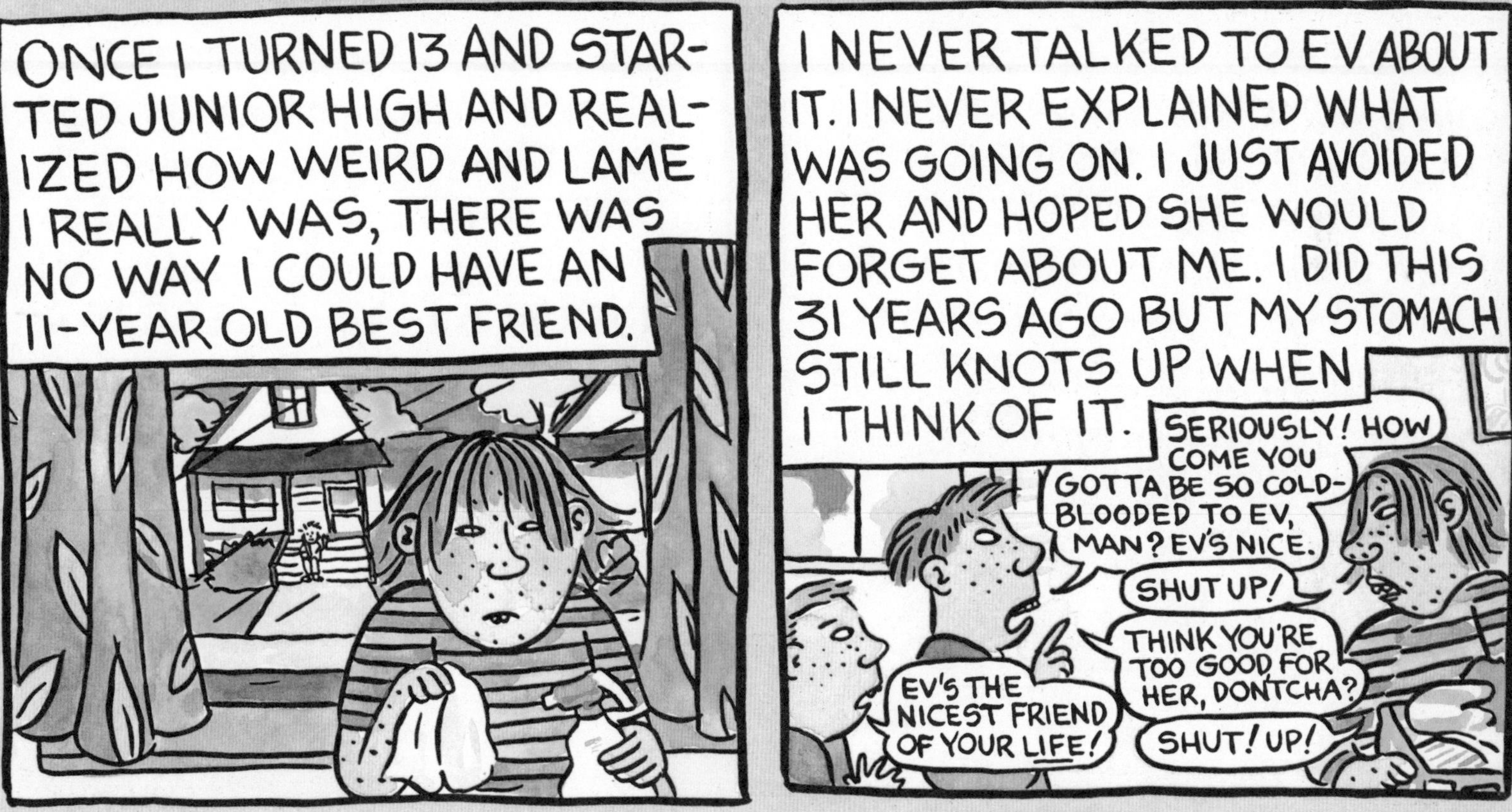
ONCE I TURNED 13 AND STARTED JUNIOR HIGH AND REALIZED HOW WEIRD AND LAME I REALLY WAS, THERE WAS NO WAY I COULD HAVE AN 11-YEAR OLD BEST FRIEND.
I NEVER TALKED TO EV ABOUT IT. I NEVER EXPLAINED WHAT WAS GOING ON. I JUST AVOIDED HER AND HOPED SHE WOULD FORGET ABOUT ME. I DID THIS 31 YEARS AGO BUT MY STOMACH STILL KNOTS UP WHEN I THINK OF IT.
SERIOUSLY! HOW COME YOU GOTTA BE SO COLD-BLOODED TO EV, MAN? EV'S NICE.
SHUT UP!
THINK YOU'RE TOO GOOD FOR HER, DONTCHA?
EV'S THE NICEST FRIEND OF YOUR LIFE!
SHUT! UP!

IT WASN'T ONLY THAT SHE WAS YOUNGER. SOMETHING HAD HAPPENED INSIDE OF ME. I DIDN'T HAVE A NAME FOR IT. MAYBE IT WAS THE THING THAT HITS WHEN YOU STOP BELIEVING IN MAGIC.

ONE DAY YOU JUST NOTICE SOMETHING IS GONE. POSSIBILITY IS GONE. IT'S SO GONE THAT EVERYONE AROUND YOU SEEMS LIKE AN IDIOT OR A LIAR. THERE IS A MOOD THAT SETS IN.

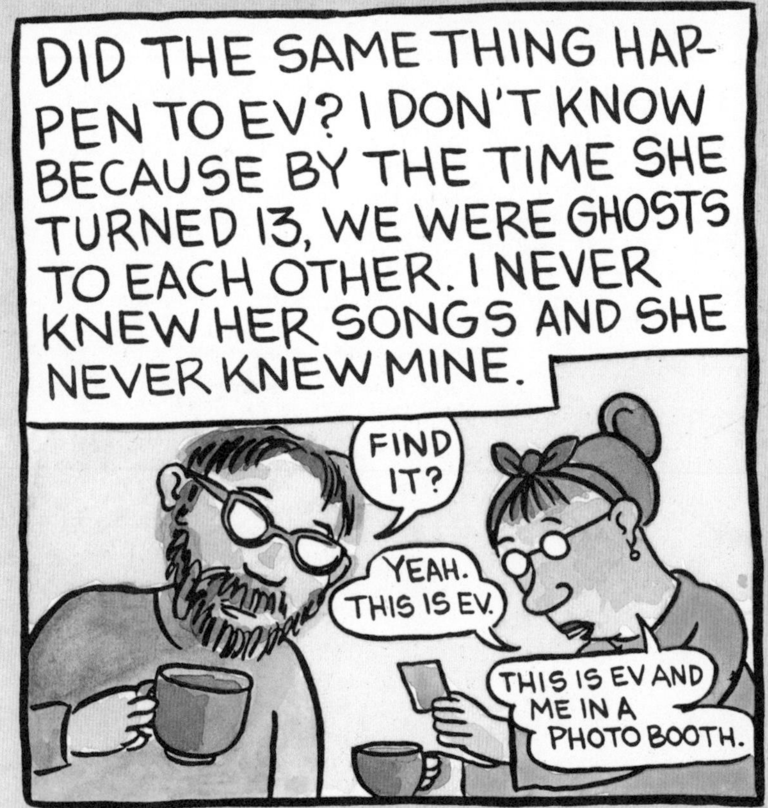
DID THE SAME THING HAPPEN TO EV? I DON'T KNOW BECAUSE BY THE TIME SHE TURNED 13, WE WERE GHOSTS TO EACH OTHER. I NEVER KNEW HER SONGS AND SHE NEVER KNEW MINE.
FIND IT?
YEAH. THIS IS EV.
THIS IS EV AND ME IN A PHOTO BOOTH.

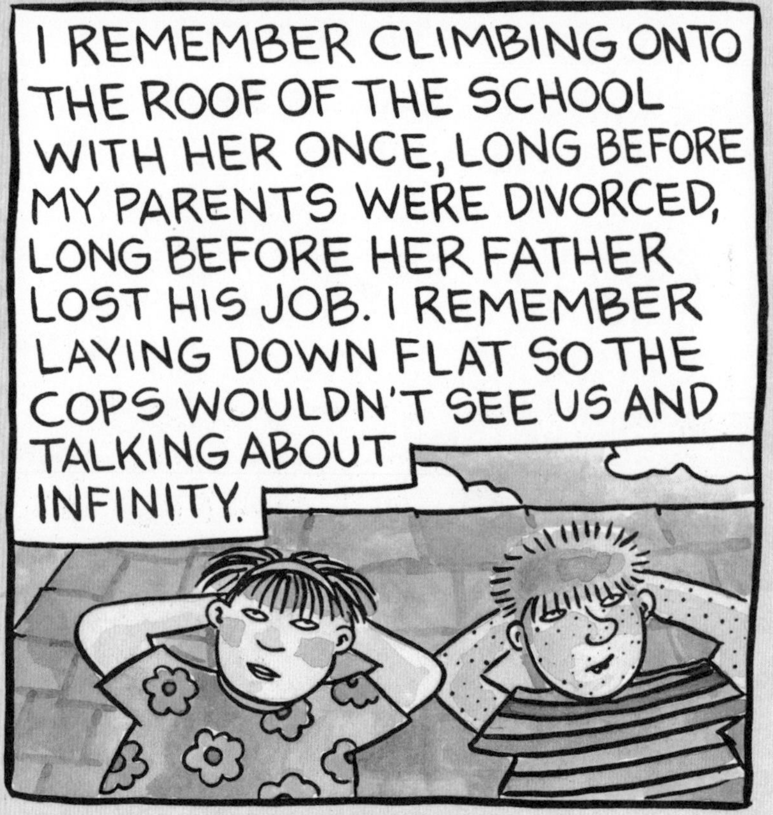
I REMEMBER CLIMBING ONTO THE ROOF OF THE SCHOOL WITH HER ONCE, LONG BEFORE MY PARENTS WERE DIVORCED, LONG BEFORE HER FATHER LOST HIS JOB. I REMEMBER LAYING DOWN FLAT SO THE COPS WOULDN'T SEE US AND TALKING ABOUT INFINITY.

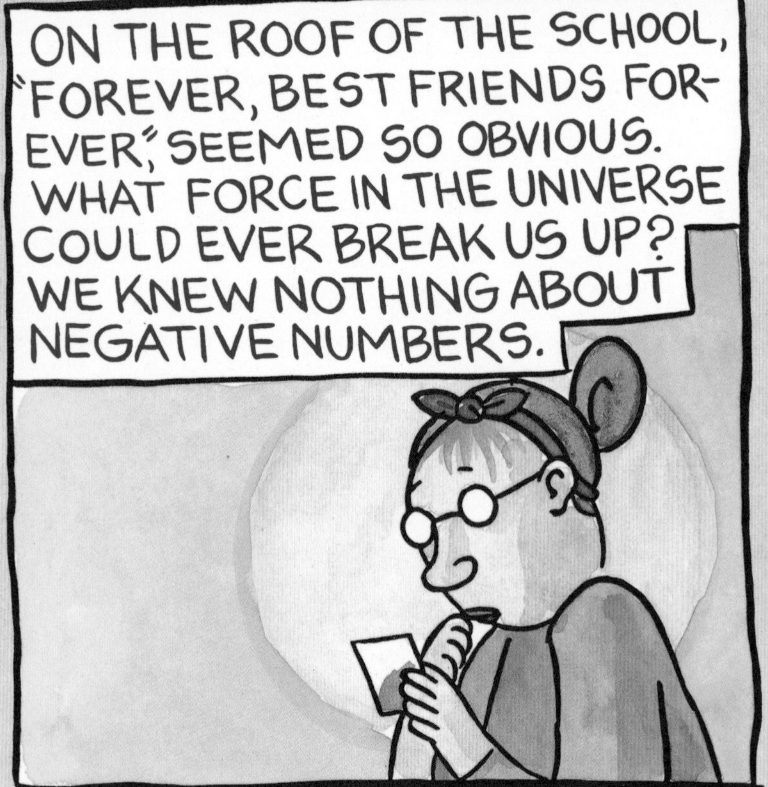
ON THE ROOF OF THE SCHOOL, "FOREVER, BEST FRIENDS FOREVER," SEEMED SO OBVIOUS. WHAT FORCE IN THE UNIVERSE COULD EVER BREAK US UP? WE KNEW NOTHING ABOUT NEGATIVE NUMBERS.

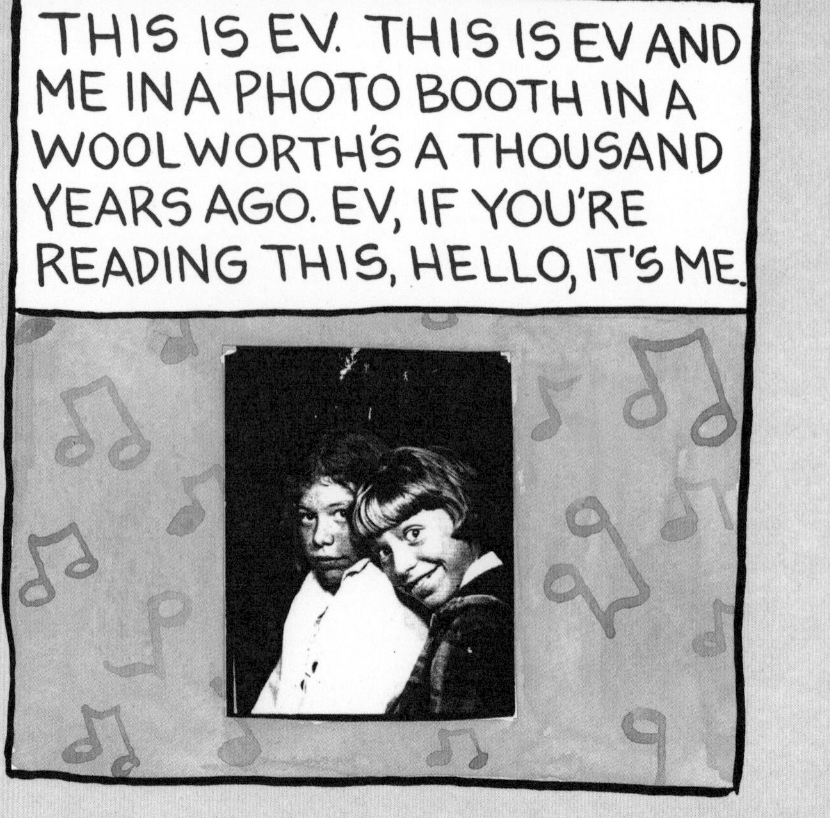
THIS IS EV. THIS IS EV AND ME IN A PHOTO BOOTH IN A WOOLWORTH'S A THOUSAND YEARS AGO. EV, IF YOU'RE READING THIS, HELLO, IT'S ME.

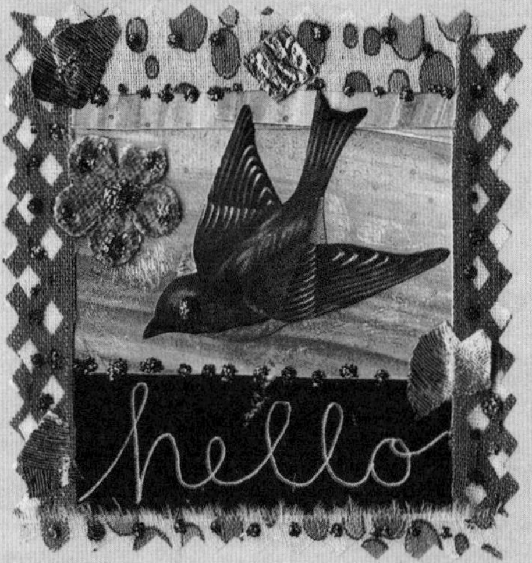
hello

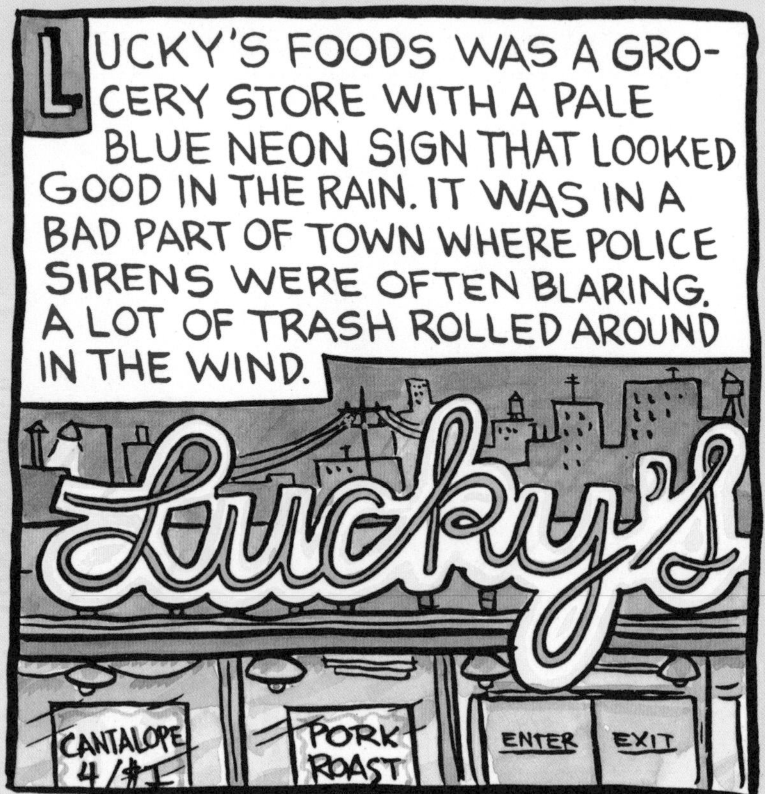
LUCKY'S FOODS WAS A GROCERY STORE WITH A PALE BLUE NEON SIGN THAT LOOKED GOOD IN THE RAIN. IT WAS IN A BAD PART OF TOWN WHERE POLICE SIRENS WERE OFTEN BLARING. A LOT OF TRASH ROLLED AROUND IN THE WIND.
Lucky's
CANTALOPE 4/$1
PORK ROAST
ENTER
EXIT

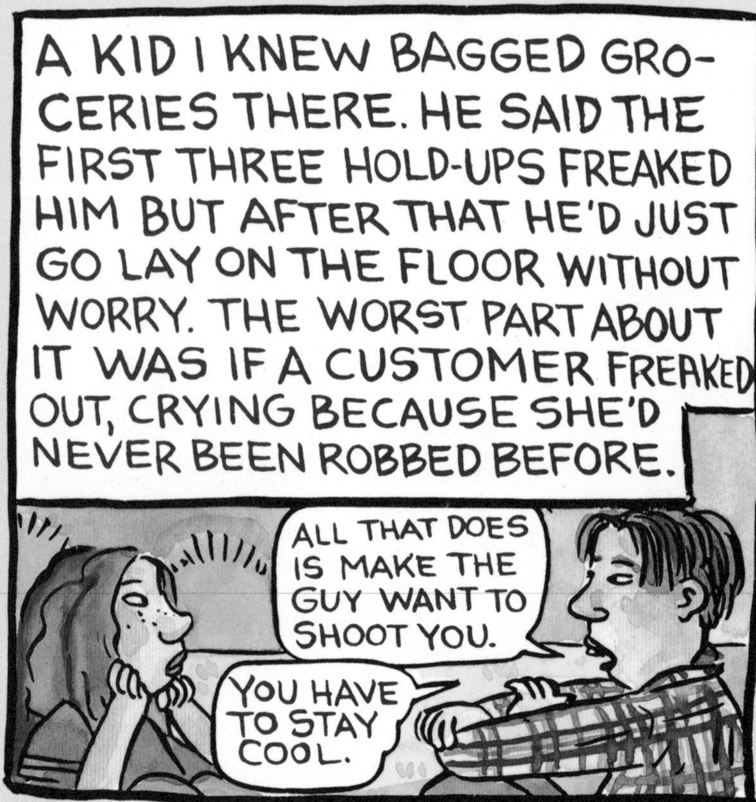
A KID I KNEW BAGGED GROCERIES THERE. HE SAID THE FIRST THREE HOLD-UPS FREAKED HIM BUT AFTER THAT HE'D JUST GO LAY ON THE FLOOR WITHOUT WORRY. THE WORST PART ABOUT IT WAS IF A CUSTOMER FREAKED OUT, CRYING BECAUSE SHE'D NEVER BEEN ROBBED BEFORE.
ALL THAT DOES IS MAKE THE GUY WANT TO SHOOT YOU.
YOU HAVE TO STAY COOL.

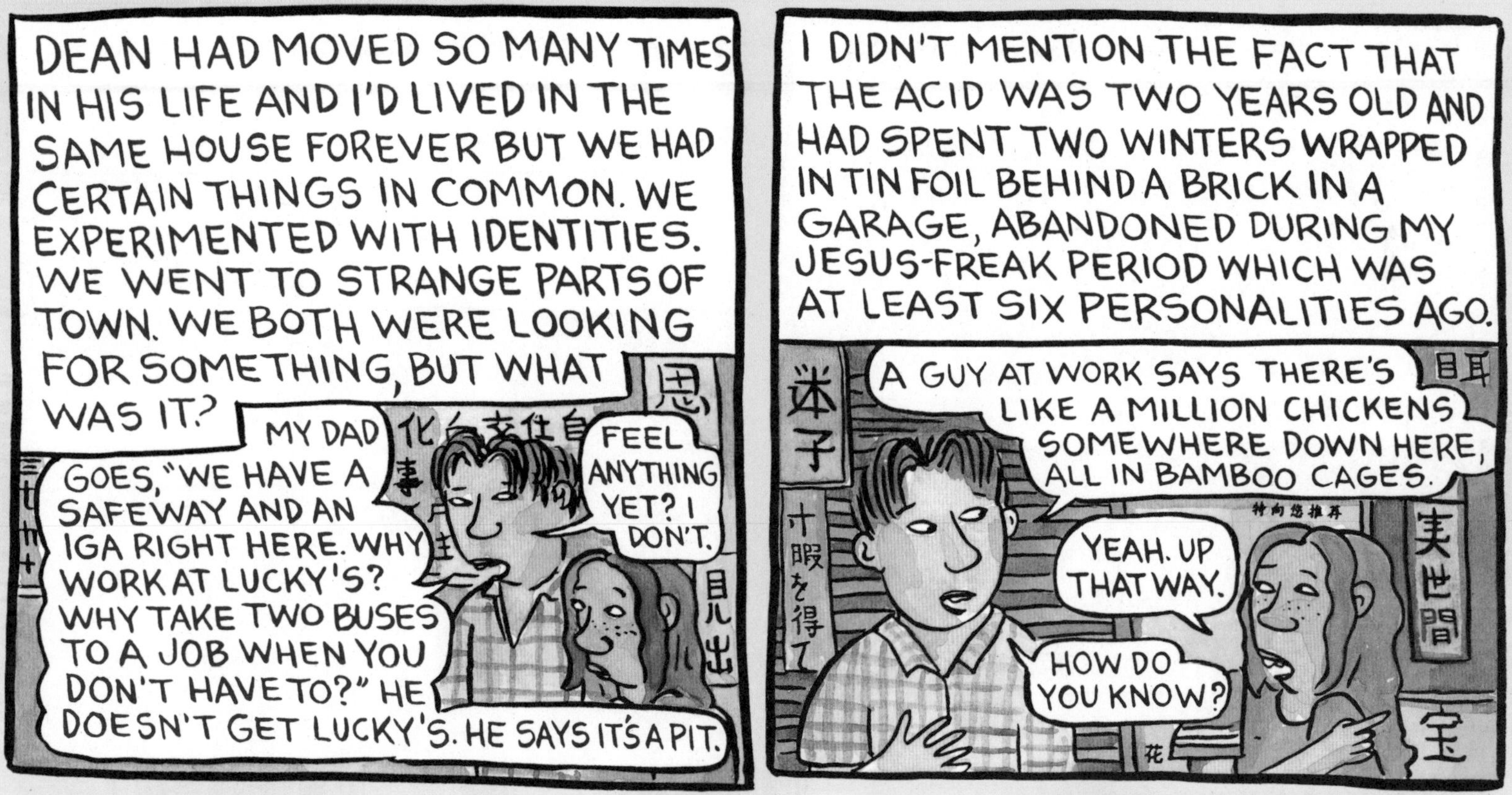
DEAN HAD MOVED SO MANY TIMES IN HIS LIFE AND I'D LIVED IN THE SAME HOUSE FOREVER BUT WE HAD CERTAIN THINGS IN COMMON. WE EXPERIMENTED WITH IDENTITIES. WE WENT TO STRANGE PARTS OF TOWN. WE BOTH WERE LOOKING FOR SOMETHING, BUT WHAT WAS IT?
MY DAD GOES, "WE HAVE A SAFEWAY AND AN IGA RIGHT HERE. WHY WORK AT LUCKY'S? WHY TAKE TWO BUSES TO A JOB WHEN YOU DON'T HAVE TO?" HE DOESN'T GET LUCKY'S. HE SAYS IT'S A PIT.
FEEL ANYTHING YET? I DON'T.
I DIDN'T MENTION THE FACT THAT THE ACID WAS TWO YEARS OLD AND HAD SPENT TWO WINTERS WRAPPED IN TIN FOIL BEHIND A BRICK IN A GARAGE, ABANDONED DURING MY JESUS-FREAK PERIOD WHICH WAS AT LEAST SIX PERSONALITIES AGO.
A GUY AT WORK SAYS THERE'S LIKE A MILLION CHICKENS SOMEWHERE DOWN HERE, ALL IN BAMBOO CAGES.
YEAH. UP THAT WAY.
HOW DO YOU KNOW?

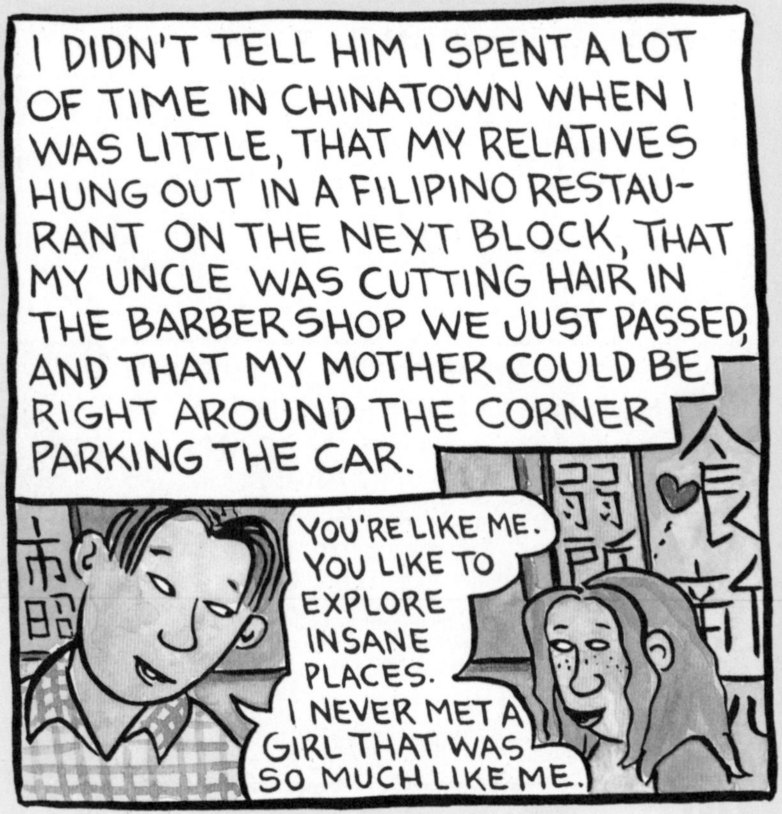
I DIDN'T TELL HIM I SPENT A LOT OF TIME IN CHINATOWN WHEN I WAS LITTLE, THAT MY RELATIVES HUNG OUT IN A FILIPINO RESTAU-RANT ON THE NEXT BLOCK, THAT MY UNCLE WAS CUTTING HAIR IN THE BARBER SHOP WE JUST PASSED, AND THAT MY MOTHER COULD BE RIGHT AROUND THE CORNER PARKING THE CAR.
YOU'RE LIKE ME. YOU LIKE TO EXPLORE INSANE PLACES. I NEVER MET A GIRL THAT WAS SO MUCH LIKE ME.

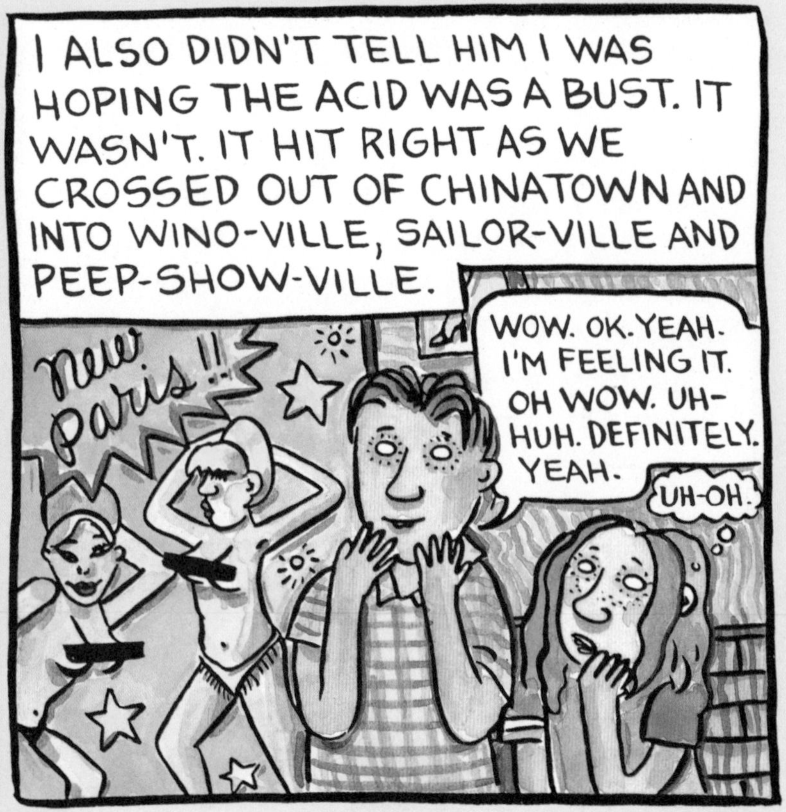
I ALSO DIDN'T TELL HIM I WAS HOPING THE ACID WAS A BUST. IT WASN'T. IT HIT RIGHT AS WE CROSSED OUT OF CHINATOWN AND INTO WINO-VILLE, SAILOR-VILLE AND PEEP-SHOW-VILLE.
new Paris!!
WOW. OK. YEAH. I'M FEELING IT. OH WOW. UH-HUH. DEFINITELY. YEAH.
UH-OH.

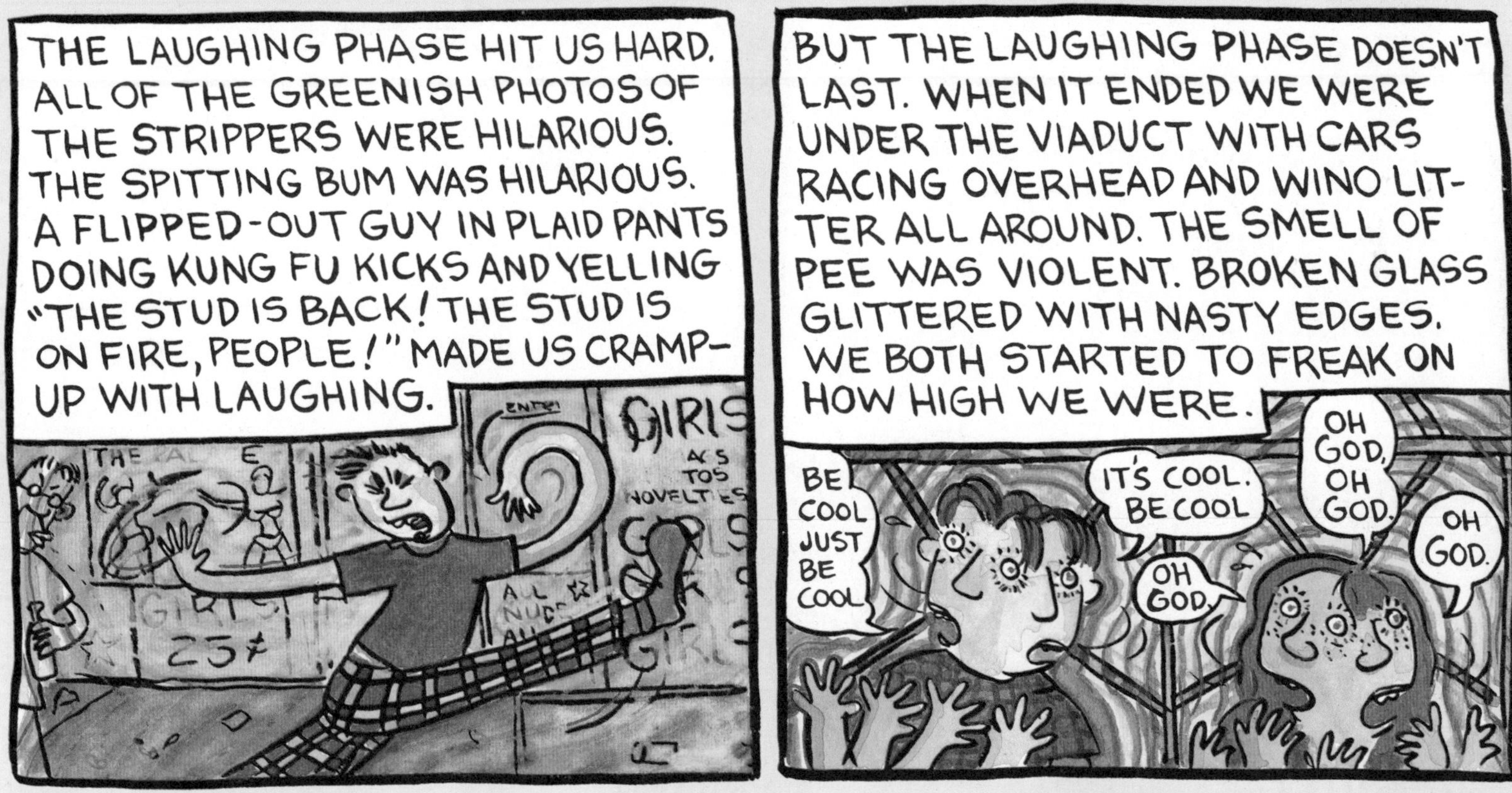
THE LAUGHING PHASE HIT US HARD. ALL OF THE GREENISH PHOTOS OF THE STRIPPERS WERE HILARIOUS. THE SPITTING BUM WAS HILARIOUS. A FLIPPED-OUT GUY IN PLAID PANTS DOING KUNG FU KICKS AND YELLING "THE STUD IS BACK! THE STUD IS ON FIRE, PEOPLE!" MADE US CRAMP-UP WITH LAUGHING.
25¢
BUT THE LAUGHING PHASE DOESN'T LAST. WHEN IT ENDED WE WERE UNDER THE VIADUCT WITH CARS RACING OVERHEAD AND WINO LITTER ALL AROUND. THE SMELL OF PEE WAS VIOLENT. BROKEN GLASS GLITTERED WITH NASTY EDGES. WE BOTH STARTED TO FREAK ON HOW HIGH WE WERE.
BE COOL JUST BE COOL
IT'S COOL. BE COOL
OH GOD.
OH GOD, OH GOD.
OH GOD.

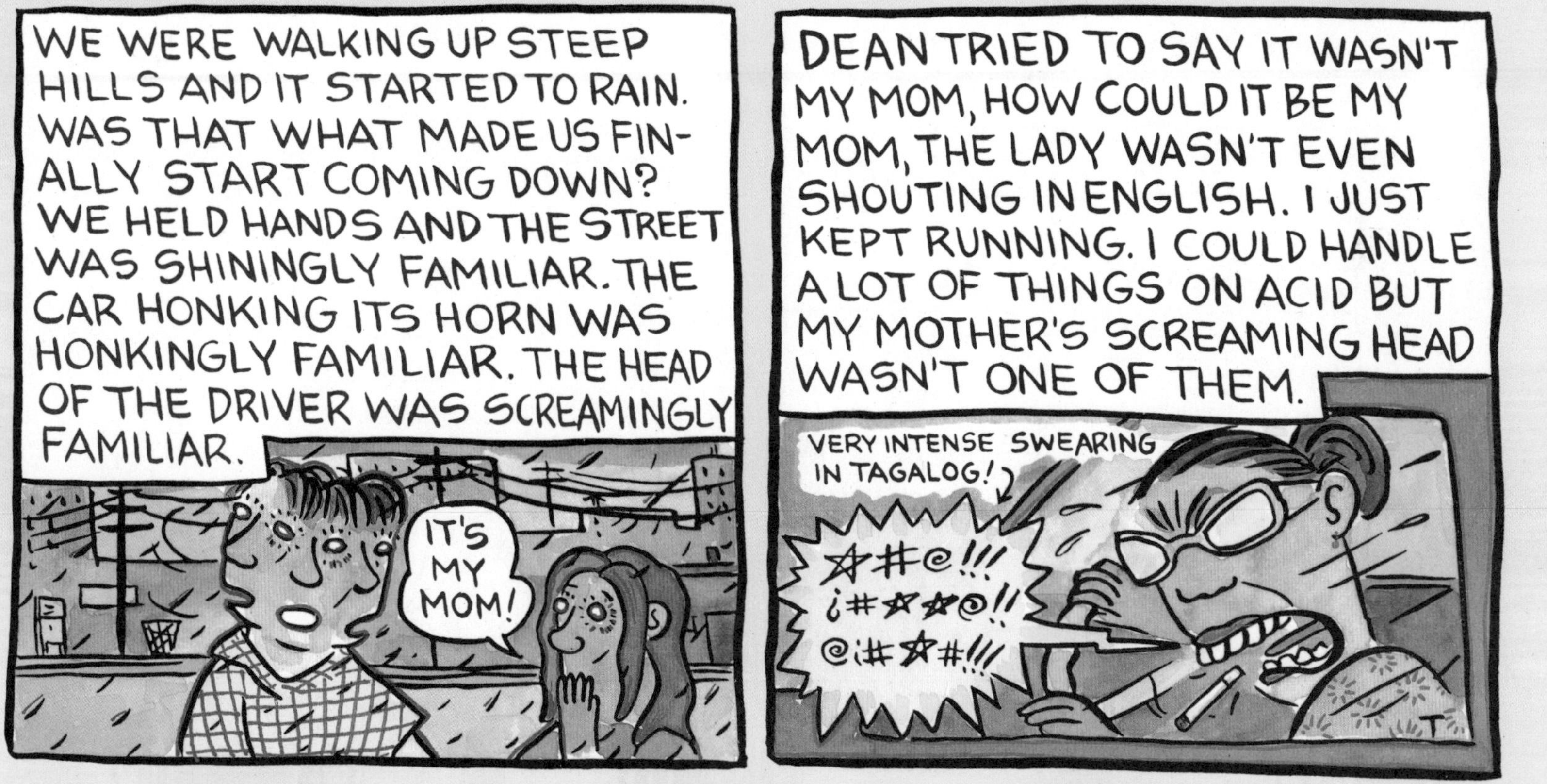
WE WERE WALKING UP STEEP HILLS AND IT STARTED TO RAIN. WAS THAT WHAT MADE US FIN-ALLY START COMING DOWN? WE HELD HANDS AND THE STREET WAS SHININGLY FAMILIAR. THE CAR HONKING ITS HORN WAS HONKINGLY FAMILIAR. THE HEAD OF THE DRIVER WAS SCREAMINGLY FAMILIAR.
IT'S MY MOM!
DEAN TRIED TO SAY IT WASN'T MY MOM, HOW COULD IT BE MY MOM, THE LADY WASN'T EVEN SHOUTING IN ENGLISH. I JUST KEPT RUNNING. I COULD HANDLE A LOT OF THINGS ON ACID BUT MY MOTHER'S SCREAMING HEAD WASN'T ONE OF THEM.
VERY INTENSE SWEARING IN TAGALOG!

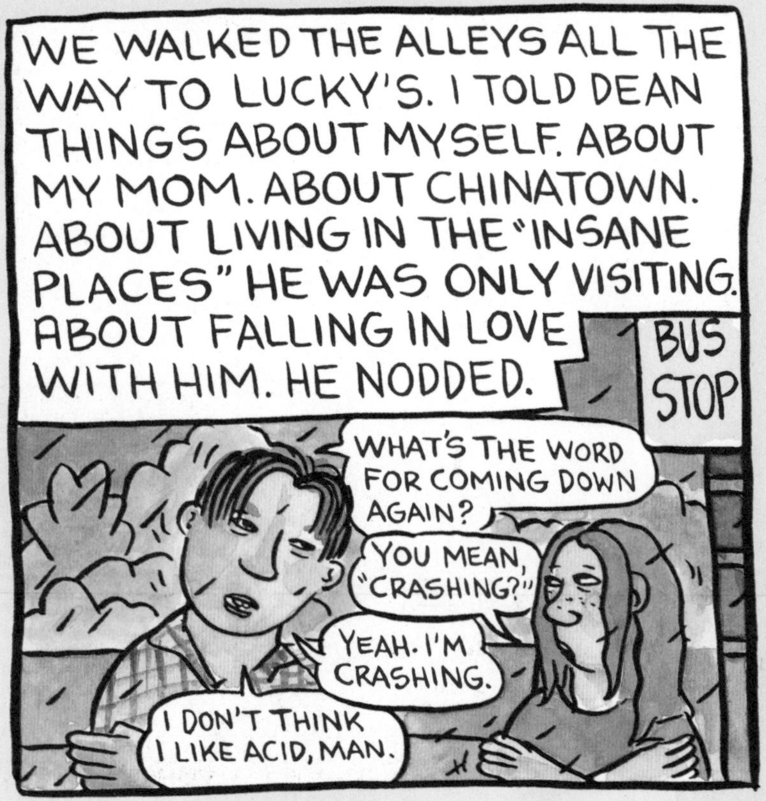
WE WALKED THE ALLEYS ALL THE WAY TO LUCKY'S. I TOLD DEAN THINGS ABOUT MYSELF. ABOUT MY MOM. ABOUT CHINATOWN. ABOUT LIVING IN THE "INSANE PLACES" HE WAS ONLY VISITING. ABOUT FALLING IN LOVE WITH HIM. HE NODDED.
BUS STOP
WHAT'S THE WORD FOR COMING DOWN AGAIN?
YOU MEAN, "CRASHING?"
YEAH. I'M CRASHING.
I DON'T THINK I LIKE ACID, MAN.

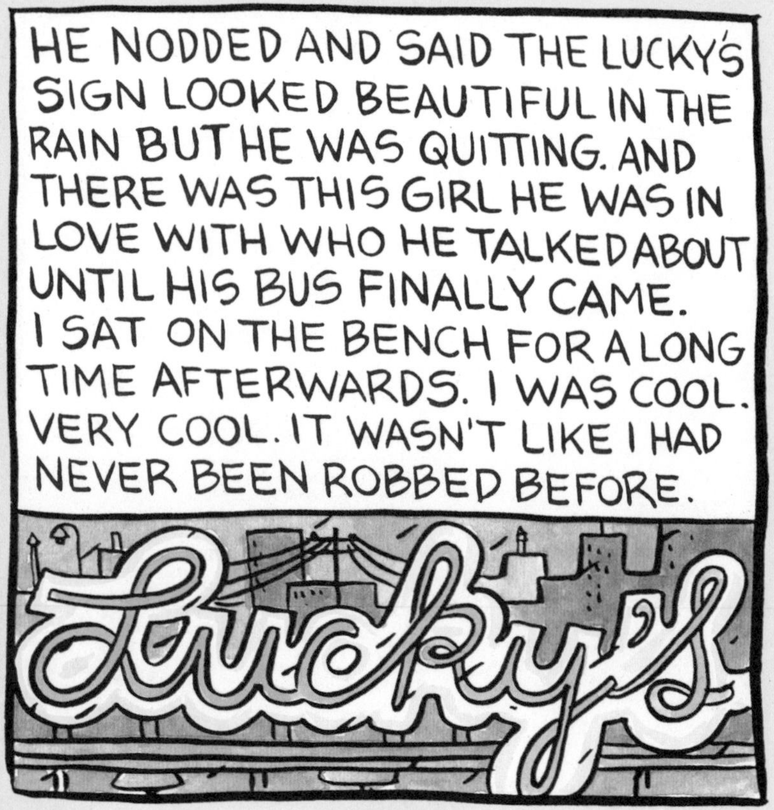
HE NODDED AND SAID THE LUCKY'S SIGN LOOKED BEAUTIFUL IN THE RAIN BUT HE WAS QUITTING. AND THERE WAS THIS GIRL HE WAS IN LOVE WITH WHO HE TALKED ABOUT UNTIL HIS BUS FINALLY CAME. I SAT ON THE BENCH FOR A LONG TIME AFTERWARDS. I WAS COOL. VERY COOL. IT WASN'T LIKE I HAD NEVER BEEN ROBBED BEFORE.
Lucky's

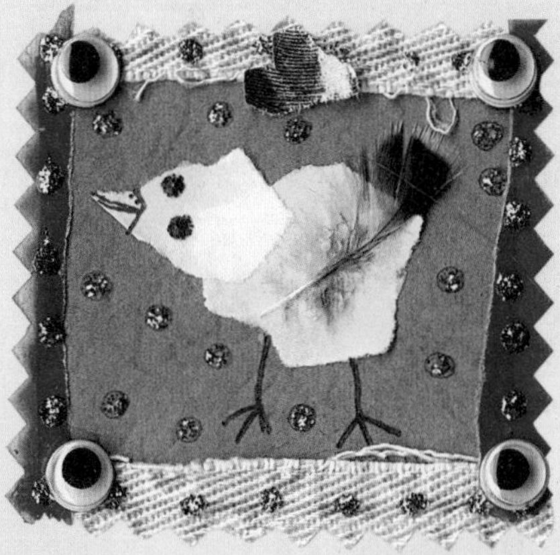

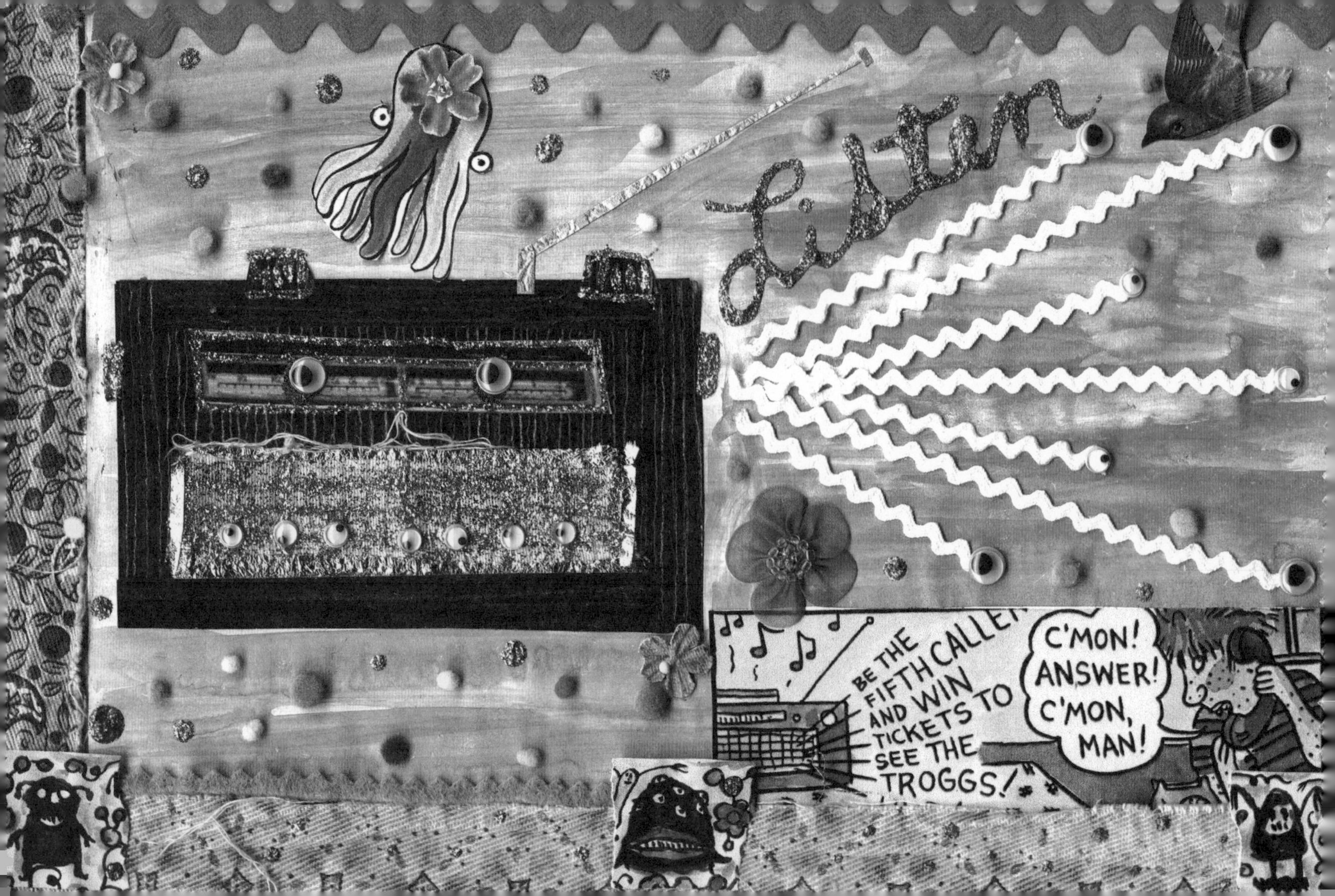
Listen
BE THE FIFTH CALLER AND WIN TICKETS TO SEE THE TROGGS!
C'MON! ANSWER! C'MON, MAN!

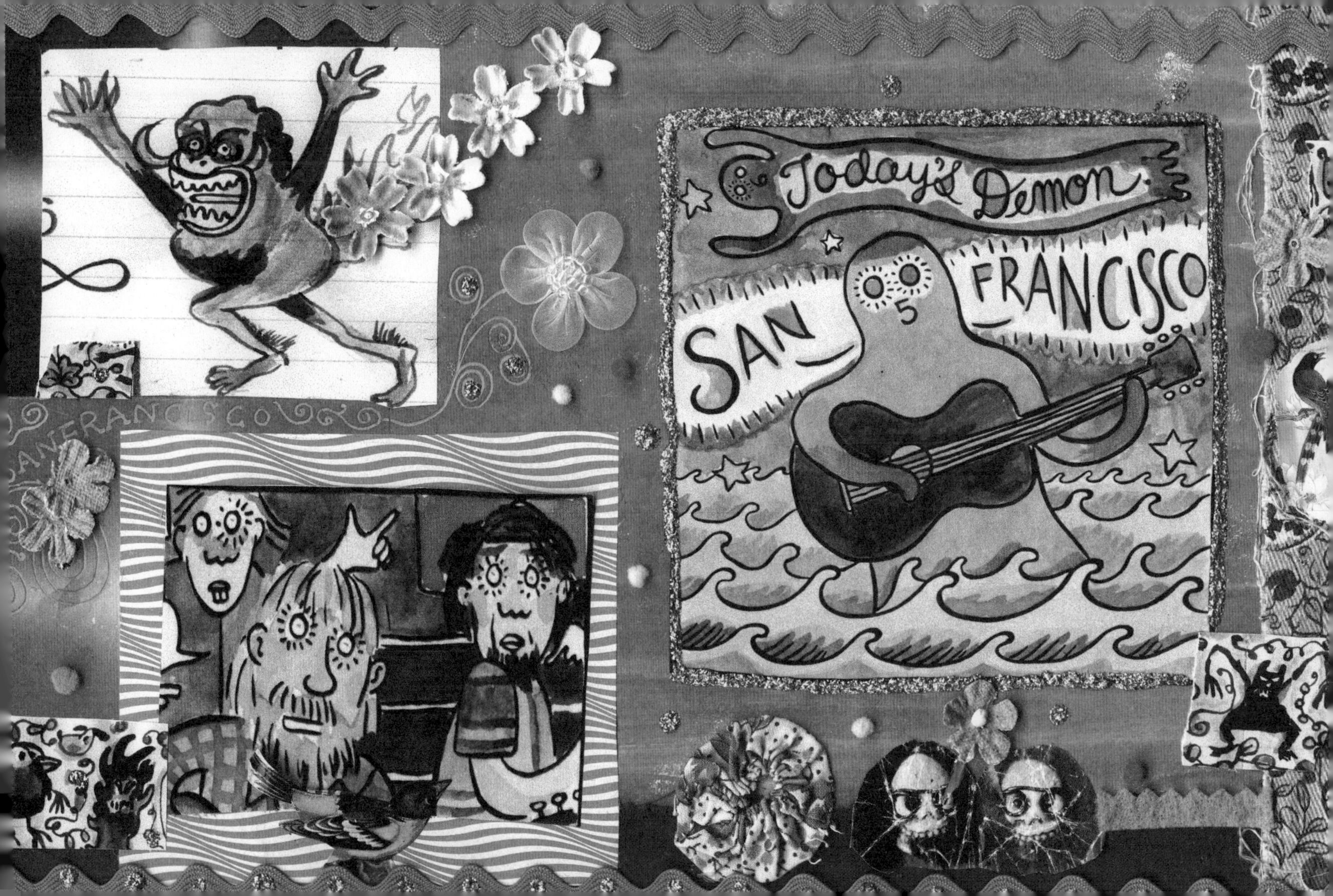

Today's Demon
SAN FRANCISCO
5

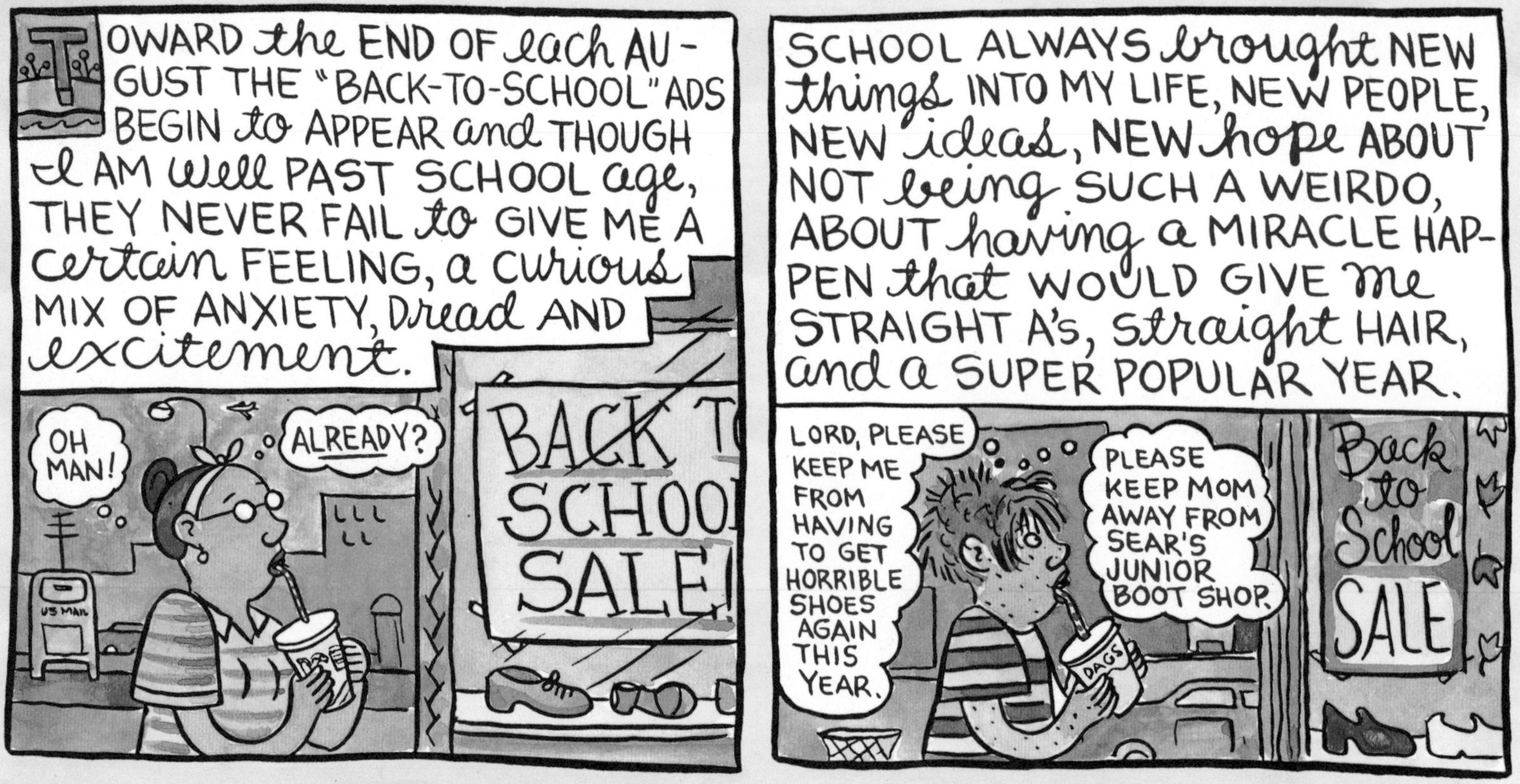
TOWARD the END OF each AUGUST THE "BACK-TO-SCHOOL" ADS BEGIN to APPEAR and THOUGH I AM well PAST SCHOOL age, THEY NEVER FAIL to GIVE ME A certain FEELING, a curious MIX OF ANXIETY, Dread AND excitement.
OH MAN!
ALREADY?
US MAIL
BACK T
SCHOO
SALE
SCHOOL ALWAYS brought NEW things INTO MY LIFE, NEW PEOPLE, NEW ideas, NEW hope ABOUT NOT being SUCH A WEIRDO, ABOUT having a MIRACLE HAPPEN that WOULD GIVE me STRAIGHT A's, straight HAIR, and a SUPER POPULAR YEAR.
LORD, PLEASE KEEP ME FROM HAVING TO GET HORRIBLE SHOES AGAIN THIS YEAR.
PLEASE KEEP MOM AWAY FROM SEAR'S JUNIOR BOOT SHOP.
DAGS
Back to School SALE

125

DURING *the* DAY I WAS *still* A KID. *I* HUNG *around* THE USUAL PEOPLE, PLAYED *the* USUAL KICKBALL GAME, *Drank* THE USUAL GREEN KOOL-AID AND *waited* FOR *the* ICE CREAM *man*.

MY BEST FRIEND. SHE WAS 2 YEARS YOUNGER)

YOU GONNA DO LIKE SHONITA AND THEM WHEN YOU START 7TH GRADE?

DO LIKE WHAT?

GET WEIRD TO PEOPLE.

LIKE HOW?

LIKE HOW THEY DON'T PLAY NOTHING AND THEY ALWAYS KEEP GOING OTHER PLACES.

MY BEST FRIEND GLADYS *was about* TO START 5TH GRADE. SHE WAS A VERY COOL PERSON *and* OUR AGE DIFFERENCE *never mattered* TO ME BEFORE. BUT DURING THOSE *last* WEEKS OF *summer* I WAS STARTING *to* FEEL SICK ABOUT *it*.

(SHE WAS TINY FOR HER AGE)

YOU GONNA DO LIKE THAT?

GET ALL TEENAGERISH?

ARE YA?

YA GONNA QUIT HANGING AROUND WITH ME?

127

129

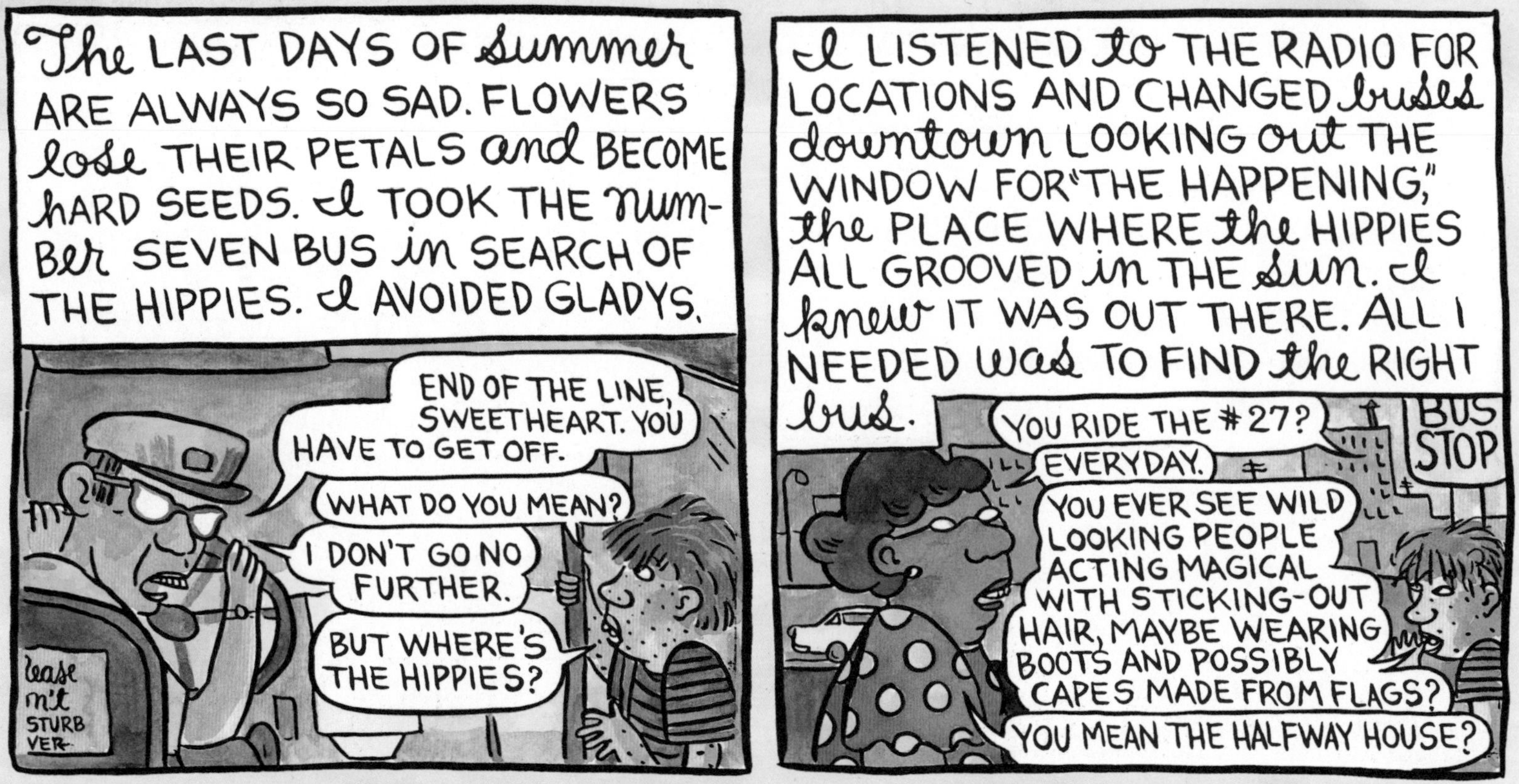
The LAST DAYS OF Summer ARE ALWAYS SO SAD. FLOWERS lose THEIR PETALS and BECOME hARD SEEDS. I TOOK THE number SEVEN BUS in SEARCH OF THE HIPPIES. I AVOIDED GLADYS.
END OF THE LINE, SWEETHEART. YOU HAVE TO GET OFF.
WHAT DO YOU MEAN?
I DON'T GO NO FURTHER.
BUT WHERE'S THE HIPPIES?
I LISTENED to THE RADIO FOR LOCATIONS AND CHANGED buses downtown LOOKING out THE WINDOW FOR "THE HAPPENING," the PLACE WHERE the HIPPIES ALL GROOVED in THE sun. I knew IT WAS OUT THERE. ALL I NEEDED was TO FIND the RIGHT bus.
BUS STOP
YOU RIDE THE #27?
EVERYDAY.
YOU EVER SEE WILD LOOKING PEOPLE ACTING MAGICAL WITH STICKING-OUT HAIR, MAYBE WEARING BOOTS AND POSSIBLY CAPES MADE FROM FLAGS?
YOU MEAN THE HALFWAY HOUSE?

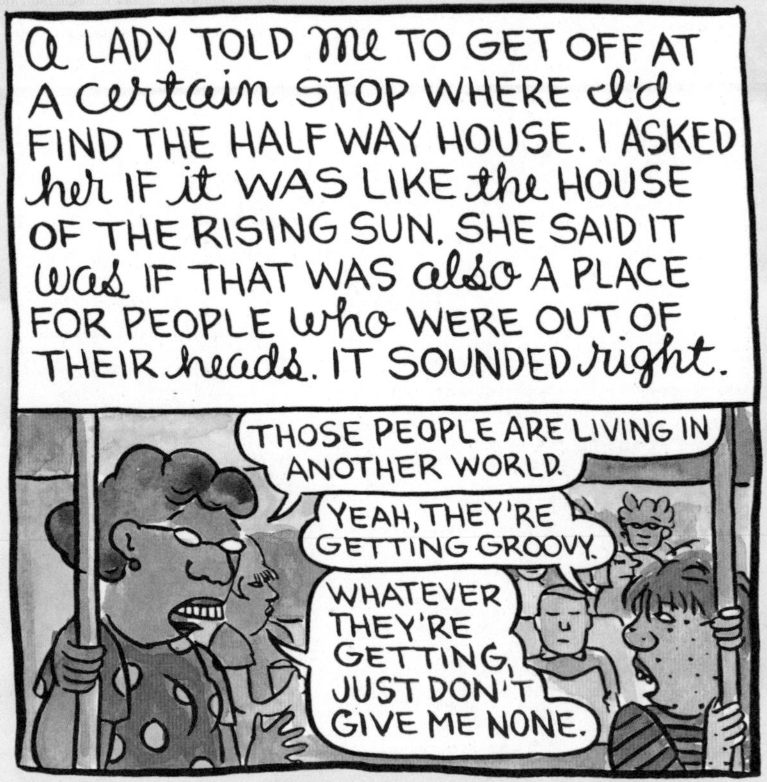
a LADY TOLD me TO GET OFF AT A certain STOP WHERE I'd FIND THE HALF WAY HOUSE. I ASKED her IF it WAS LIKE the HOUSE OF THE RISING SUN. SHE SAID IT was IF THAT WAS also A PLACE FOR PEOPLE who WERE OUT OF THEIR heads. IT SOUNDED right.
THOSE PEOPLE ARE LIVING IN ANOTHER WORLD.
YEAH, THEY'RE GETTING GROOVY.
WHATEVER THEY'RE GETTING, JUST DON'T GIVE ME NONE.

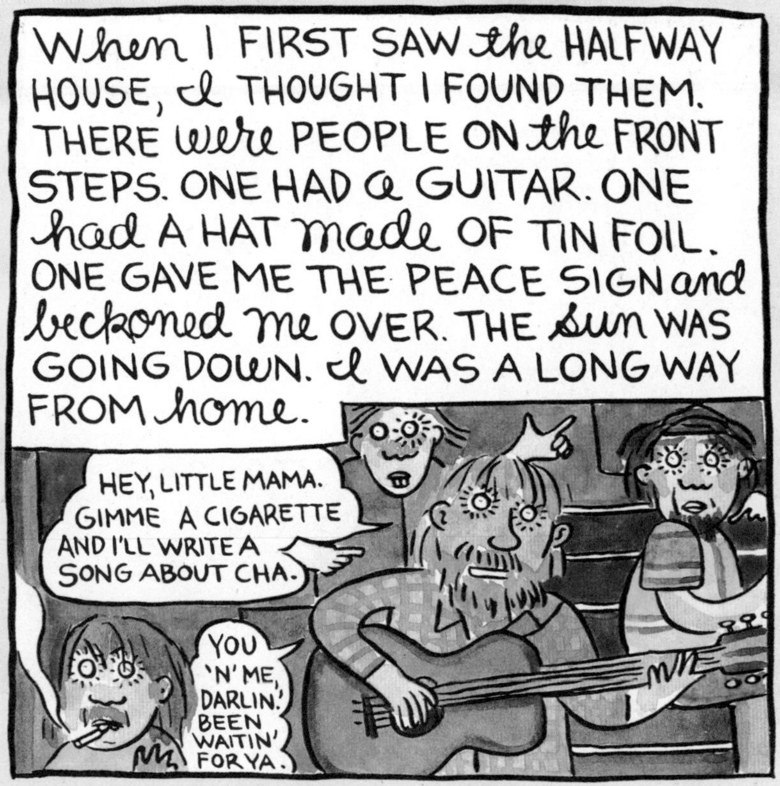
When I FIRST SAW the HALFWAY HOUSE, I THOUGHT I FOUND THEM. THERE were PEOPLE ON the FRONT STEPS. ONE HAD a GUITAR. ONE had A HAT made OF TIN FOIL. ONE GAVE ME THE PEACE SIGN and beckoned me OVER. THE sun WAS GOING DOWN. I WAS A LONG WAY FROM home.
HEY, LITTLE MAMA. GIMME A CIGARETTE AND I'LL WRITE A SONG ABOUT CHA.
YOU 'N' ME, DARLIN'. BEEN WAITIN' FOR YA.

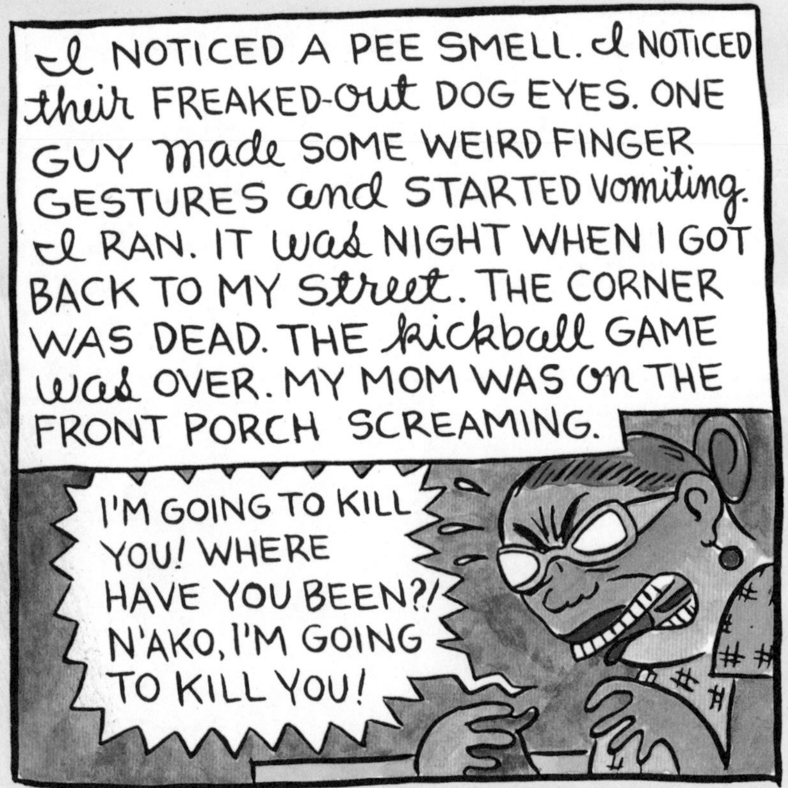
I NOTICED A PEE SMELL. I NOTICED their FREAKED-out DOG EYES. ONE GUY made SOME WEIRD FINGER GESTURES and STARTED vomiting. I RAN. IT was NIGHT WHEN I GOT BACK TO MY street. THE CORNER WAS DEAD. THE kickball GAME was OVER. MY MOM WAS on THE FRONT PORCH SCREAMING.
I'M GOING TO KILL YOU! WHERE HAVE YOU BEEN?! N'AKO, I'M GOING TO KILL YOU!

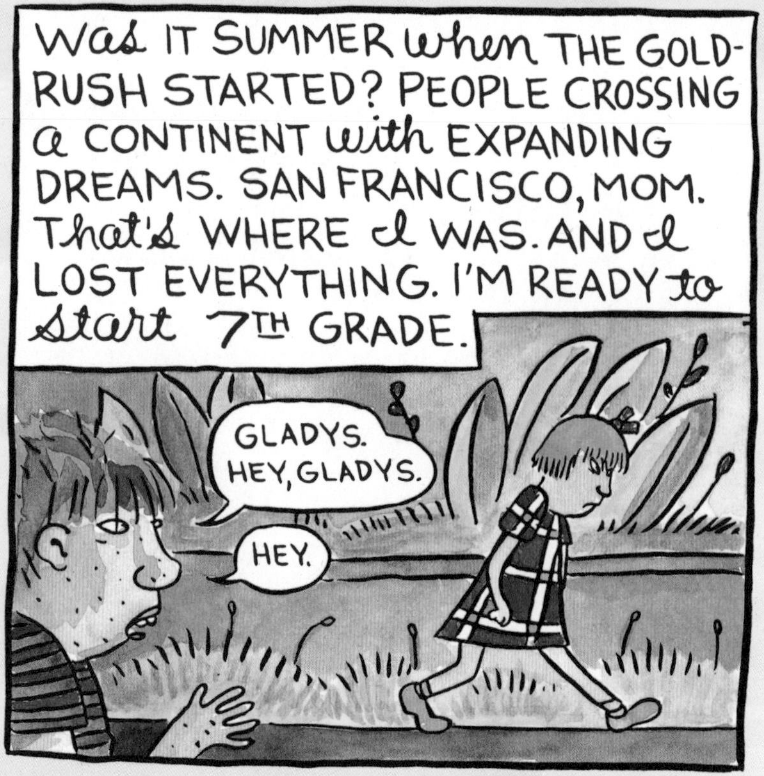
Was IT SUMMER when THE GOLD-RUSH STARTED? PEOPLE CROSSING a CONTINENT with EXPANDING DREAMS. SAN FRANCISCO, MOM. That's WHERE I WAS. AND I LOST EVERYTHING. I'M READY to start 7TH GRADE.
GLADYS. HEY, GLADYS.
HEY.

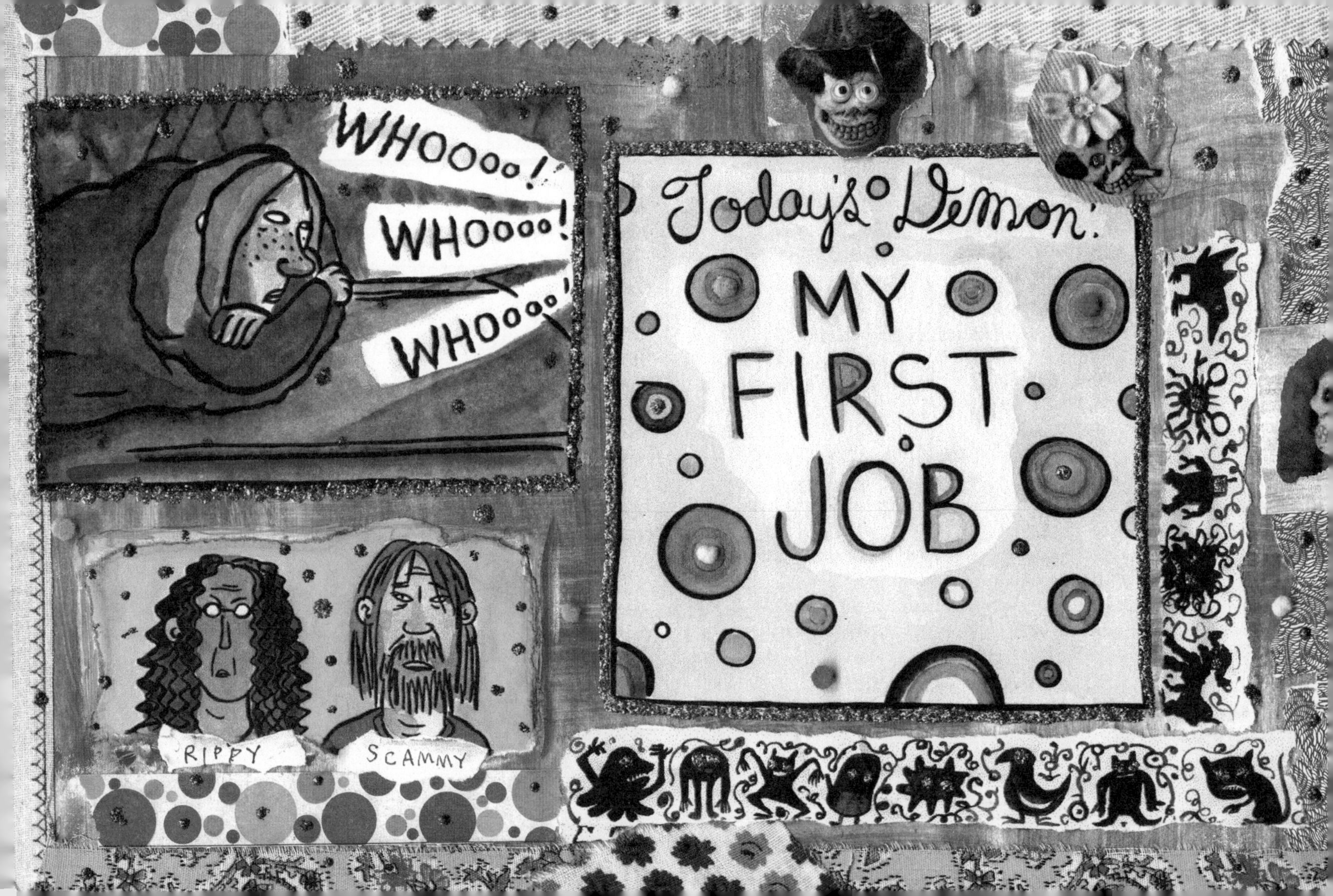

WHOOoo!
WHOOoo!
WHOOoo!
RIPPY
SCAMMY
Today's Demon:
MY FIRST JOB

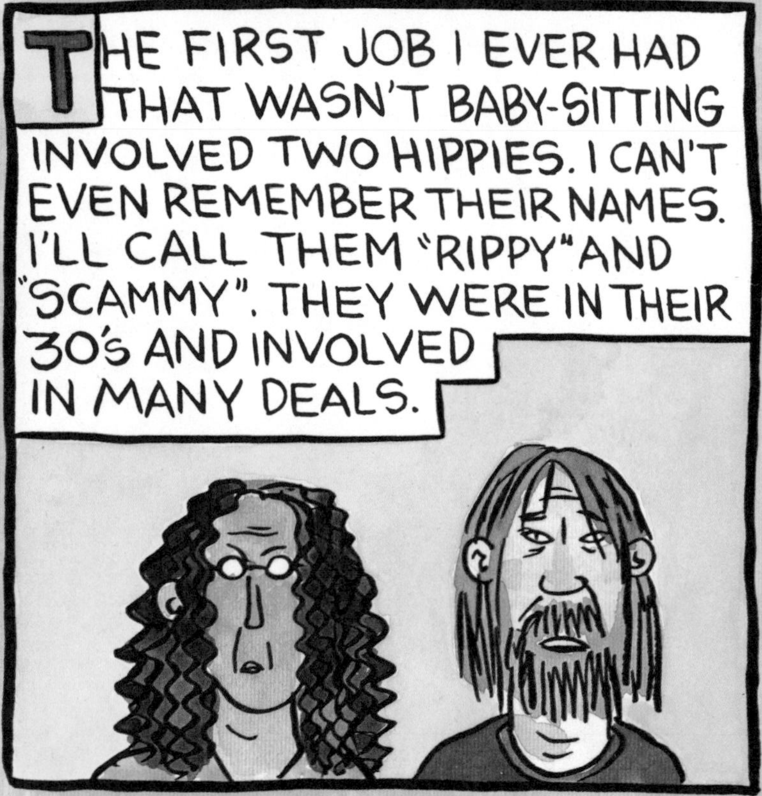
THE FIRST JOB I EVER HAD THAT WASN'T BABY-SITTING INVOLVED TWO HIPPIES. I CAN'T EVEN REMEMBER THEIR NAMES. I'LL CALL THEM "RIPPY" AND "SCAMMY". THEY WERE IN THEIR 30'S AND INVOLVED IN MANY DEALS.

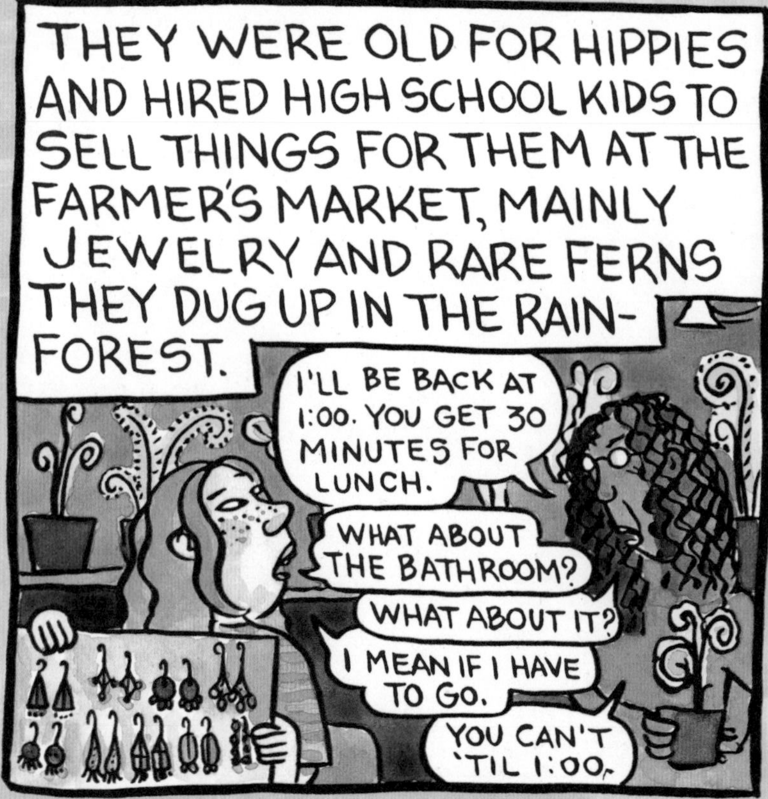
THEY WERE OLD FOR HIPPIES AND HIRED HIGH SCHOOL KIDS TO SELL THINGS FOR THEM AT THE FARMER'S MARKET, MAINLY JEWELRY AND RARE FERNS THEY DUG UP IN THE RAIN-FOREST.
I'LL BE BACK AT 1:00. YOU GET 30 MINUTES FOR LUNCH.
WHAT ABOUT THE BATHROOM?
WHAT ABOUT IT?
I MEAN IF I HAVE TO GO.
YOU CAN'T 'TIL 1:00.

137

141

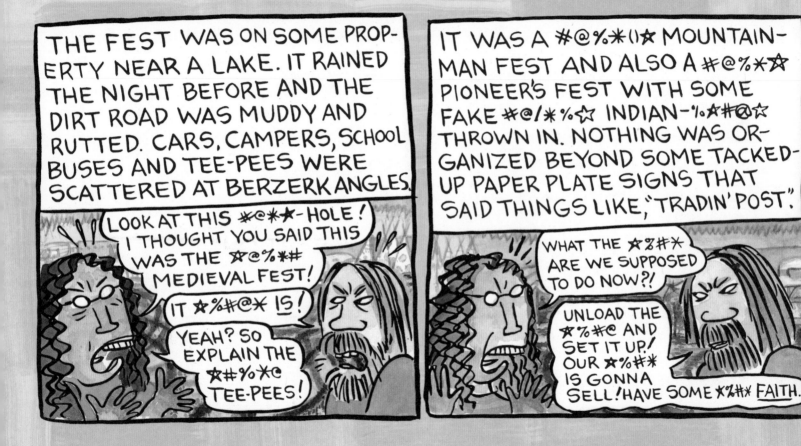

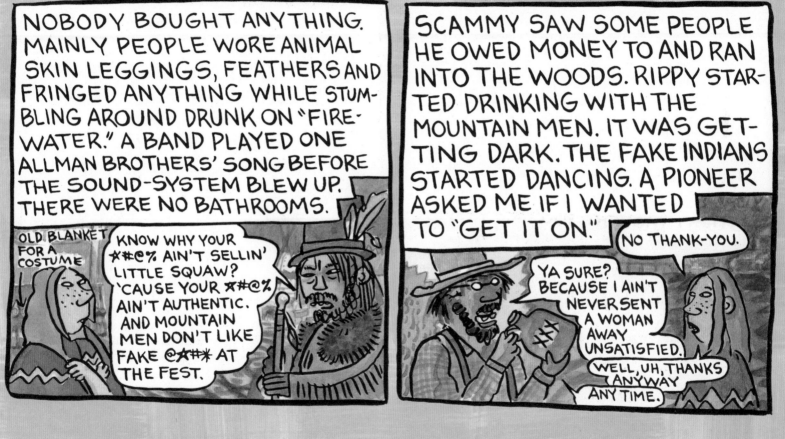

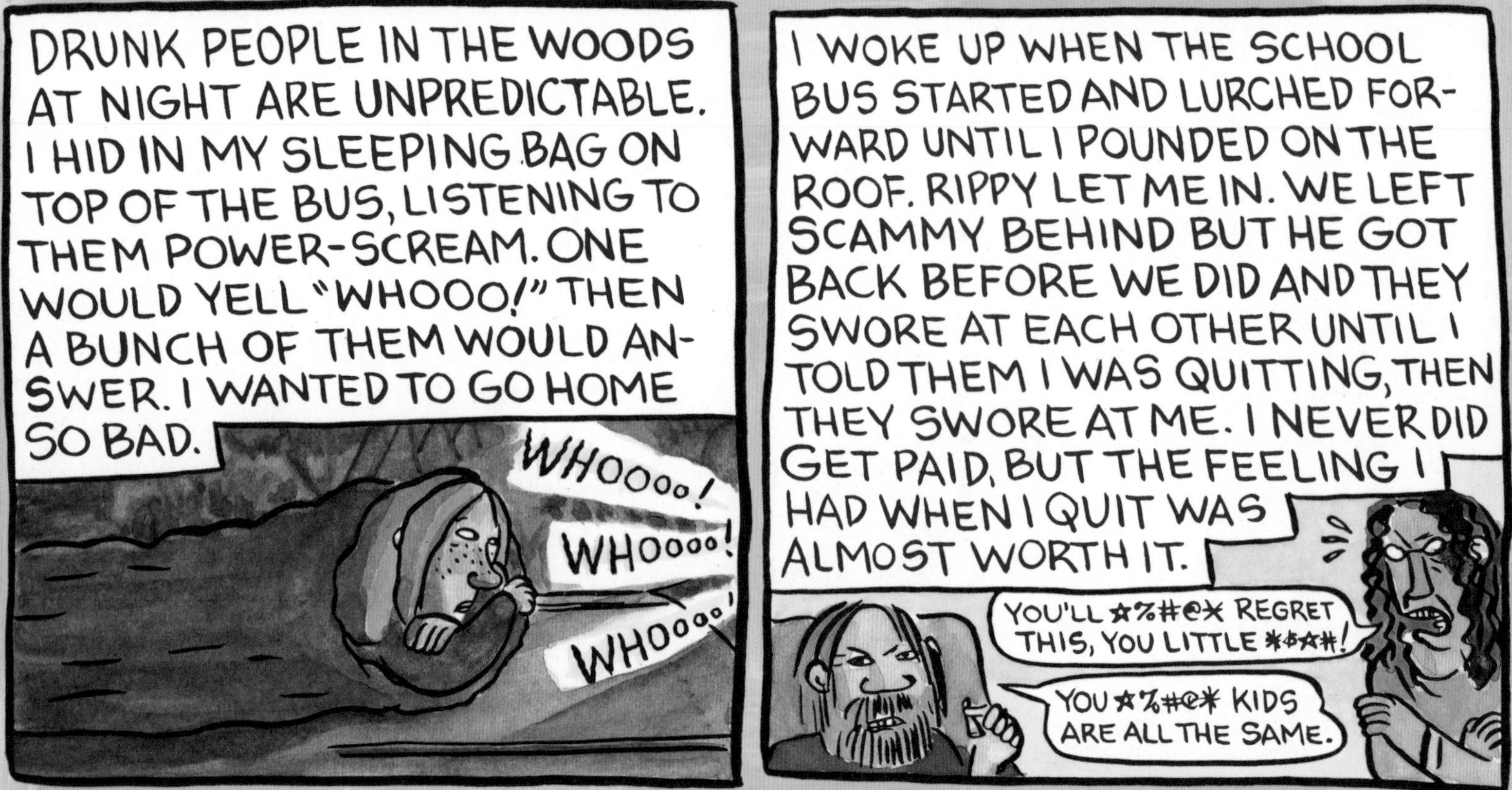
DRUNK PEOPLE IN THE WOODS AT NIGHT ARE UNPREDICTABLE. I HID IN MY SLEEPING BAG ON TOP OF THE BUS, LISTENING TO THEM POWER-SCREAM. ONE WOULD YELL "WHOOO!" THEN A BUNCH OF THEM WOULD ANSWER. I WANTED TO GO HOME SO BAD.
WHOooo!
WHOooo!
WHOooo!
I WOKE UP WHEN THE SCHOOL BUS STARTED AND LURCHED FORWARD UNTIL I POUNDED ON THE ROOF. RIPPY LET ME IN. WE LEFT SCAMMY BEHIND BUT HE GOT BACK BEFORE WE DID AND THEY SWORE AT EACH OTHER UNTIL I TOLD THEM I WAS QUITTING, THEN THEY SWORE AT ME. I NEVER DID GET PAID, BUT THE FEELING I HAD WHEN I QUIT WAS ALMOST WORTH IT.
YOU'LL *%#@* REGRET THIS, YOU LITTLE *$*#!
YOU *%#@* KIDS ARE ALL THE SAME.

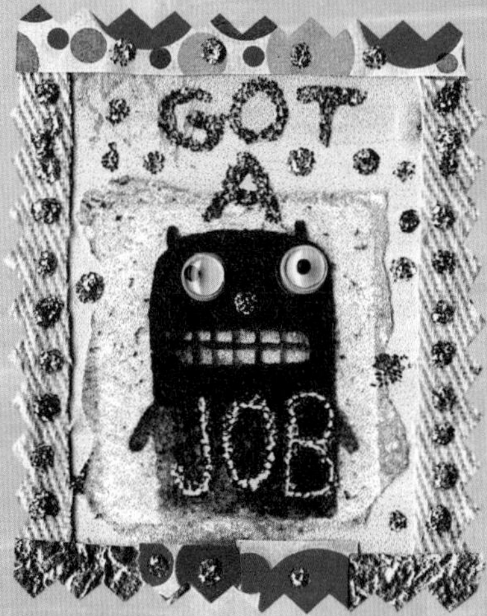
GOT
A
JOB

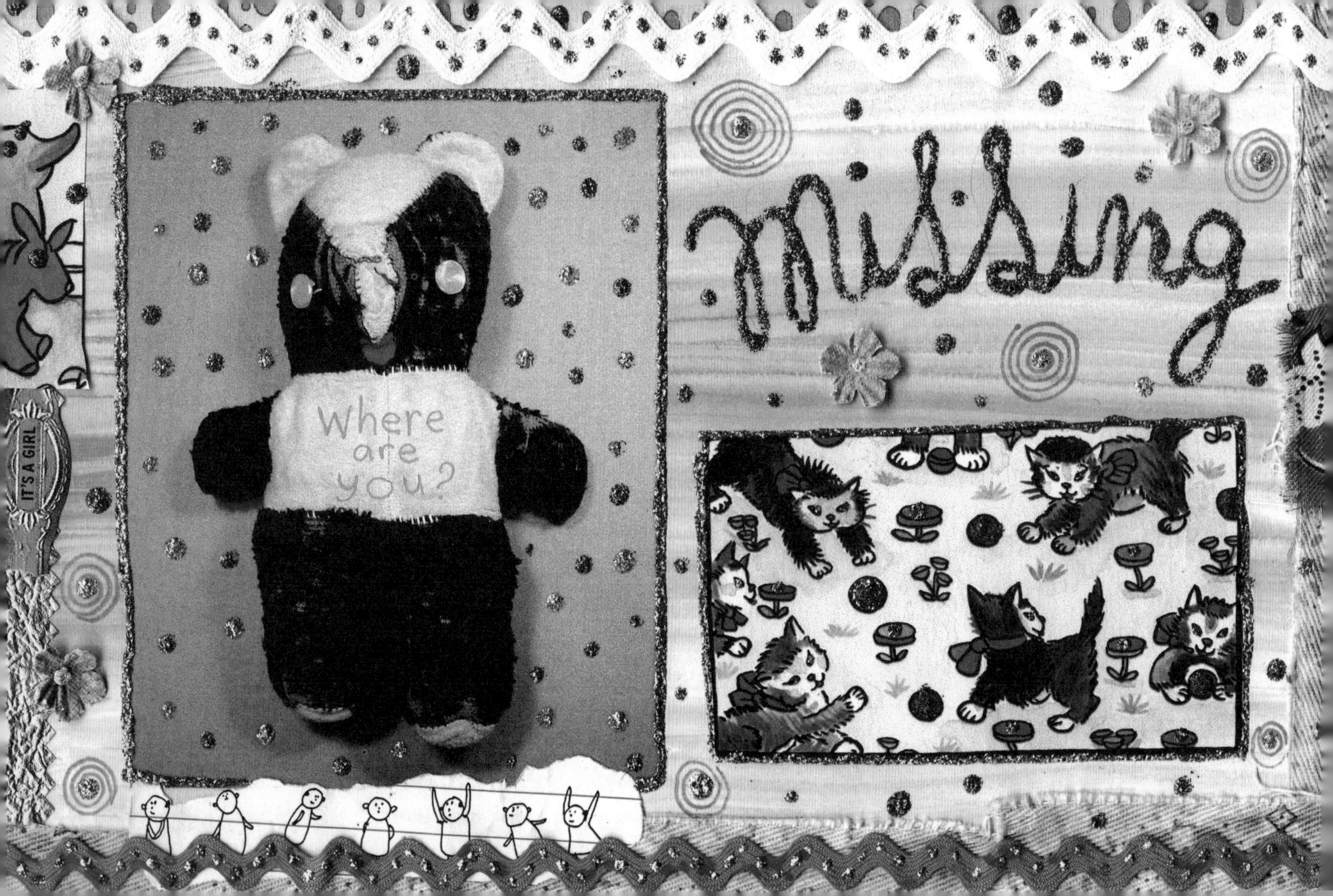
Missing
Where are you?
IT'S A GIRL

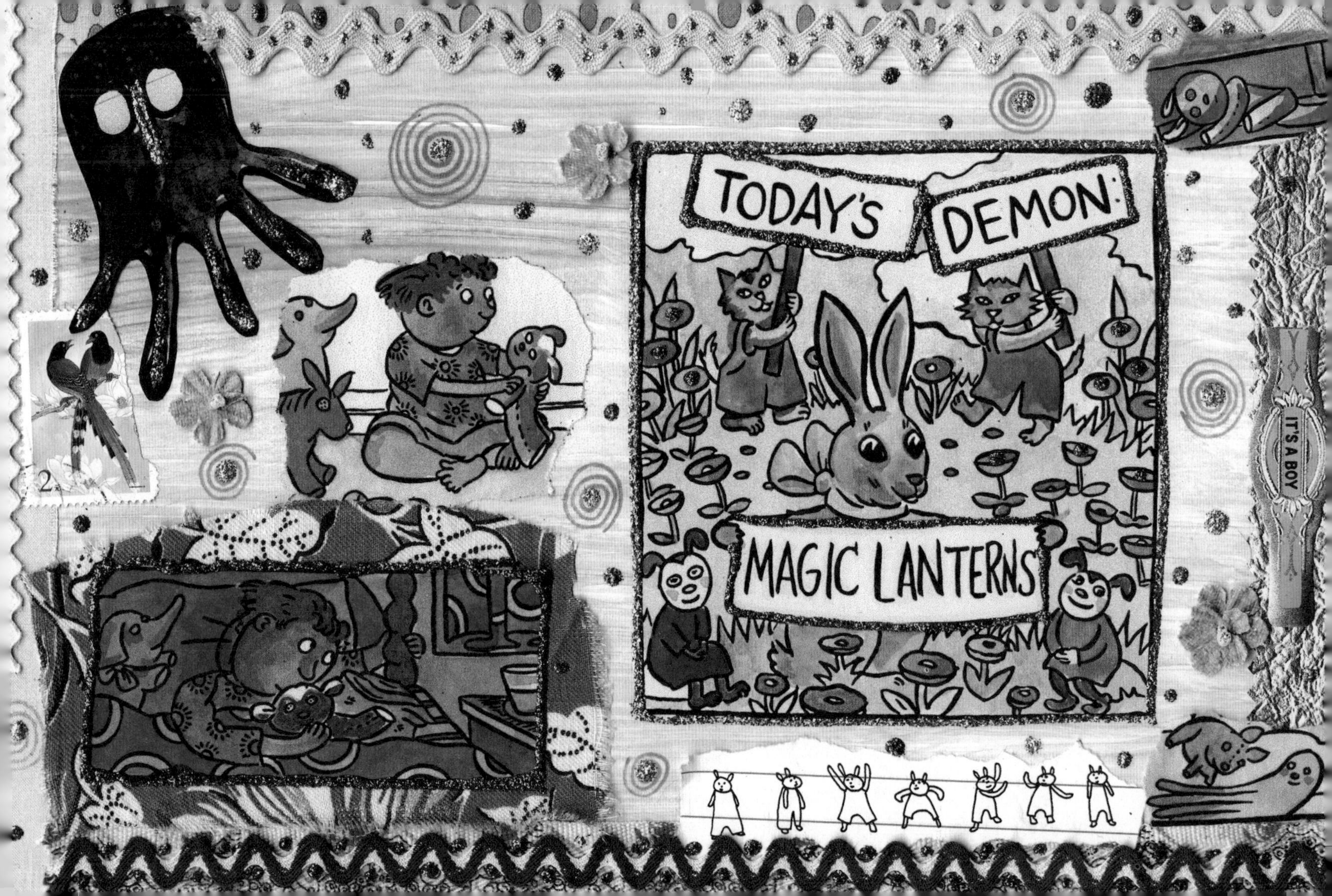
TODAY'S
DEMON:
MAGIC LANTERNS
IT'S A BOY

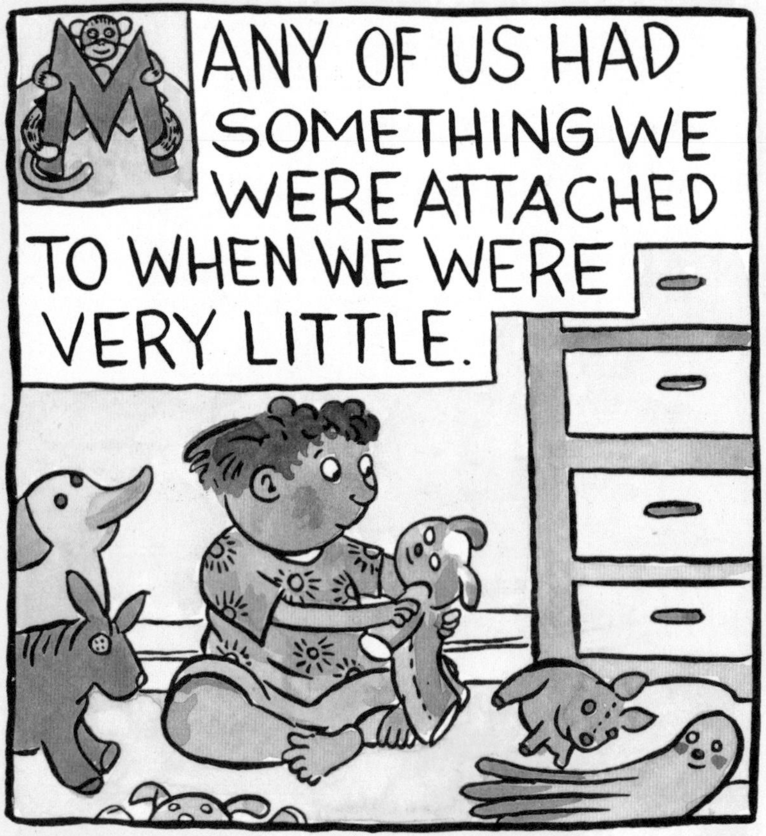
MANY OF US HAD SOMETHING WE WERE ATTACHED TO WHEN WE WERE VERY LITTLE.

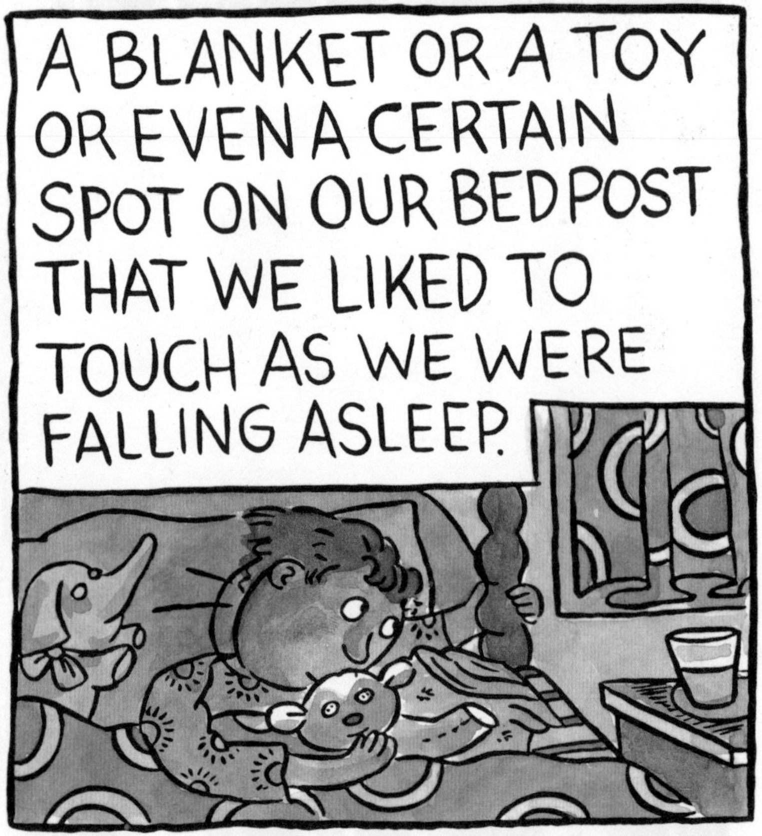
A BLANKET OR A TOY OR EVEN A CERTAIN SPOT ON OUR BEDPOST THAT WE LIKED TO TOUCH AS WE WERE FALLING ASLEEP.

149

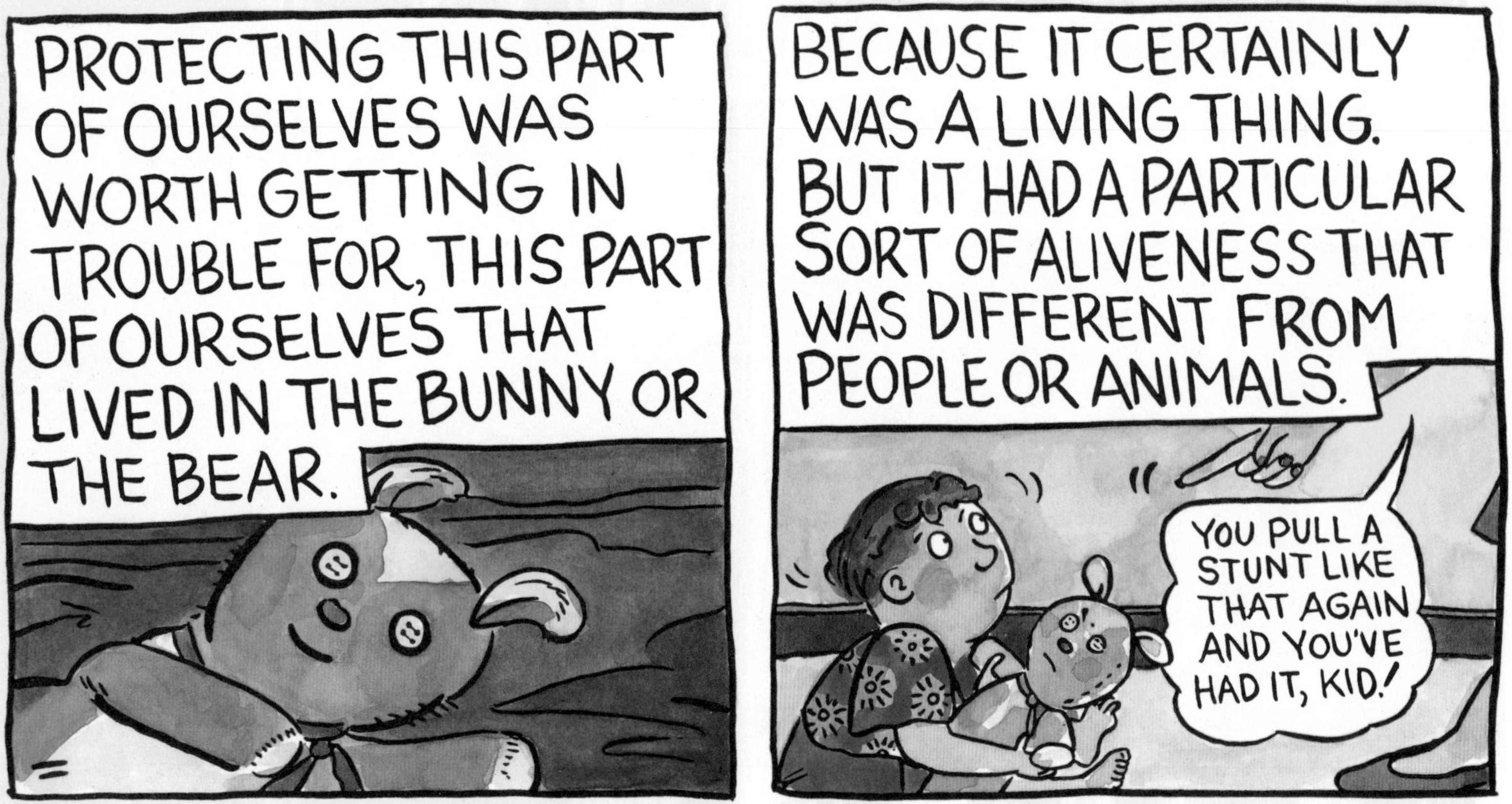
PROTECTING THIS PART OF OURSELVES WAS WORTH GETTING IN TROUBLE FOR, THIS PART OF OURSELVES THAT LIVED IN THE BUNNY OR THE BEAR.
BECAUSE IT CERTAINLY WAS A LIVING THING. BUT IT HAD A PARTICULAR SORT OF ALIVENESS THAT WAS DIFFERENT FROM PEOPLE OR ANIMALS.
YOU PULL A STUNT LIKE THAT AGAIN AND YOU'VE HAD IT, KID!

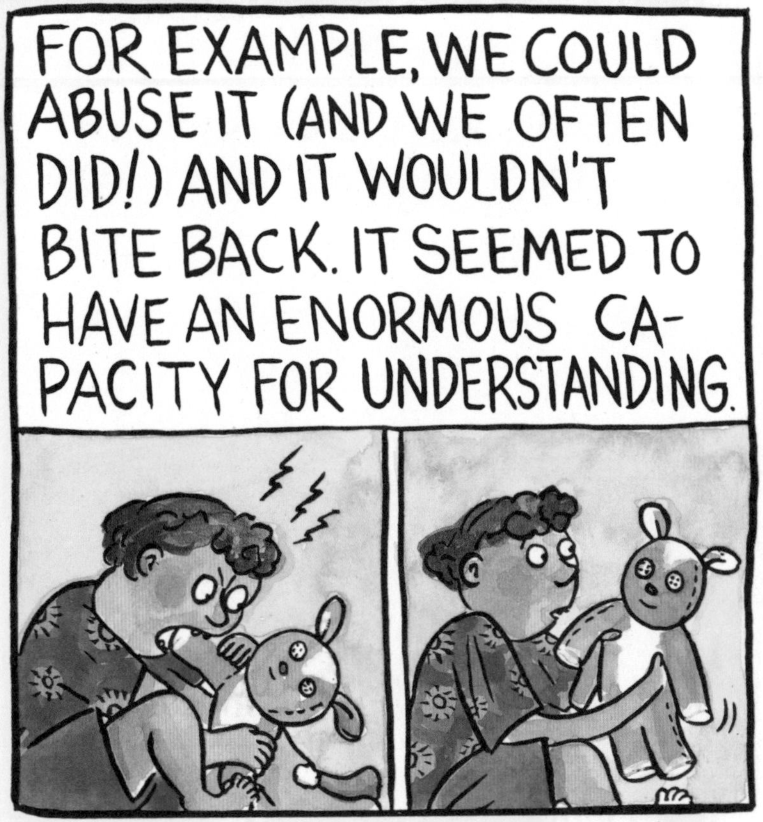
FOR EXAMPLE, WE COULD ABUSE IT (AND WE OFTEN DID!) AND IT WOULDN'T BITE BACK. IT SEEMED TO HAVE AN ENORMOUS CAPACITY FOR UNDERSTANDING.

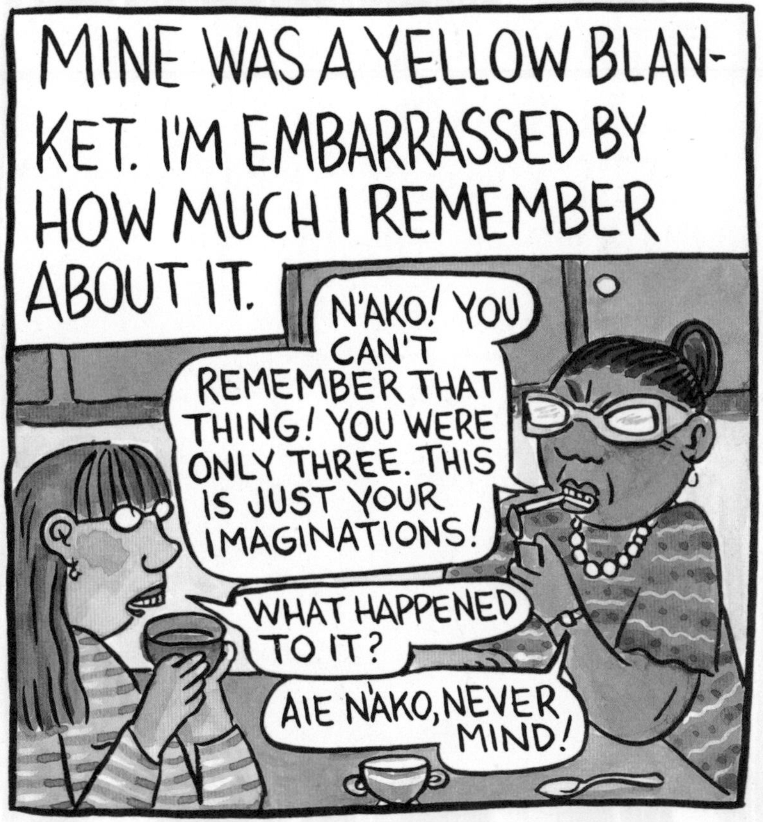
MINE WAS A YELLOW BLANKET. I'M EMBARRASSED BY HOW MUCH I REMEMBER ABOUT IT.
N'AKO! YOU CAN'T REMEMBER THAT THING! YOU WERE ONLY THREE. THIS IS JUST YOUR IMAGINATIONS!
WHAT HAPPENED TO IT?
AIE N'AKO, NEVER MIND!

IT HAD GRAY AND BLACK KITTENS ON IT AND THEY WERE CHASING RED BALLS THROUGH THE FLOWERS. I KNEW THOSE KITTENS WELL.

SOME ADULTS ARE MADE NERVOUS BY SUCH PASSIONATE ATTACHMENT IN A CHILD. THEY GIVE REASONS FOR STOPPING IT THAT SOUND SENSIBLE, AT LEAST TO THEMSELVES.

THAT THING WAS A RAG! IT WAS FILTHY! I WAS ASHAMED FOR YOU! YOU WERE TOO OLD! N'AKO, YOU LOOKED STUPID! YOU WANT PEOPLE TO SAY YOU'RE DIRTY AND STUPID?

AND THERE WERE BROTHERS OR SISTERS OR COUSINS WHO ENJOYED THE SUDDEN POWER THEY COULD HAVE OVER US BY MESSING WITH SOMETHING THAT SEEMED LIKE NOTHING TO THEM.

WHAT'S THE BIG DEAL ABOUT THIS STUPID BEAR?

HUH? WHAT'S THE BIG DEAL?

AND THEN THERE ARE THE ACCIDENTS. THINGS DROP. THINGS ARE LEFT BEHIND. THE TWINS, THE LOVERS, THE CHILD AND ITS MOTHER ARE SEPARATED. WHAT LOOKED LIKE A RAG CONTAINED ALL THESE THINGS AND MORE.

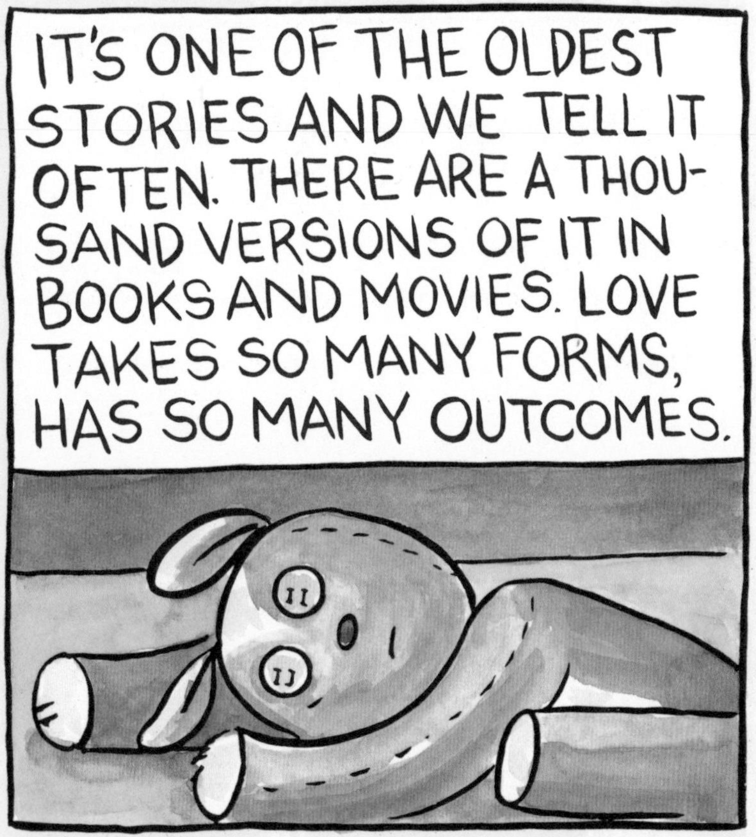
IT'S ONE OF THE OLDEST STORIES AND WE TELL IT OFTEN. THERE ARE A THOUSAND VERSIONS OF IT IN BOOKS AND MOVIES. LOVE TAKES SO MANY FORMS, HAS SO MANY OUTCOMES.

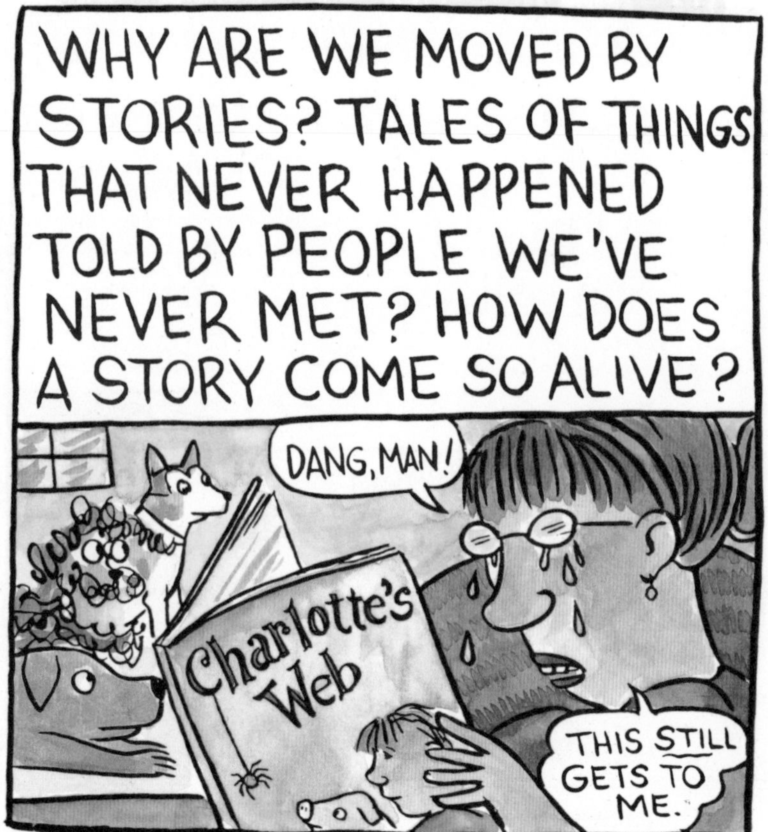
WHY ARE WE MOVED BY STORIES? TALES OF THINGS THAT NEVER HAPPENED TOLD BY PEOPLE WE'VE NEVER MET? HOW DOES A STORY COME SO ALIVE?
DANG, MAN!
Charlotte's Web
THIS STILL GETS TO ME.

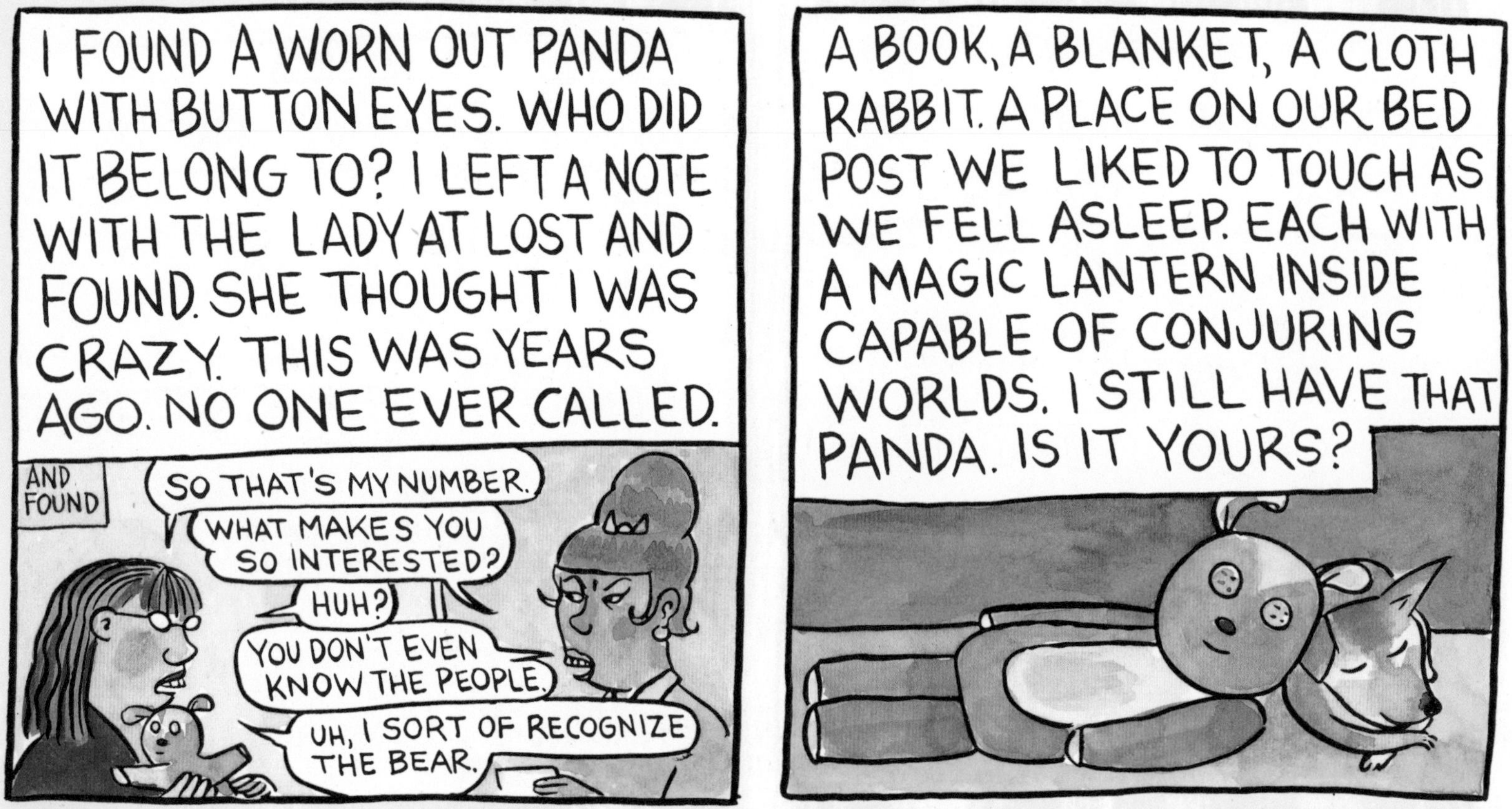
I FOUND A WORN OUT PANDA WITH BUTTON EYES. WHO DID IT BELONG TO? I LEFT A NOTE WITH THE LADY AT LOST AND FOUND. SHE THOUGHT I WAS CRAZY. THIS WAS YEARS AGO. NO ONE EVER CALLED.
AND FOUND
SO THAT'S MY NUMBER.
WHAT MAKES YOU SO INTERESTED?
HUH?
YOU DON'T EVEN KNOW THE PEOPLE.
UH, I SORT OF RECOGNIZE THE BEAR.
A BOOK, A BLANKET, A CLOTH RABBIT. A PLACE ON OUR BED POST WE LIKED TO TOUCH AS WE FELL ASLEEP. EACH WITH A MAGIC LANTERN INSIDE CAPABLE OF CONJURING WORLDS. I STILL HAVE THAT PANDA. IS IT YOURS?

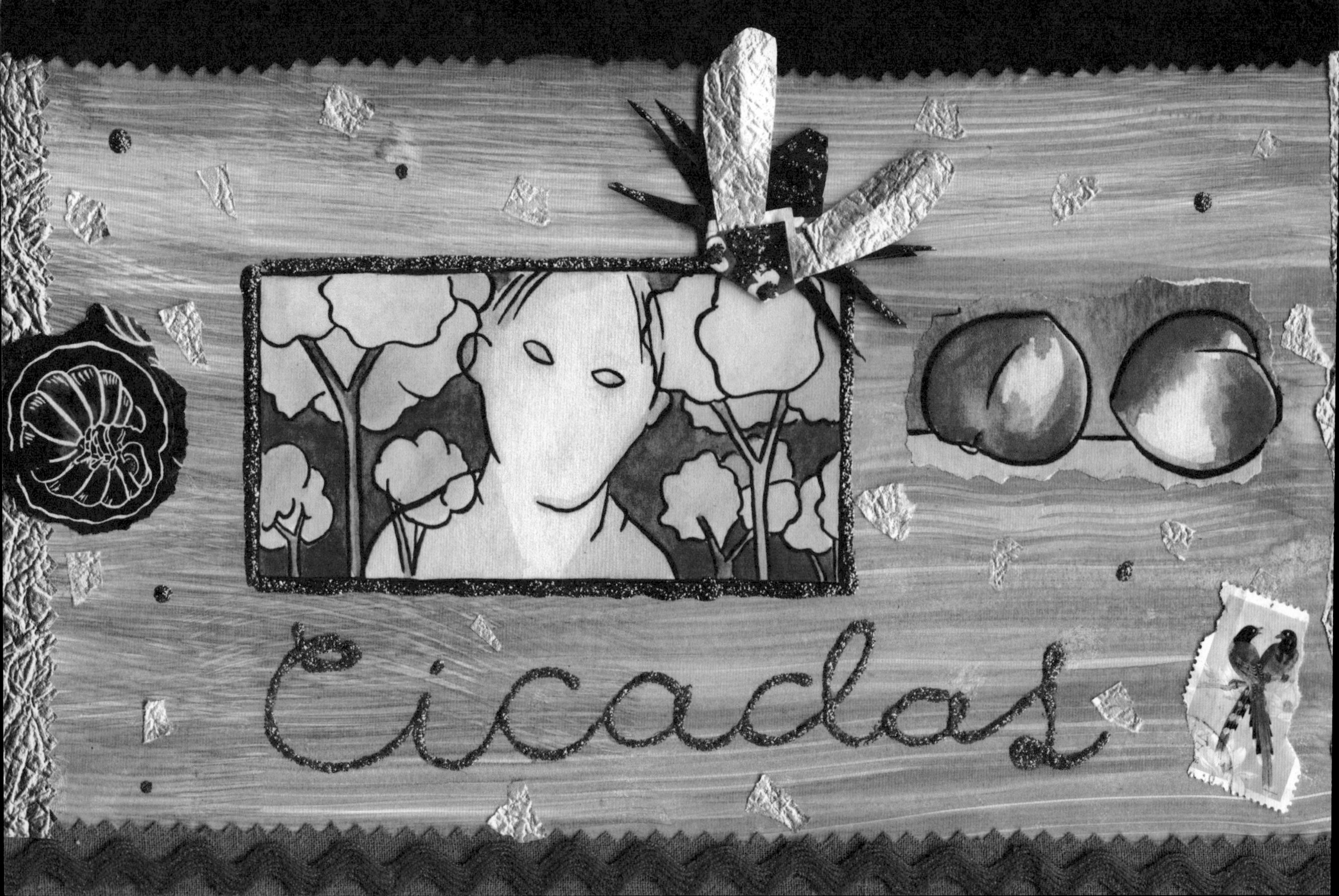
Cicadas

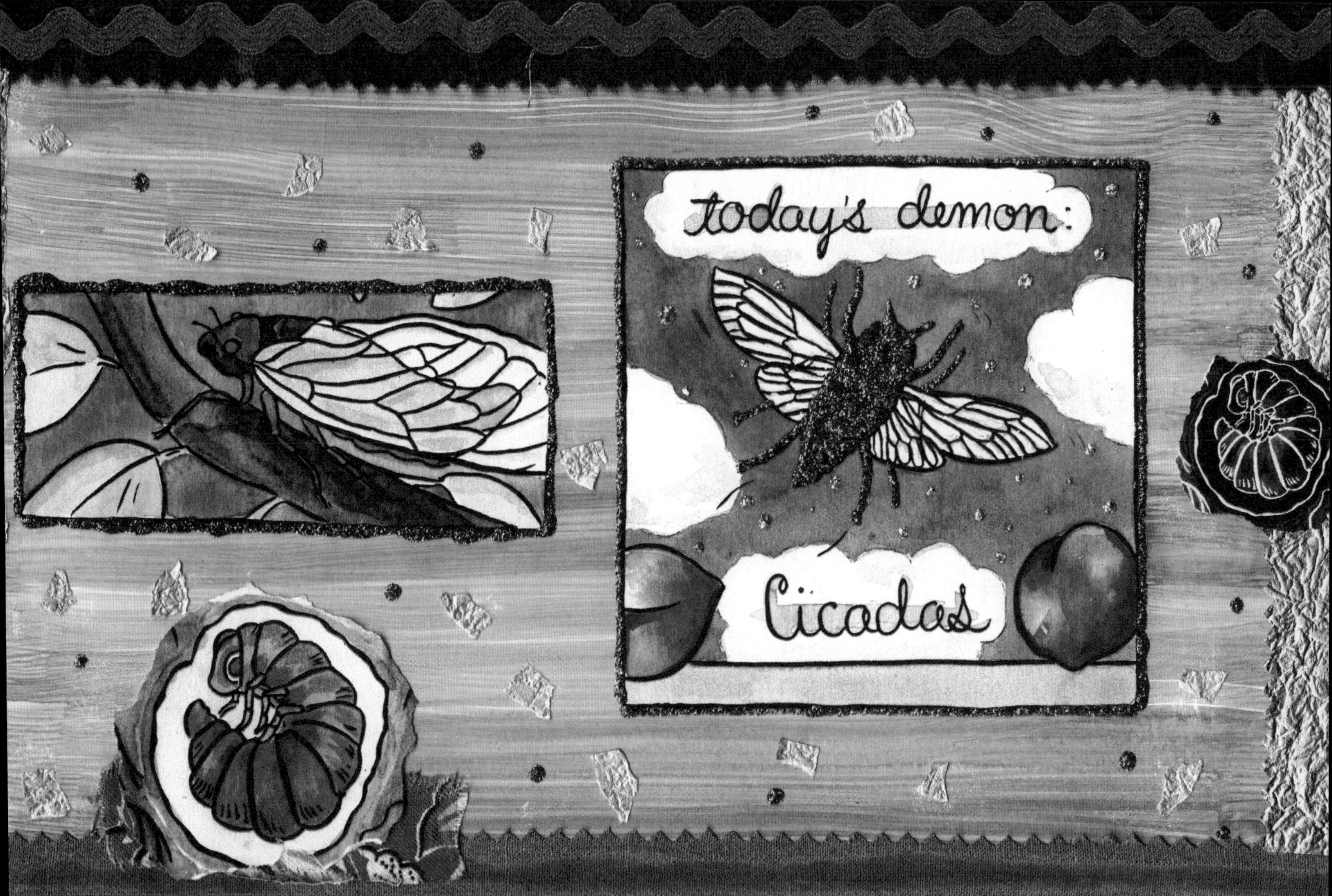
today's demon:
Cicadas

hen I WAS 14 I MET A BOY WHOSE FACE I BARELY re-member NOW, ALTHOUGH I REMEMBER HE was CUTE, and WE took SPEED TOGETHER. WE GOT SOME wine ONCE and CHUGGED IT. we KISSED that DAY. HE had FRECKLES. I CAN remember THAT.

When I TRY to PICTURE HIM I SEE a CHIPPED FRONT tooth, I Sat IN THE DYING GRASS WITH him BEHIND the ROLLER rink 30 YEARS AGO. It WAS NIGHT, EARLY SEP-TEMBER. We SPLIT A CIG AND kissed A LITTLE, waiting FOR OUR FRIENDS. INSIDE THE ROLLER RINK, LAME music BLASTED.

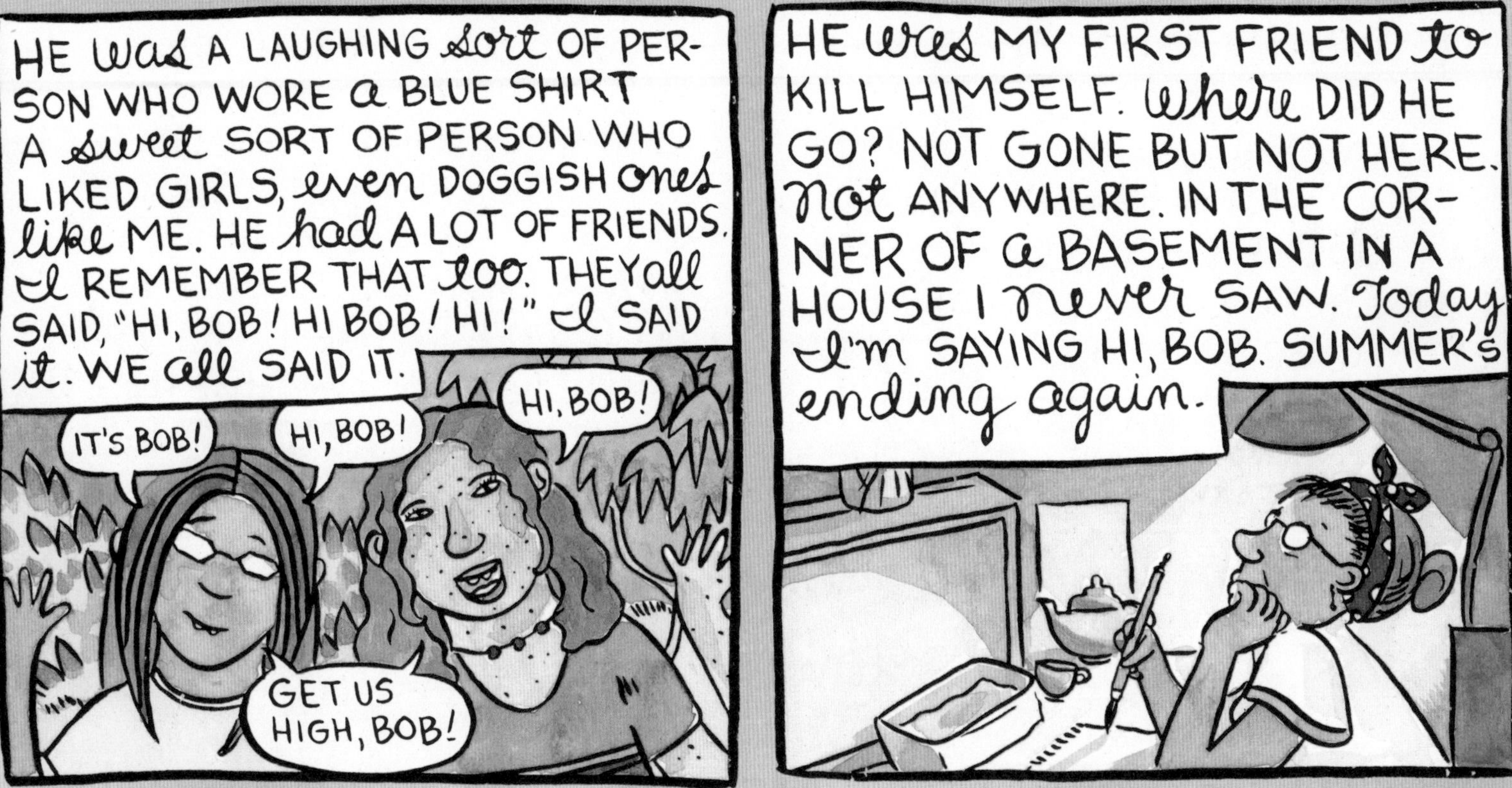
HE was A LAUGHING sort OF PERSON WHO WORE a BLUE SHIRT A sweet SORT OF PERSON WHO LIKED GIRLS, even DOGGISH ones like ME. HE had A LOT OF FRIENDS. I REMEMBER THAT too. THEY all SAID, "HI, BOB! HI BOB! HI!" I SAID it. WE all SAID IT.
IT'S BOB!
HI, BOB!
HI, BOB!
GET US HIGH, BOB!
HE was MY FIRST FRIEND to KILL HIMSELF. Where DID HE GO? NOT GONE BUT NOT HERE. Not ANYWHERE. IN THE CORNER OF a BASEMENT IN A HOUSE I never SAW. Today I'm SAYING HI, BOB. SUMMER's ending again.

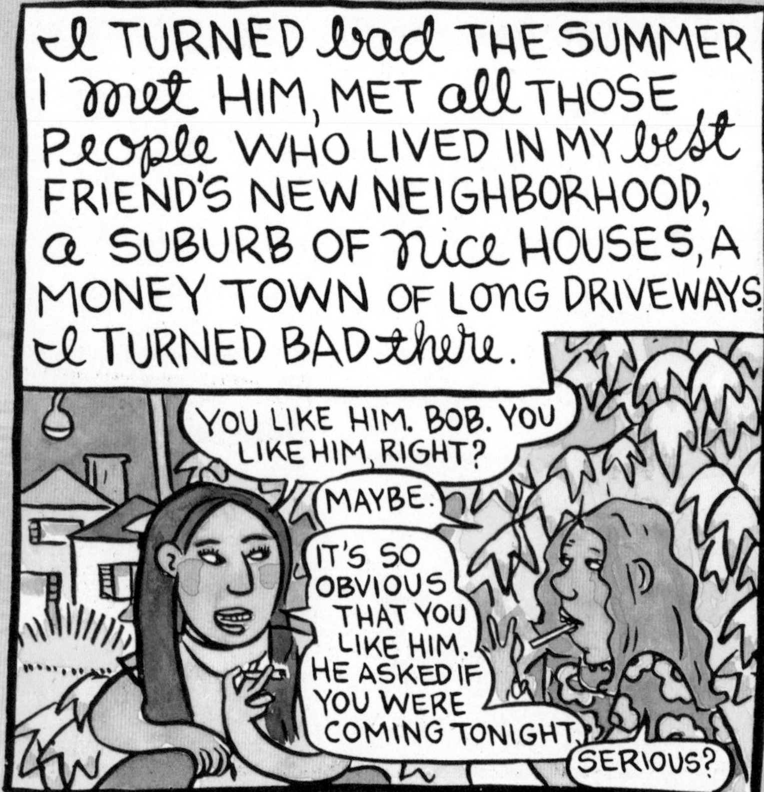
I TURNED bad THE SUMMER I met HIM, MET all THOSE people WHO LIVED IN MY best FRIEND'S NEW NEIGHBORHOOD, a SUBURB OF nice HOUSES, A MONEY TOWN OF LONG DRIVEWAYS. I TURNED BAD there.
YOU LIKE HIM. BOB. YOU LIKE HIM, RIGHT?
MAYBE.
IT'S SO OBVIOUS THAT YOU LIKE HIM. HE ASKED IF YOU WERE COMING TONIGHT.
SERIOUS?

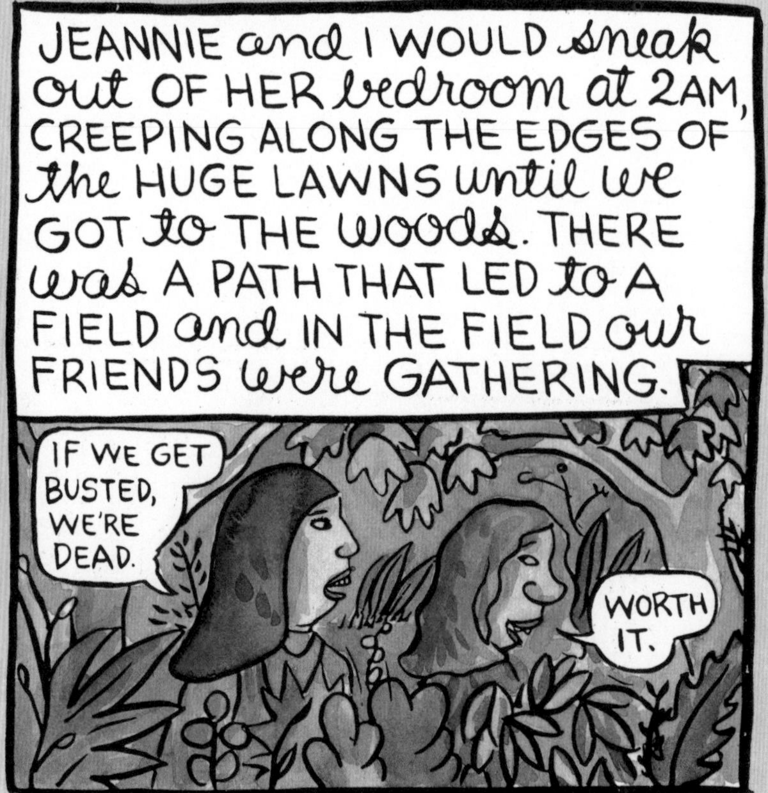
JEANNIE and I WOULD sneak out OF HER bedroom at 2AM, CREEPING ALONG THE EDGES OF the HUGE LAWNS until we GOT to THE woods. THERE was A PATH THAT LED to A FIELD and IN THE FIELD our FRIENDS were GATHERING.
IF WE GET BUSTED, WE'RE DEAD.
WORTH IT.

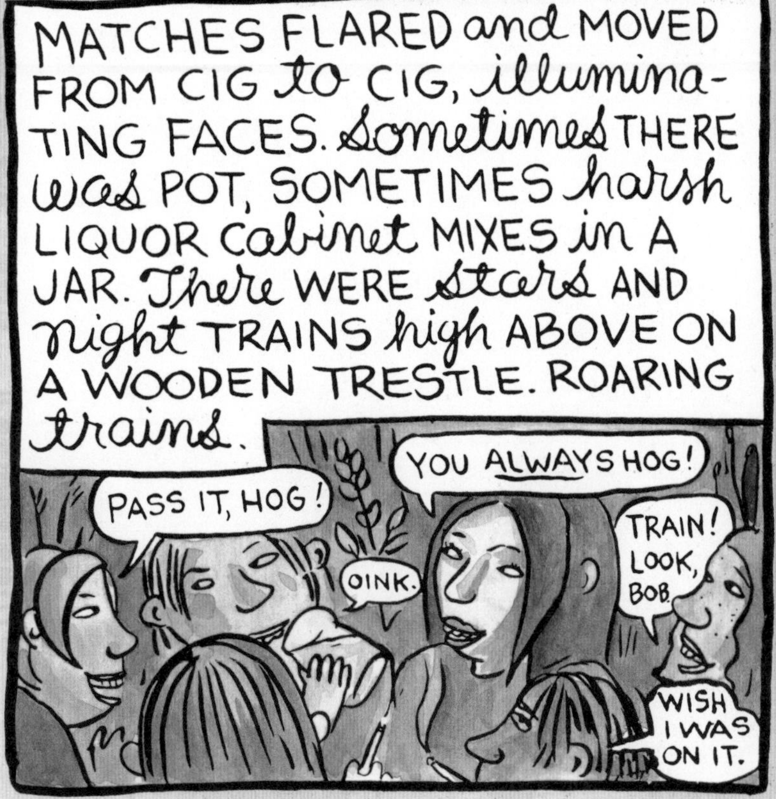
MATCHES FLARED and MOVED FROM CIG to CIG, illuminating FACES. Sometimes THERE was POT, SOMETIMES harsh LIQUOR cabinet MIXES in A JAR. There WERE stars AND night TRAINS high ABOVE ON A WOODEN TRESTLE. ROARING trains.
YOU ALWAYS HOG!
PASS IT, HOG!
OINK.
TRAIN! LOOK, BOB.
WISH I WAS ON IT.

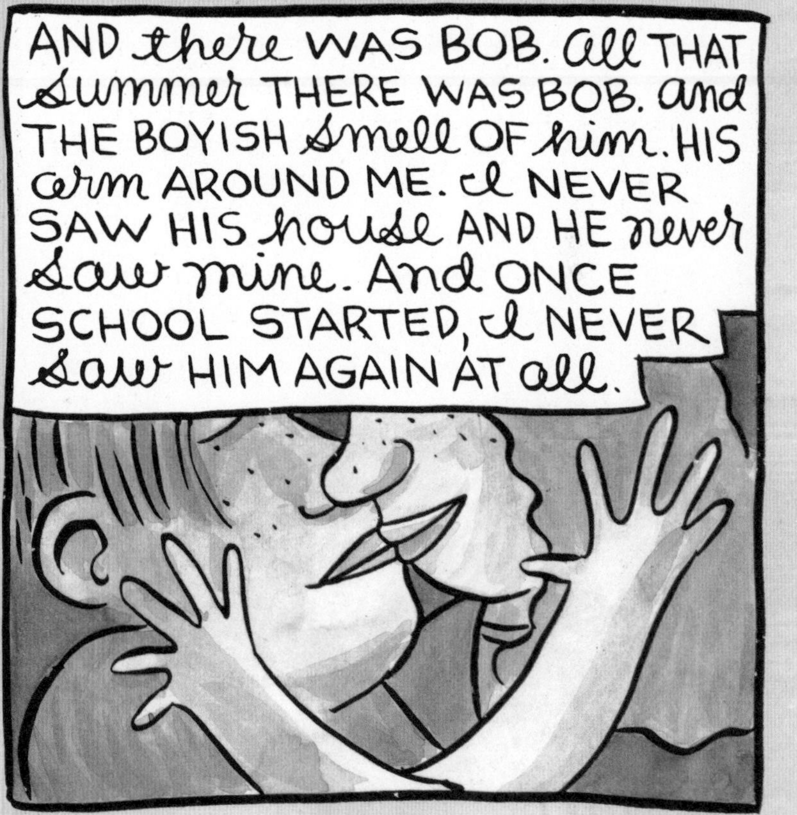
AND there WAS BOB. All THAT Summer THERE WAS BOB. and THE BOYISH Smell OF him. HIS arm AROUND ME. I NEVER SAW HIS house AND HE never saw mine. And ONCE SCHOOL STARTED, I NEVER saw HIM AGAIN AT all.

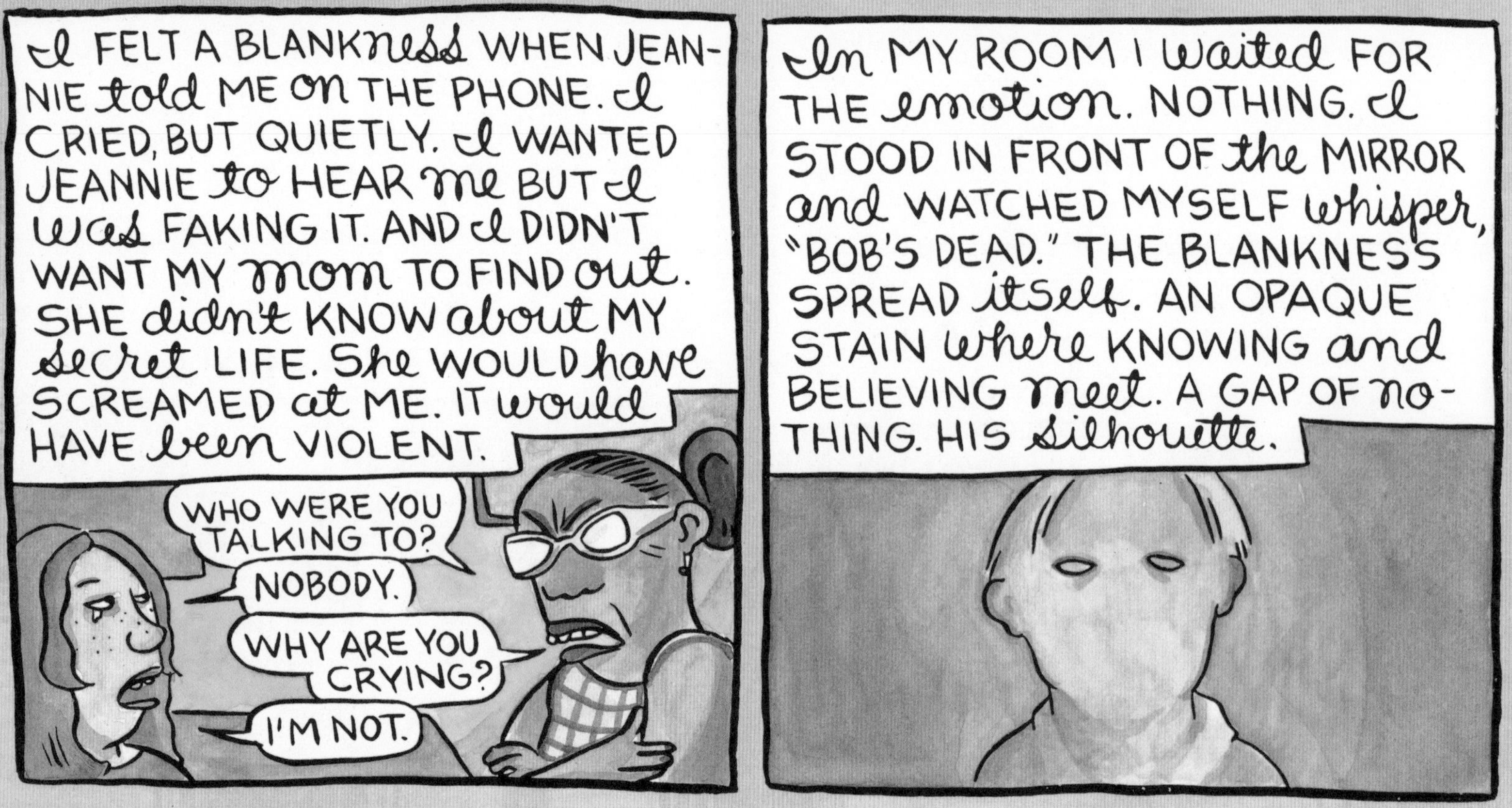
I FELT A BLANKNESS WHEN JEANNIE told ME ON THE PHONE. I CRIED, BUT QUIETLY. I WANTED JEANNIE to HEAR me BUT I was FAKING IT. AND I DIDN'T WANT MY mom TO FIND out. SHE didn't KNOW about MY secret LIFE. She WOULD have SCREAMED at ME. IT would HAVE been VIOLENT.
WHO WERE YOU TALKING TO?
NOBODY.
WHY ARE YOU CRYING?
I'M NOT.
In MY ROOM I waited FOR THE emotion. NOTHING. I STOOD IN FRONT OF the MIRROR and WATCHED MYSELF whisper, "BOB'S DEAD." THE BLANKNESS SPREAD itself. AN OPAQUE STAIN where KNOWING and BELIEVING meet. A GAP OF nothing. HIS silhouette.

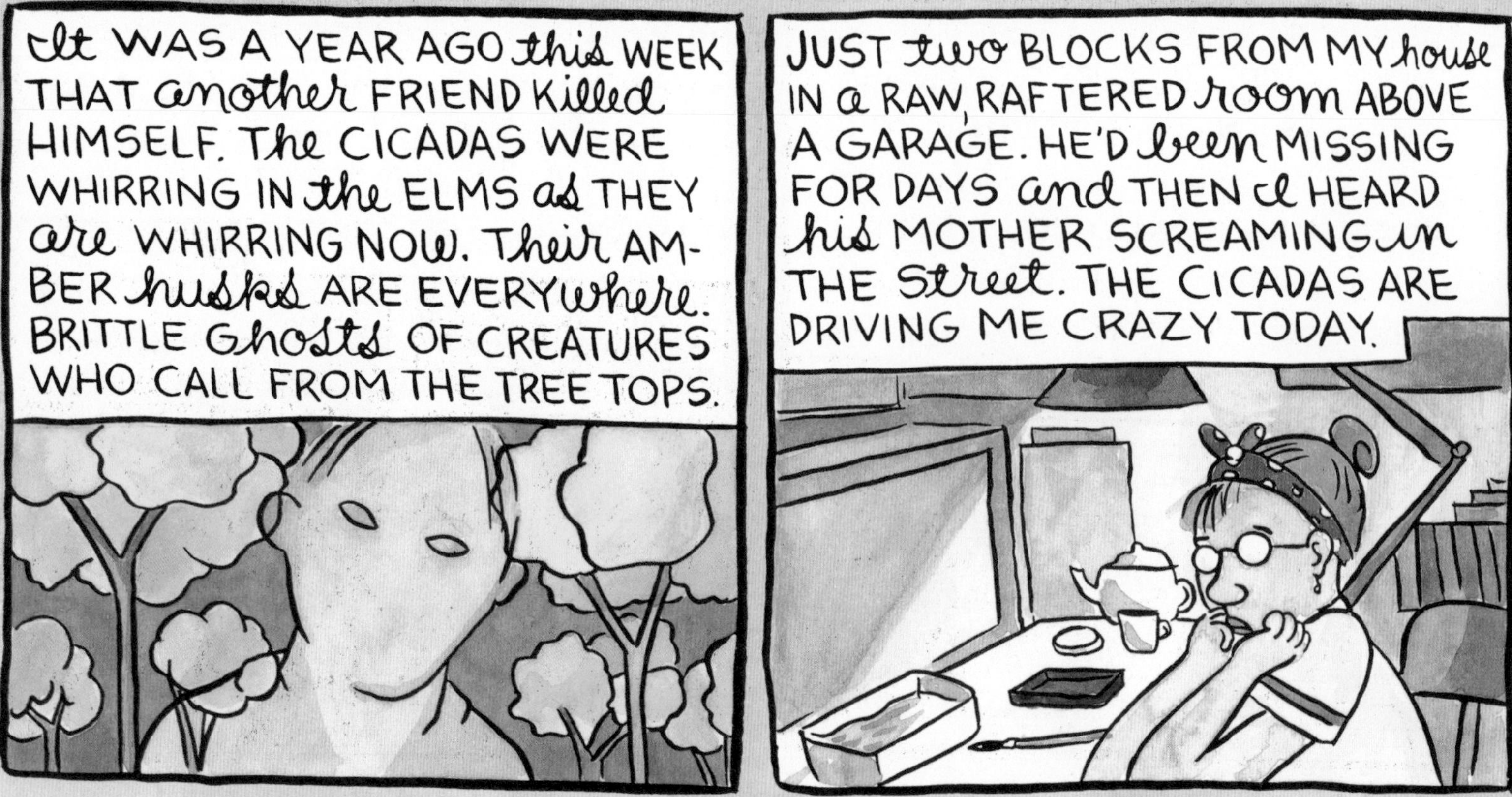
It WAS A YEAR AGO this WEEK THAT another FRIEND Killed HIMSELF. The CICADAS WERE WHIRRING IN the ELMS as THEY are WHIRRING NOW. Their AMBER husks ARE EVERYwhere. BRITTLE Ghosts OF CREATURES WHO CALL FROM THE TREE TOPS.
JUST two BLOCKS FROM MY house IN a RAW, RAFTERED room ABOVE A GARAGE. HE'D been MISSING FOR DAYS and THEN I HEARD his MOTHER SCREAMING in THE Street. THE CICADAS ARE DRIVING ME CRAZY TODAY.

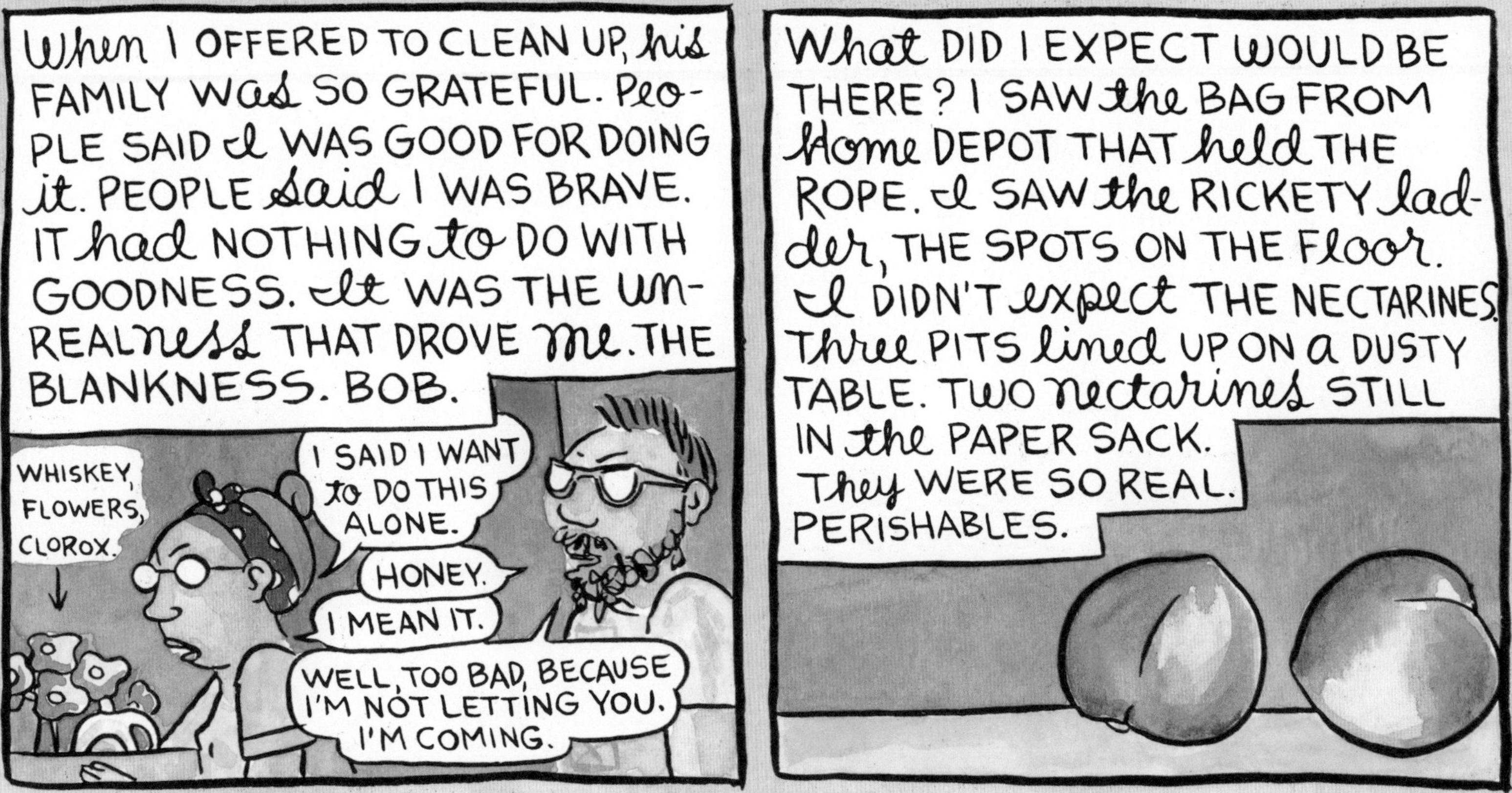
When I OFFERED TO CLEAN UP, his FAMILY was SO GRATEFUL. People SAID I WAS GOOD FOR DOING it. PEOPLE said I WAS BRAVE. IT had NOTHING to DO WITH GOODNESS. It WAS THE unREALness THAT DROVE me. THE BLANKNESS. BOB.
WHISKEY, FLOWERS, CLOROX.
I SAID I WANT to DO THIS ALONE.
HONEY.
I MEAN IT.
WELL, TOO BAD, BECAUSE I'M NOT LETTING YOU. I'M COMING.
What DID I EXPECT WOULD BE THERE? I SAW the BAG FROM Home DEPOT THAT held THE ROPE. I SAW the RICKETY ladder, THE SPOTS ON THE Floor. I DIDN'T expect THE NECTARINES. Three PITS lined UP ON a DUSTY TABLE. TWO nectarines STILL IN the PAPER SACK. They WERE SO REAL. PERISHABLES.

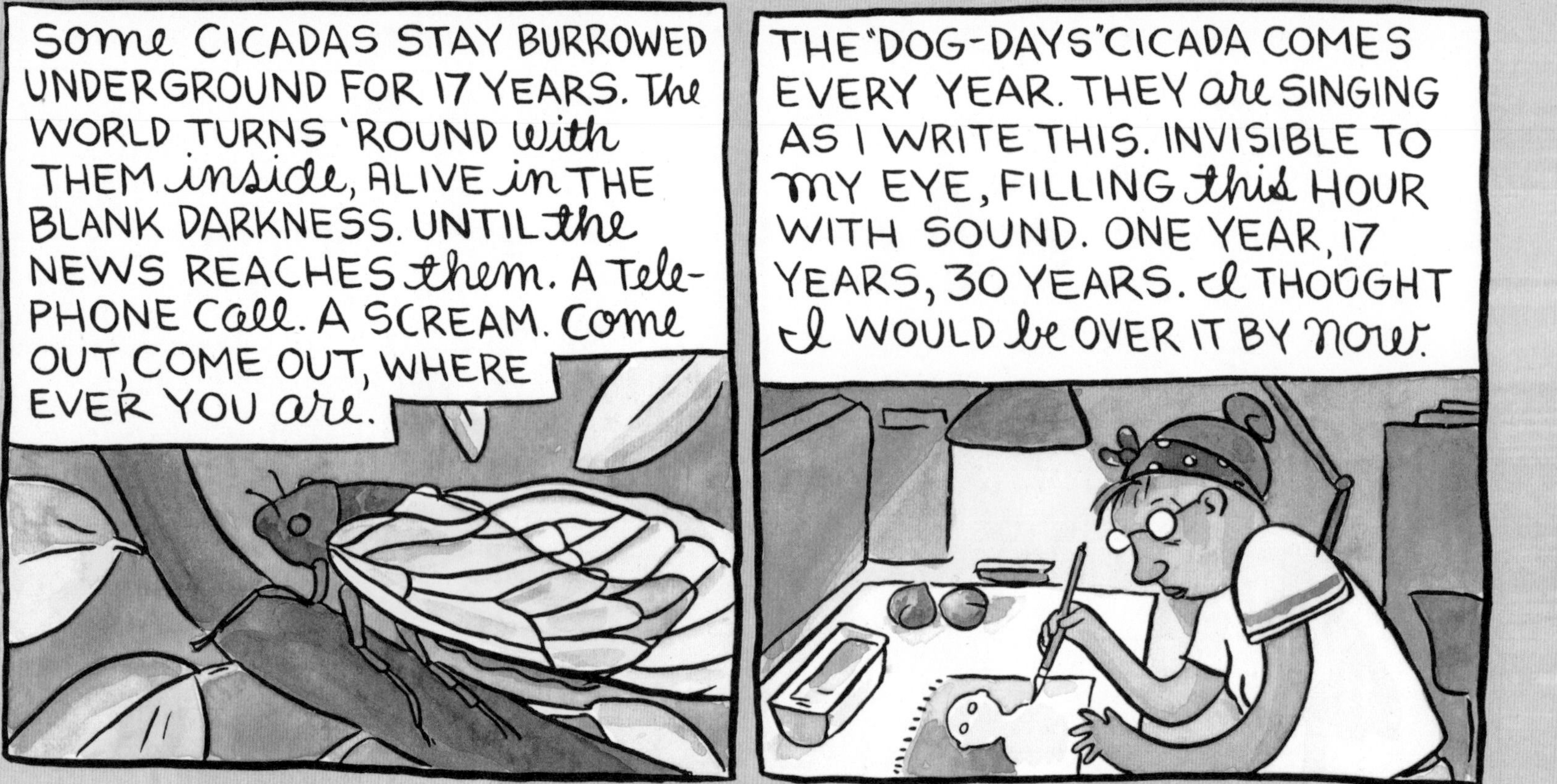
Some CICADAS STAY BURROWED UNDERGROUND FOR 17 YEARS. The WORLD TURNS 'ROUND with THEM inside, ALIVE in THE BLANK DARKNESS. UNTIL the NEWS REACHES them. A Telephone Call. A SCREAM. Come OUT, COME OUT, WHERE EVER YOU are.
THE "DOG-DAYS" CICADA COMES EVERY YEAR. THEY are SINGING AS I WRITE THIS. INVISIBLE TO my EYE, FILLING this HOUR WITH SOUND. ONE YEAR, 17 YEARS, 30 YEARS. I THOUGHT I WOULD be OVER IT BY now.

Dogs

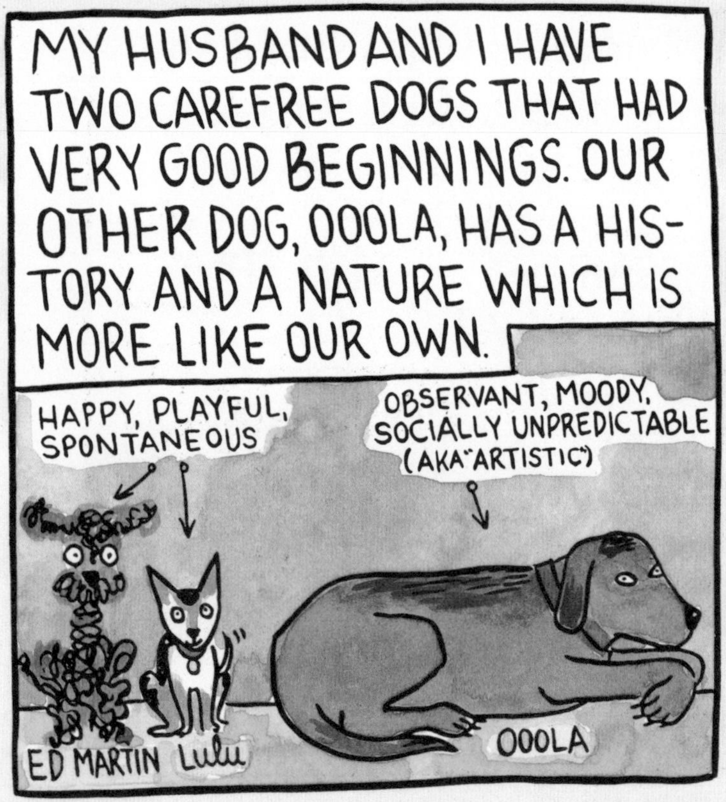
MY HUSBAND AND I HAVE TWO CAREFREE DOGS THAT HAD VERY GOOD BEGINNINGS. OUR OTHER DOG, OOOLA, HAS A HISTORY AND A NATURE WHICH IS MORE LIKE OUR OWN.
HAPPY, PLAYFUL, SPONTANEOUS
OBSERVANT, MOODY, SOCIALLY UNPREDICTABLE (AKA "ARTISTIC")
ED MARTIN
Lulu
OOOLA

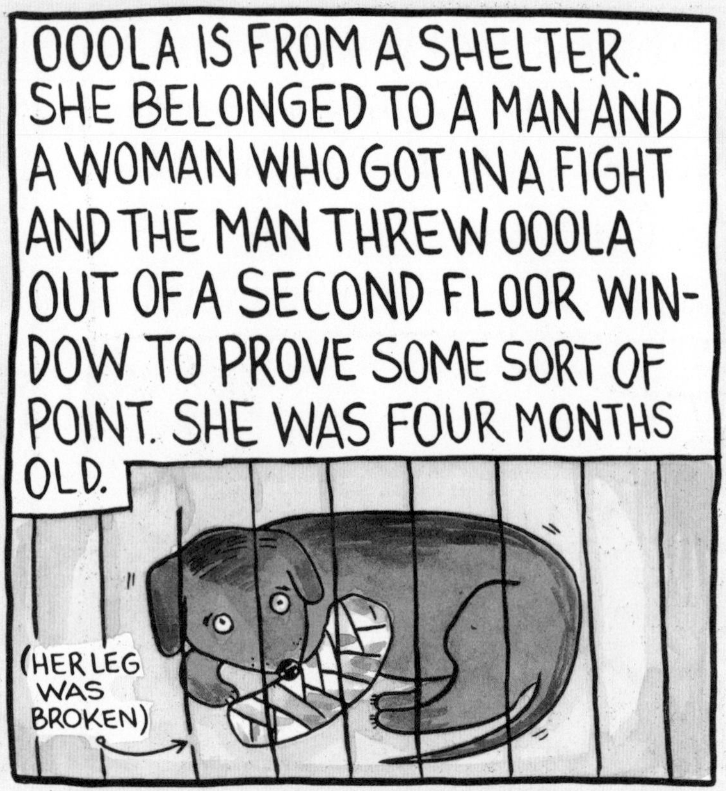
OOOLA IS FROM A SHELTER. SHE BELONGED TO A MAN AND A WOMAN WHO GOT IN A FIGHT AND THE MAN THREW OOOLA OUT OF A SECOND FLOOR WINDOW TO PROVE SOME SORT OF POINT. SHE WAS FOUR MONTHS OLD.
(HER LEG WAS BROKEN)

175

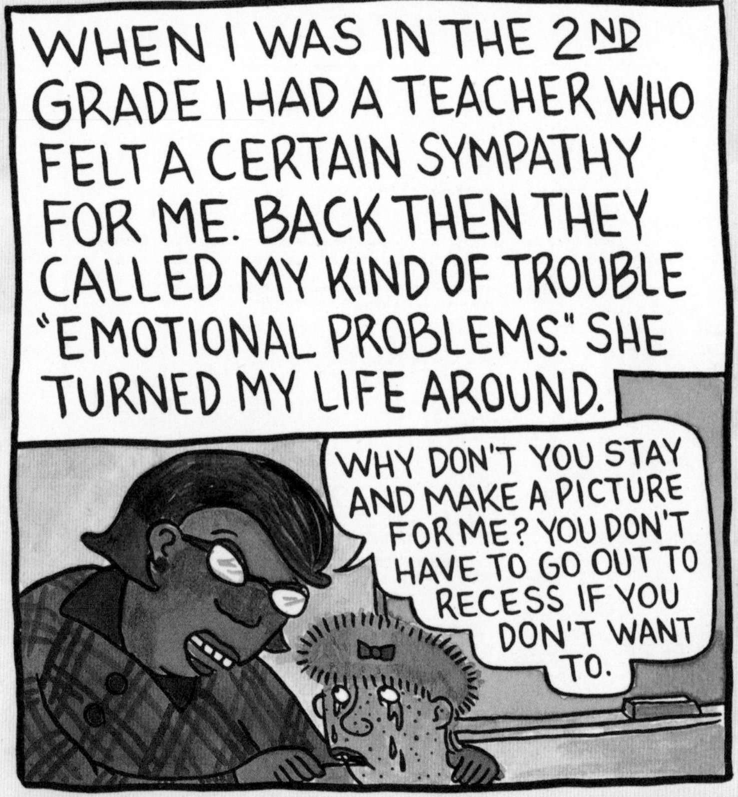
WHEN I WAS IN THE 2ND GRADE I HAD A TEACHER WHO FELT A CERTAIN SYMPATHY FOR ME. BACK THEN THEY CALLED MY KIND OF TROUBLE "EMOTIONAL PROBLEMS." SHE TURNED MY LIFE AROUND.
WHY DON'T YOU STAY AND MAKE A PICTURE FOR ME? YOU DON'T HAVE TO GO OUT TO RECESS IF YOU DON'T WANT TO.

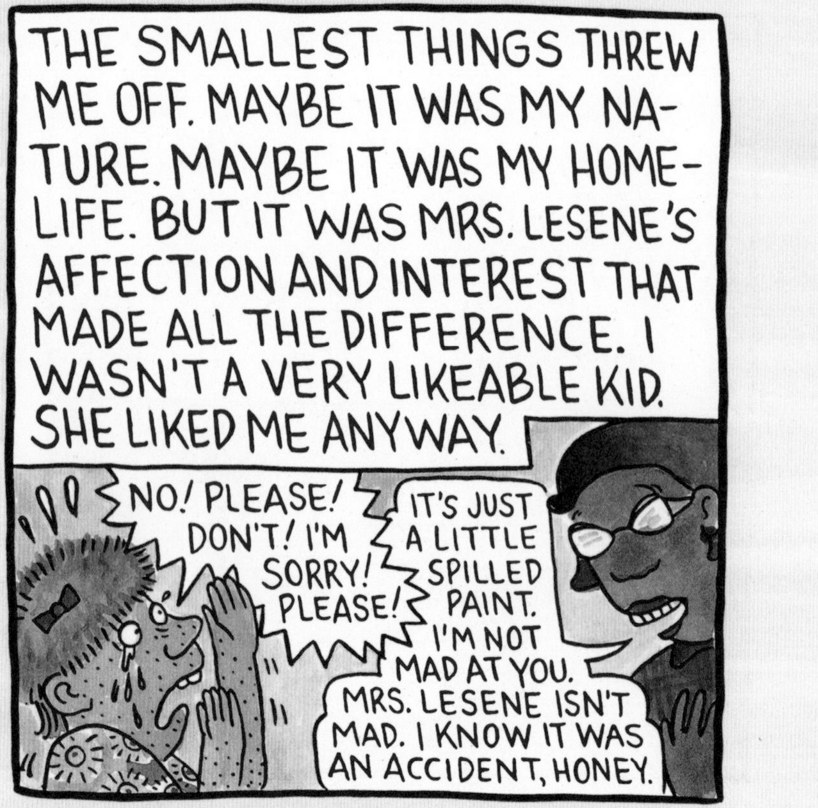
THE SMALLEST THINGS THREW ME OFF. MAYBE IT WAS MY NATURE. MAYBE IT WAS MY HOME-LIFE. BUT IT WAS MRS. LESENE'S AFFECTION AND INTEREST THAT MADE ALL THE DIFFERENCE. I WASN'T A VERY LIKEABLE KID. SHE LIKED ME ANYWAY.
NO! PLEASE! DON'T! I'M SORRY! PLEASE!
IT'S JUST A LITTLE SPILLED PAINT. I'M NOT MAD AT YOU. MRS. LESENE ISN'T MAD. I KNOW IT WAS AN ACCIDENT, HONEY.

177

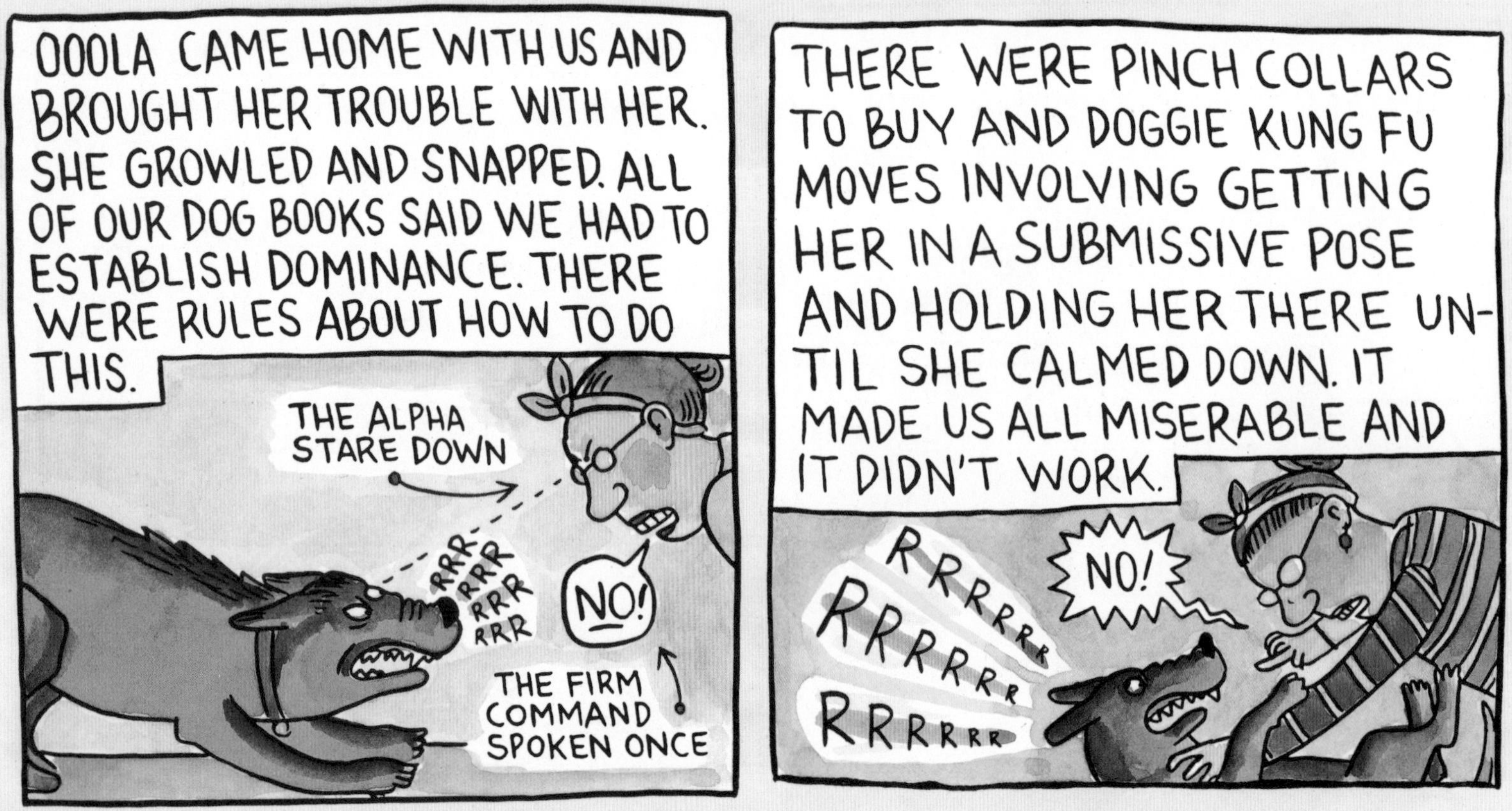
OOOLA CAME HOME WITH US AND BROUGHT HER TROUBLE WITH HER. SHE GROWLED AND SNAPPED. ALL OF OUR DOG BOOKS SAID WE HAD TO ESTABLISH DOMINANCE. THERE WERE RULES ABOUT HOW TO DO THIS.
THE ALPHA STARE DOWN
RRR RRR RRR RRR RRR
NO!
THE FIRM COMMAND SPOKEN ONCE
THERE WERE PINCH COLLARS TO BUY AND DOGGIE KUNG FU MOVES INVOLVING GETTING HER IN A SUBMISSIVE POSE AND HOLDING HER THERE UNTIL SHE CALMED DOWN. IT MADE US ALL MISERABLE AND IT DIDN'T WORK.
RRRRRRR
RRRRRRRR
RRRRRRR
NO!

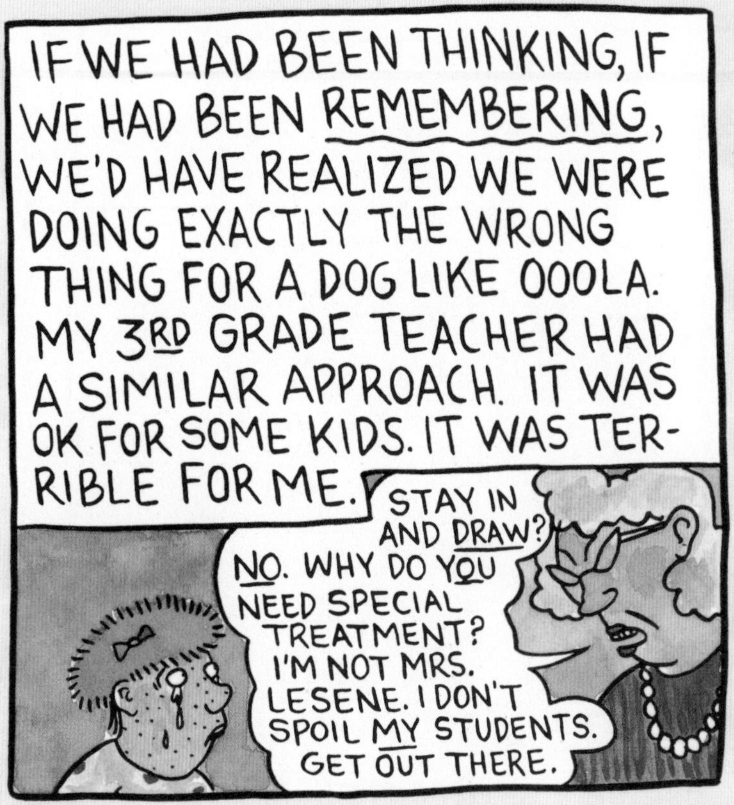
IF WE HAD BEEN THINKING, IF WE HAD BEEN REMEMBERING, WE'D HAVE REALIZED WE WERE DOING EXACTLY THE WRONG THING FOR A DOG LIKE OOOLA. MY 3RD GRADE TEACHER HAD A SIMILAR APPROACH. IT WAS OK FOR SOME KIDS. IT WAS TERRIBLE FOR ME.
STAY IN AND DRAW?
NO. WHY DO YOU NEED SPECIAL TREATMENT? I'M NOT MRS. LESENE. I DON'T SPOIL MY STUDENTS. GET OUT THERE.

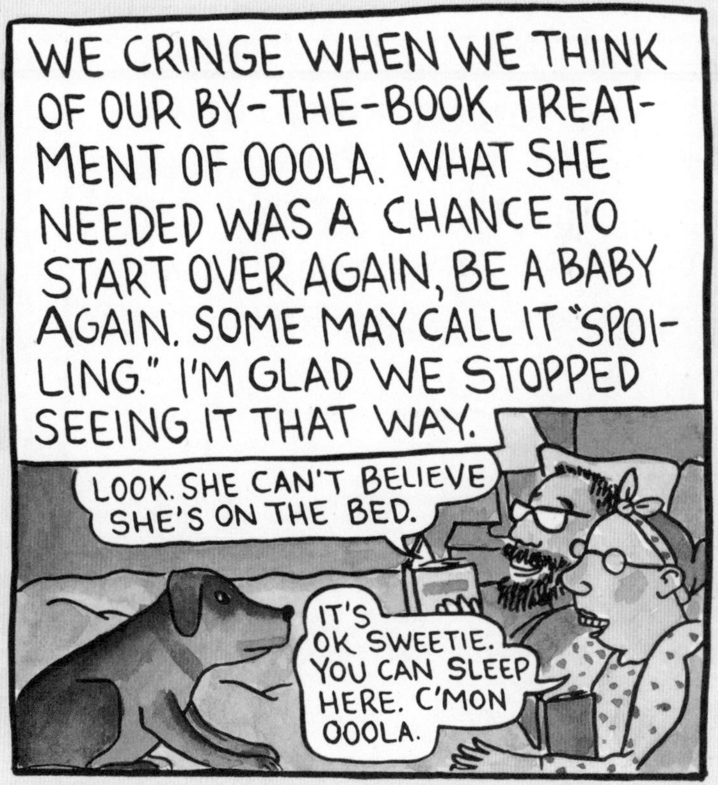
WE CRINGE WHEN WE THINK OF OUR BY-THE-BOOK TREATMENT OF OOOLA. WHAT SHE NEEDED WAS A CHANCE TO START OVER AGAIN, BE A BABY AGAIN. SOME MAY CALL IT "SPOILING." I'M GLAD WE STOPPED SEEING IT THAT WAY.
LOOK. SHE CAN'T BELIEVE SHE'S ON THE BED.
IT'S OK SWEETIE. YOU CAN SLEEP HERE. C'MON OOOLA.

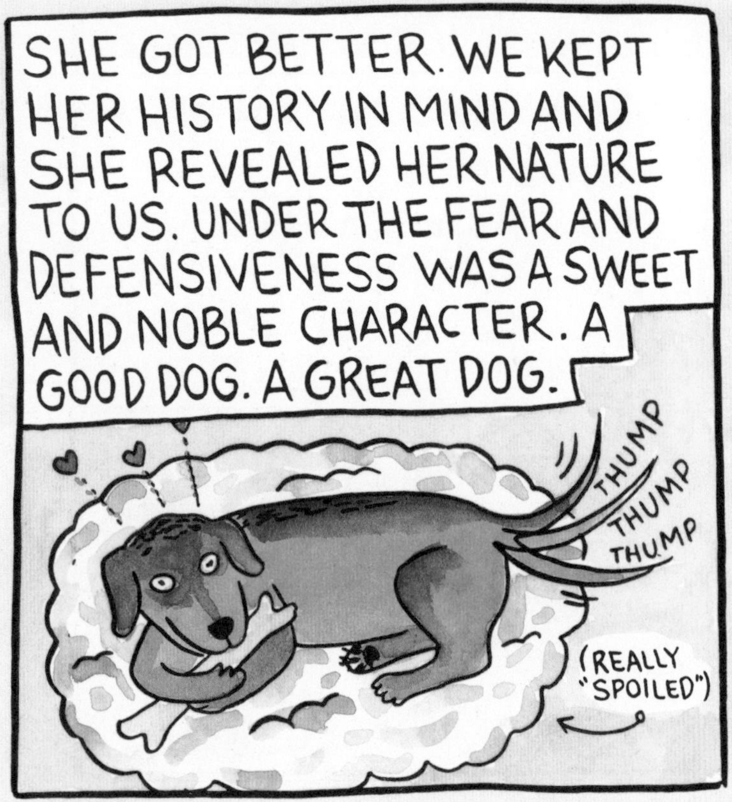
SHE GOT BETTER. WE KEPT HER HISTORY IN MIND AND SHE REVEALED HER NATURE TO US. UNDER THE FEAR AND DEFENSIVENESS WAS A SWEET AND NOBLE CHARACTER. A GOOD DOG. A GREAT DOG.
THUMP
THUMP
THUMP
(REALLY "SPOILED")

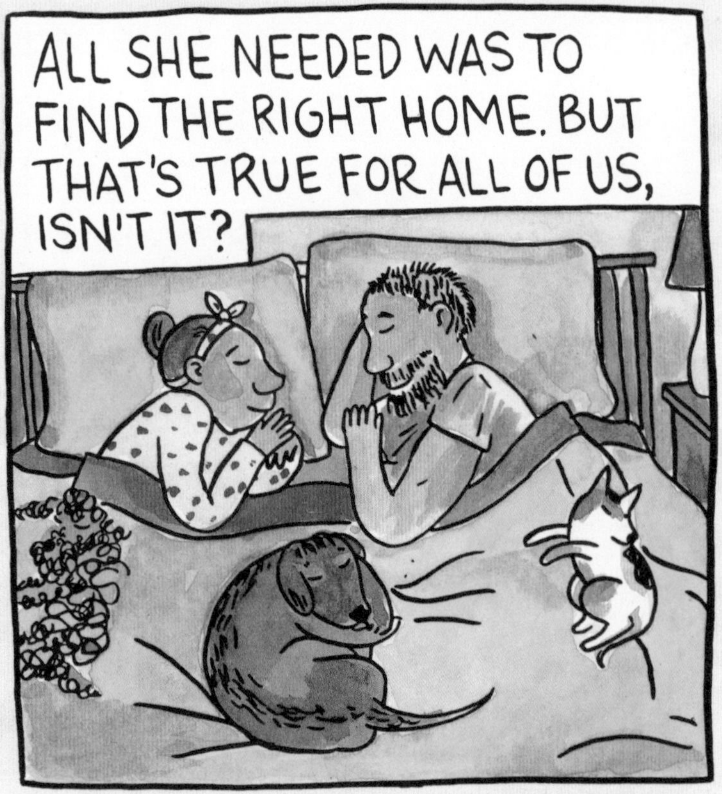
ALL SHE NEEDED WAS TO FIND THE RIGHT HOME. BUT THAT'S TRUE FOR ALL OF US, ISN'T IT?

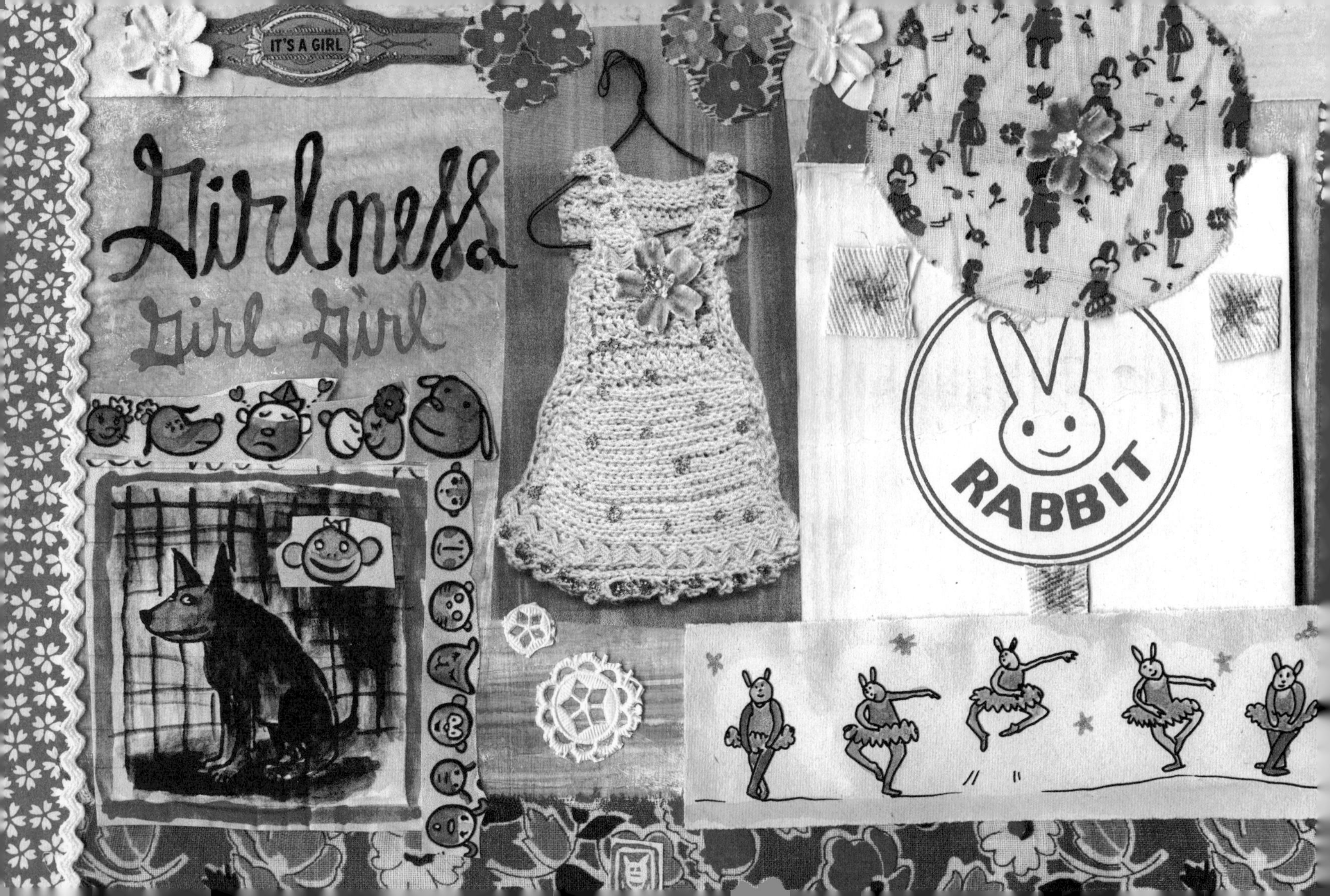

IT'S A GIRL
Girlness
Girl Girl
RABBIT

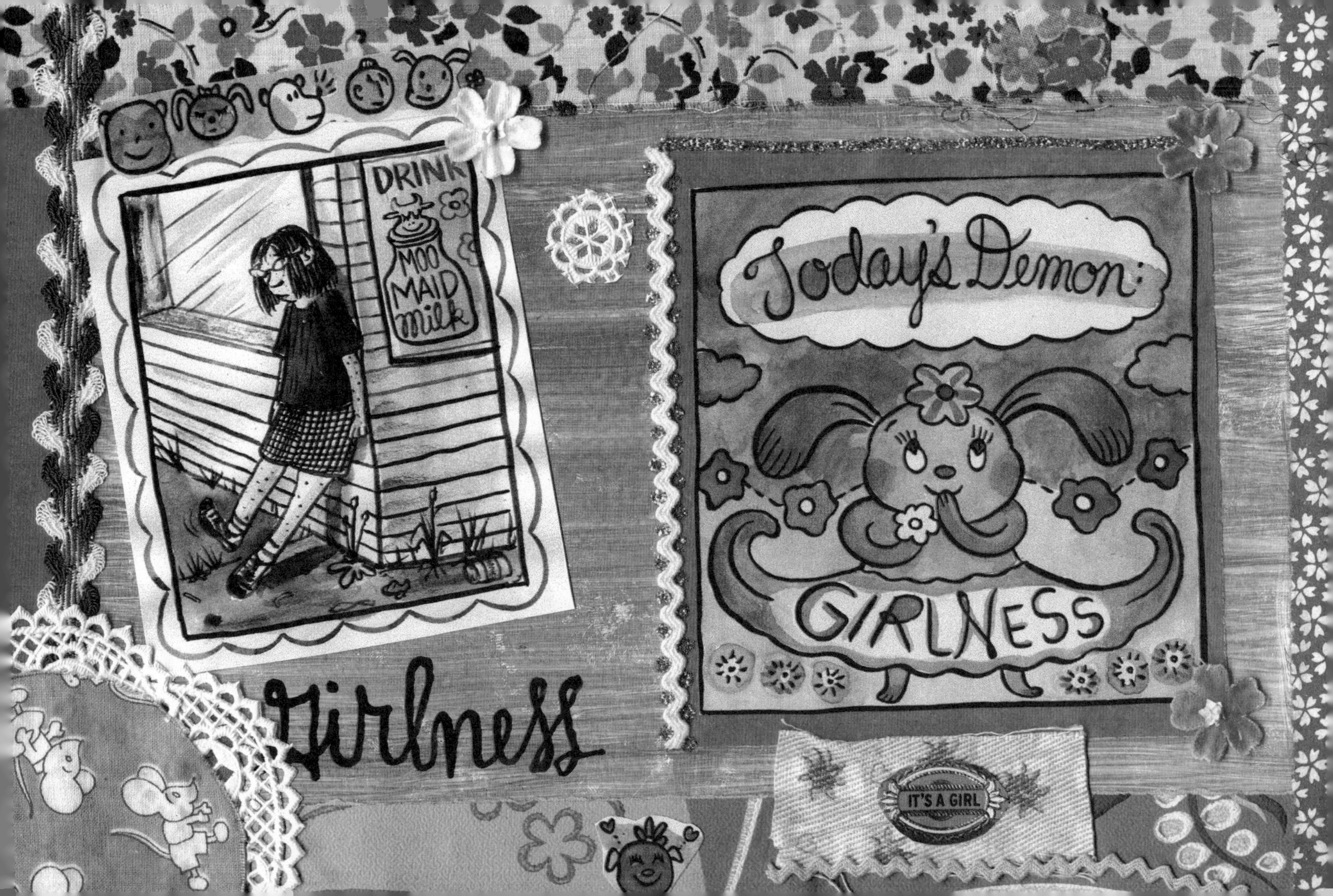

DRINK
MOO MAID milk
Today's Demon:
GIRLNESS
Girlness
IT'S A GIRL

185

187

189

WHICH *was* WORSE? GIRLNESS THAT WAS INSISTED UPON OR GIRLNESS THAT *was* FORBIDDEN? FRILLY CLOTHES YOU COULDN'T PLAY IN *or* RATTY CLOTHES YOU *were* ASHAMED OF? HER *mom* OR MY *mom*?

IT'S BACK TO SCHOOL HELL

CAN WE GET THE PURPLISH-PINK ONE?

WHY? SO YOU CAN LOOK LIKE A CORPSE? I'M THE ONE WHO HAS TO LOOK AT YOU, YOU KNOW.

NEVER MIND.

This SUMMER, A 13 YEAR *old* GIRL CAME TO STAY *with* ME. *She's* FROM *a* SMALL TOWN AND WAS EXCITED *about* SHOPPING *in* A BIG CITY. *I* GAVE UP ON SHOPPING *when* I WAS LITTLE. TO ME IT'S A NIGHT-*mare*. IT <u>WAS</u>, THAT IS, UNTIL...

LOOK!

SUPER MONKEY HEAD

I KNOW!

Back to School

OH! IT'S SO CUTE!

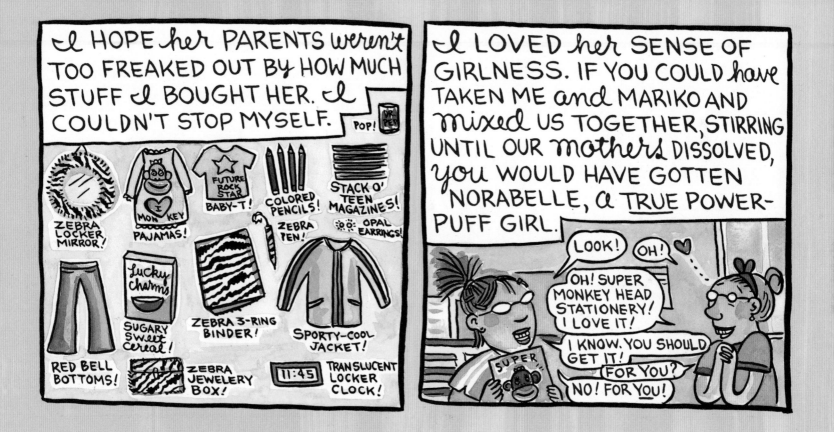

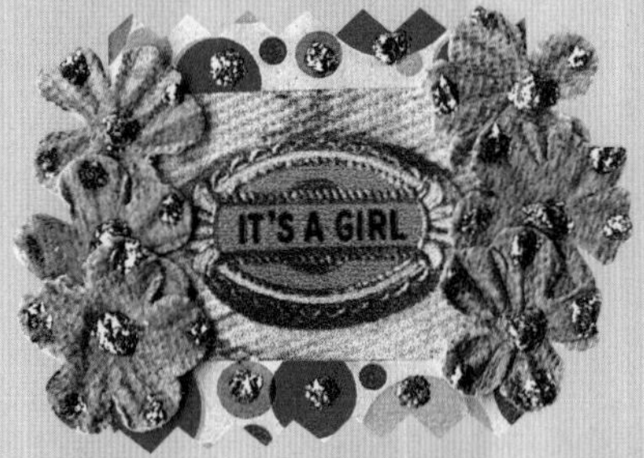
IT'S A GIRL

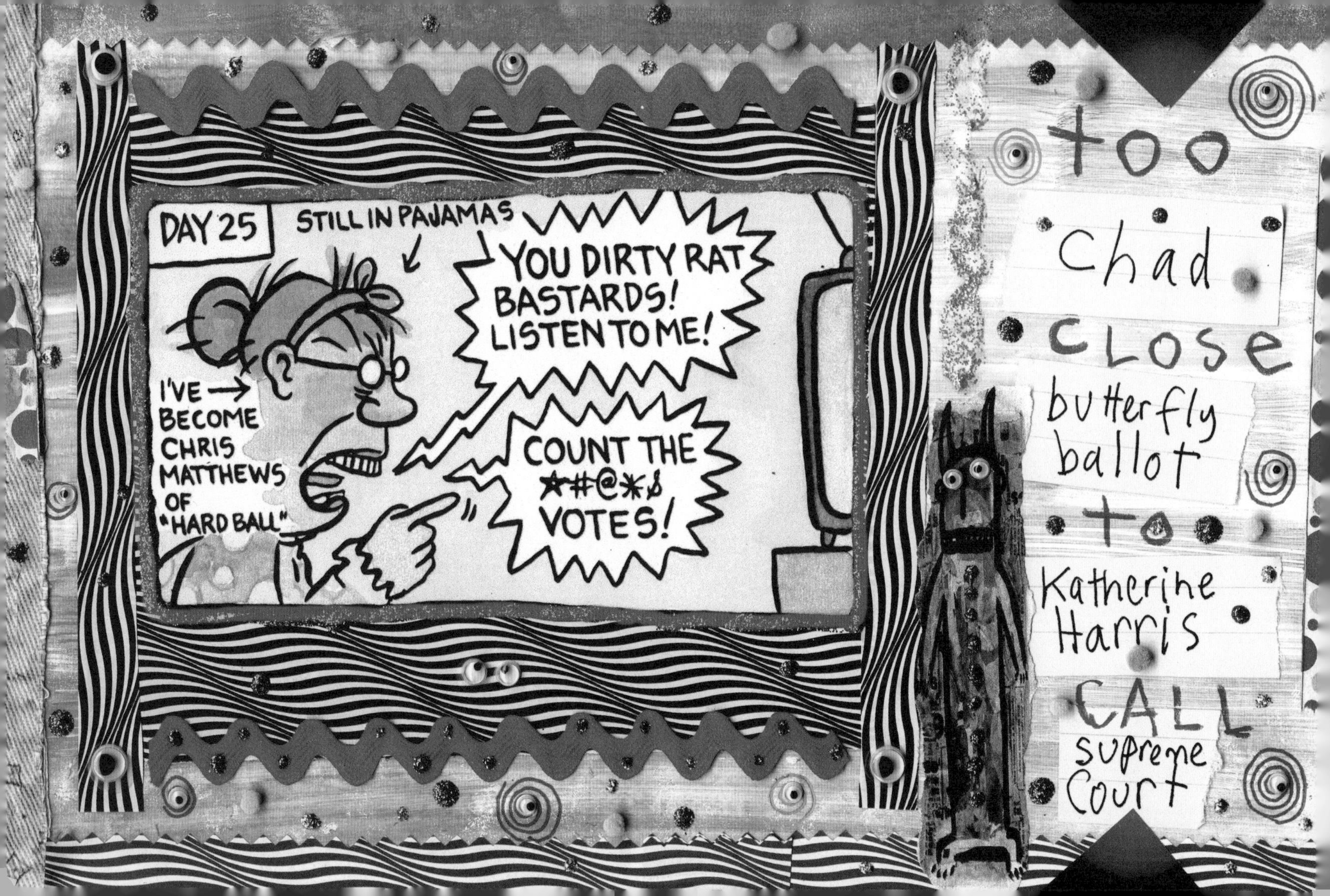
DAY 25
STILL IN PAJAMAS
YOU DIRTY RAT BASTARDS! LISTEN TO ME!
COUNT THE *#@*$ VOTES!
I'VE BECOME CHRIS MATTHEWS OF "HARD BALL"
too
chad
close
butterfly
ballot
to
Katherine
Harris
CALL
supreme
Court

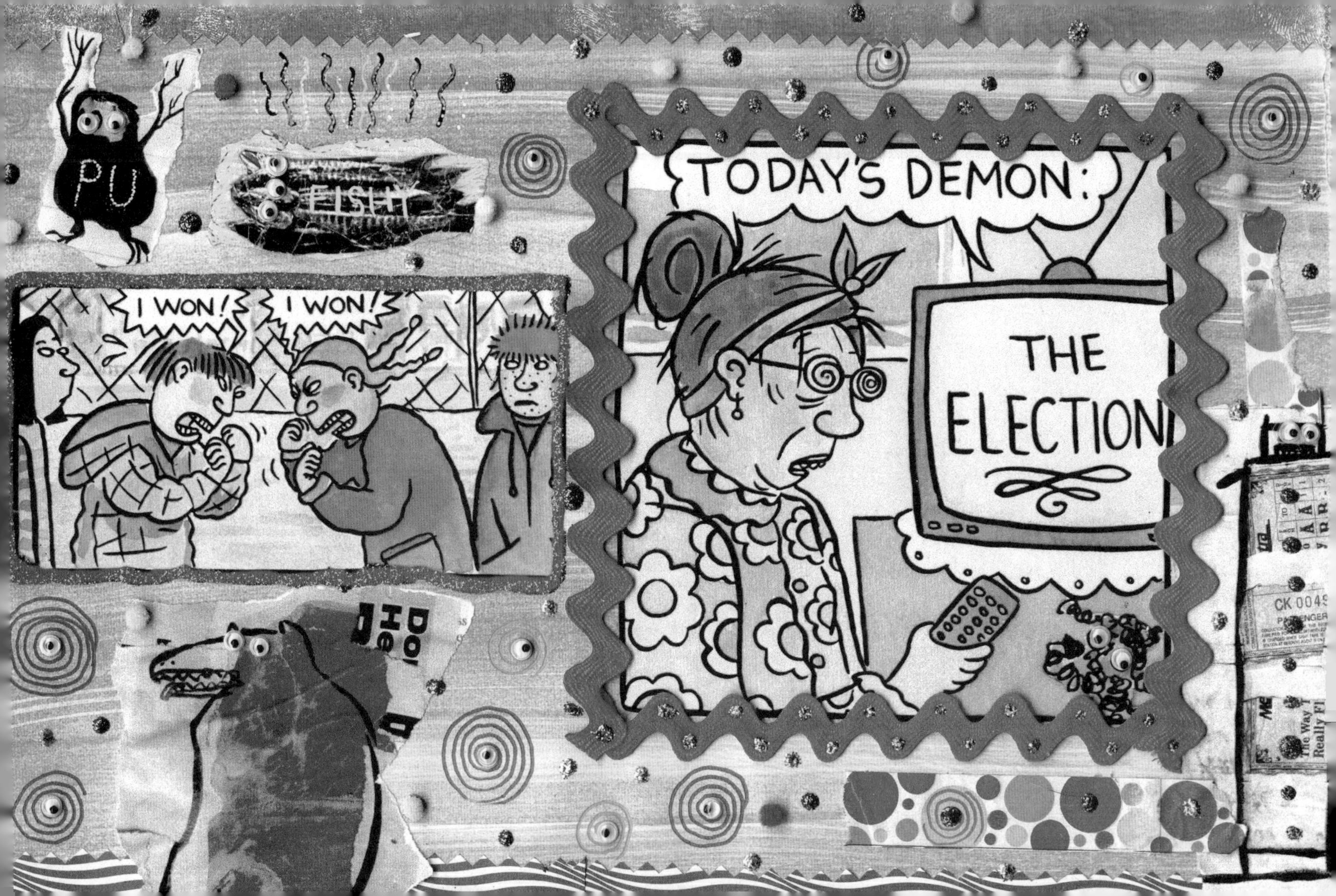

PU
FISHY
I WON!
I WON!
TODAY'S DEMON:
THE ELECTION

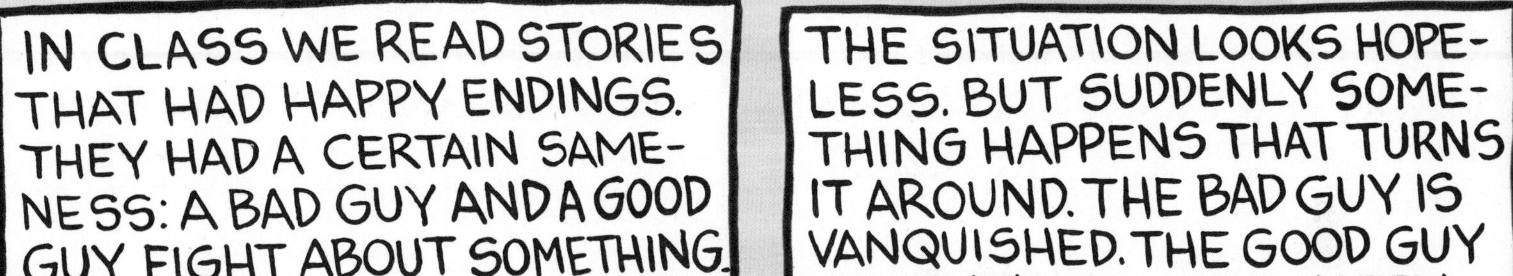
IN CLASS WE READ STORIES THAT HAD HAPPY ENDINGS. THEY HAD A CERTAIN SAMENESS: A BAD GUY AND A GOOD GUY FIGHT ABOUT SOMETHING. THE BAD GUY WINS IN AN UNFAIR WAY. EVERYONE FEELS MISERABLE. THE BAD GUY DOES HIS EVIL LAUGHTER.
HA HA HA!
NOW I AM KING!
THE SITUATION LOOKS HOPELESS. BUT SUDDENLY SOMETHING HAPPENS THAT TURNS IT AROUND. THE BAD GUY IS VANQUISHED. THE GOOD GUY WINS. IT'S CALLED A HAPPY ENDING. THERE ARE NINE MILLION STORIES LIKE THIS. WHY DO WE TELL THEM?
AND GOD BLESS US,
EVERY ONE!

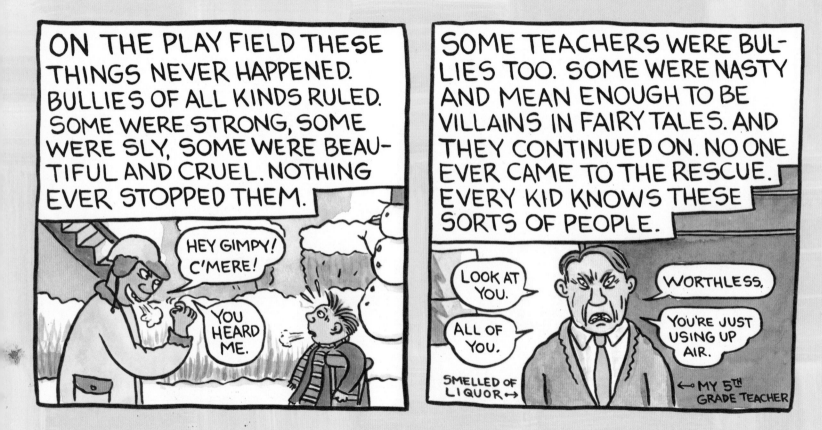

EVERY ADULT HAS SEEN THE BAD GUY WIN A THOUSAND TIMES. SO WHY DO WE TELL SO MANY STORIES WHERE THE OPPOSITE HAPPENS. GOLIATH SLAYS DAVID ON A DAILY BASIS IN REAL LIFE. I KNOW THIS. YOU KNOW THIS. AND YET...

DAY 17

WE HAVE BREAKING NEWS!

IT'S A WONDERFUL LIFE, RIGHT? RIGHT?

WRONG!

IN MY LIFE I'VE BEEN BOTH A BULLY AND A VICTIM. I NEVER COULD BULLY THOSE THAT BULLIED ME BUT I'M SURE I BULLIED OTHERS. AND WHEN I DID, I KNOW I THOUGHT I WAS IN THE RIGHT. THE BAD GUY ALWAYS DOES.

HEY, HONEY?

KATHERINE HARRIS BLOWS LYNDA'S MIND AGAIN!

DON'T TALK TO ME! CAN'T YOU SEE THE WHOLE ELECTION DEPENDS ON ME WATCHING THIS?!

SEE?

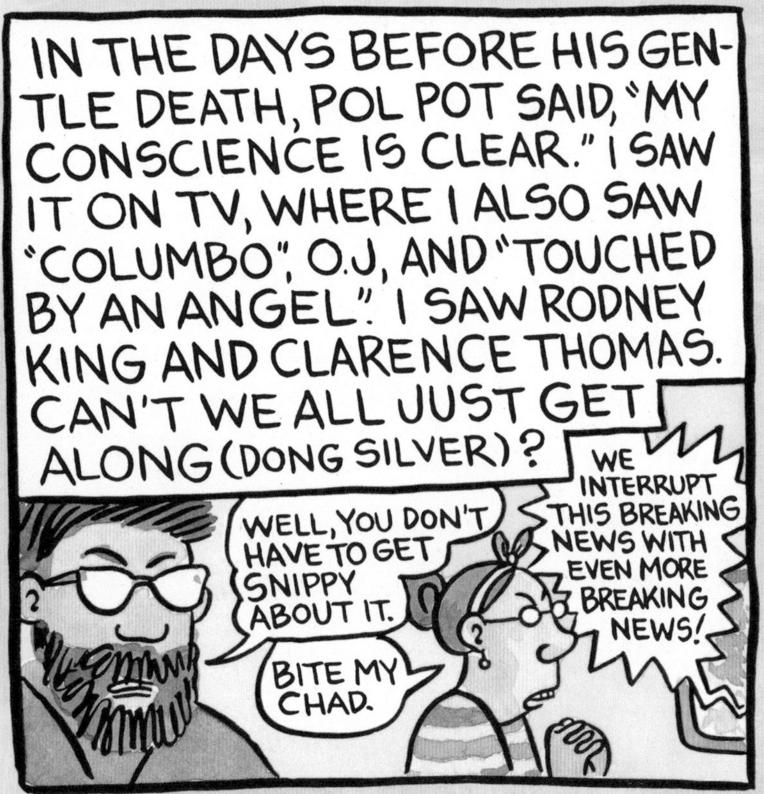
IN THE DAYS BEFORE HIS GENTLE DEATH, POL POT SAID, "MY CONSCIENCE IS CLEAR." I SAW IT ON TV, WHERE I ALSO SAW "COLUMBO", O.J, AND "TOUCHED BY AN ANGEL". I SAW RODNEY KING AND CLARENCE THOMAS. CAN'T WE ALL JUST GET ALONG (DONG SILVER)?
WE INTERRUPT THIS BREAKING NEWS WITH EVEN MORE BREAKING NEWS!
WELL, YOU DON'T HAVE TO GET SNIPPY ABOUT IT.
BITE MY CHAD.

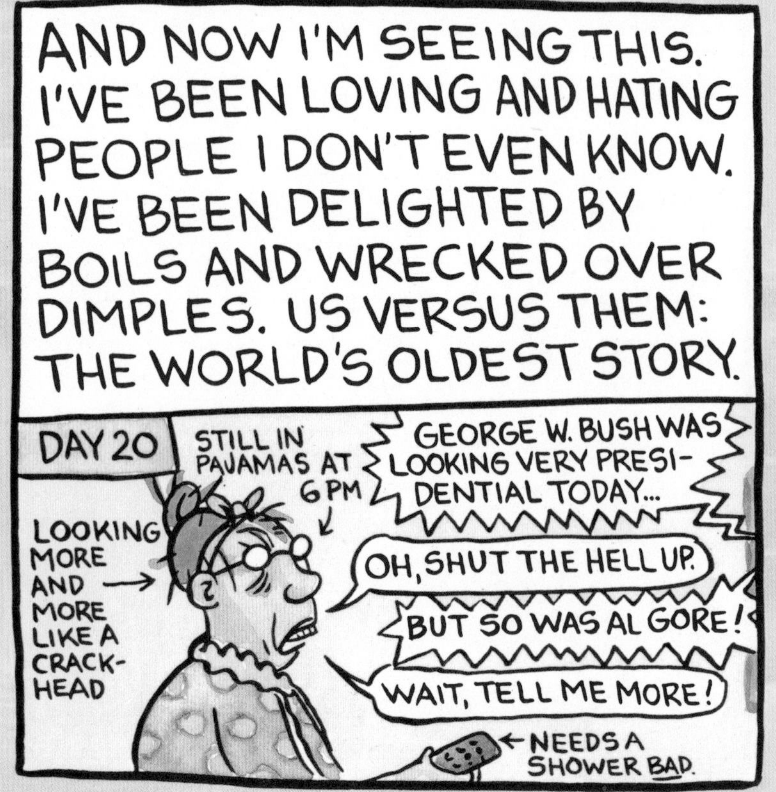
AND NOW I'M SEEING THIS. I'VE BEEN LOVING AND HATING PEOPLE I DON'T EVEN KNOW. I'VE BEEN DELIGHTED BY BOILS AND WRECKED OVER DIMPLES. US VERSUS THEM: THE WORLD'S OLDEST STORY.
DAY 20
STILL IN PAJAMAS AT 6 PM
GEORGE W. BUSH WAS LOOKING VERY PRESIDENTIAL TODAY...
LOOKING MORE AND MORE LIKE A CRACKHEAD
OH, SHUT THE HELL UP.
BUT SO WAS AL GORE!
WAIT, TELL ME MORE!
NEEDS A SHOWER BAD.

203

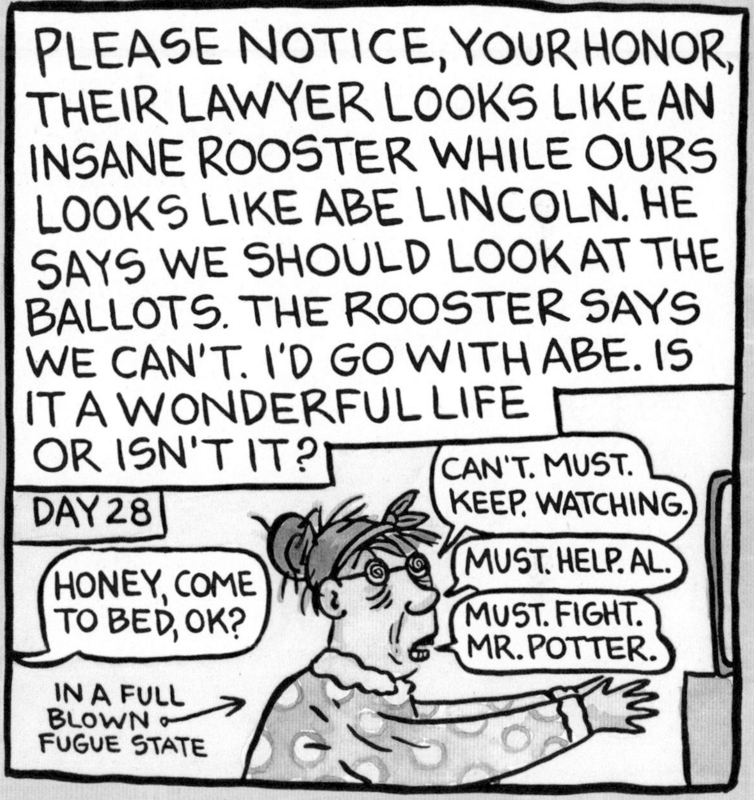

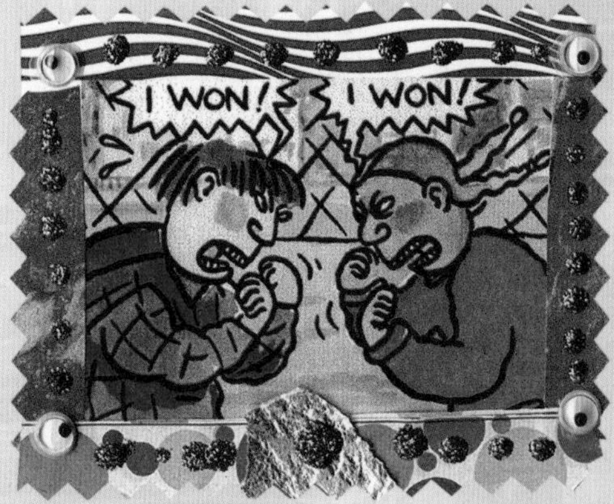
I WON!
I WON!

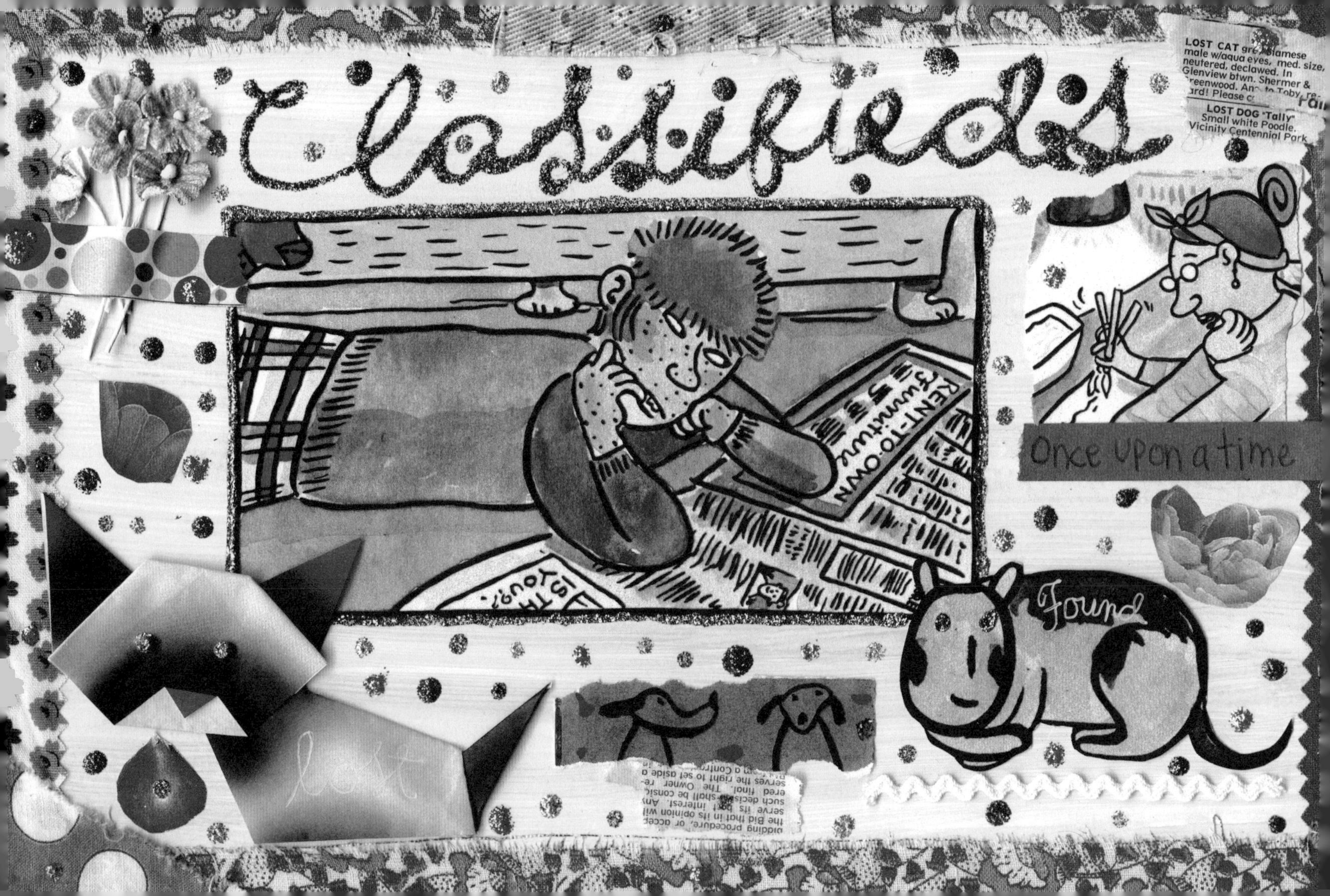
Classifieds
LOST CAT gre Siamese male w/aqua eyes, med. size, neutered, declawed. In Glenview btwn. Shermer & reenwood. Ans to Toby, re- ard! Please c
LOST DOG "Tally" Small white Poodle. Vicinity Centennial Park
RENT-TO-OWN Furniture
Once upon a time
Found
lost
bidding procedure, or accep
the Bid that in its opinion wil
serve its interest. Any
such decis shall be consic
ered final. The Owner re-
serves the right to set aside a

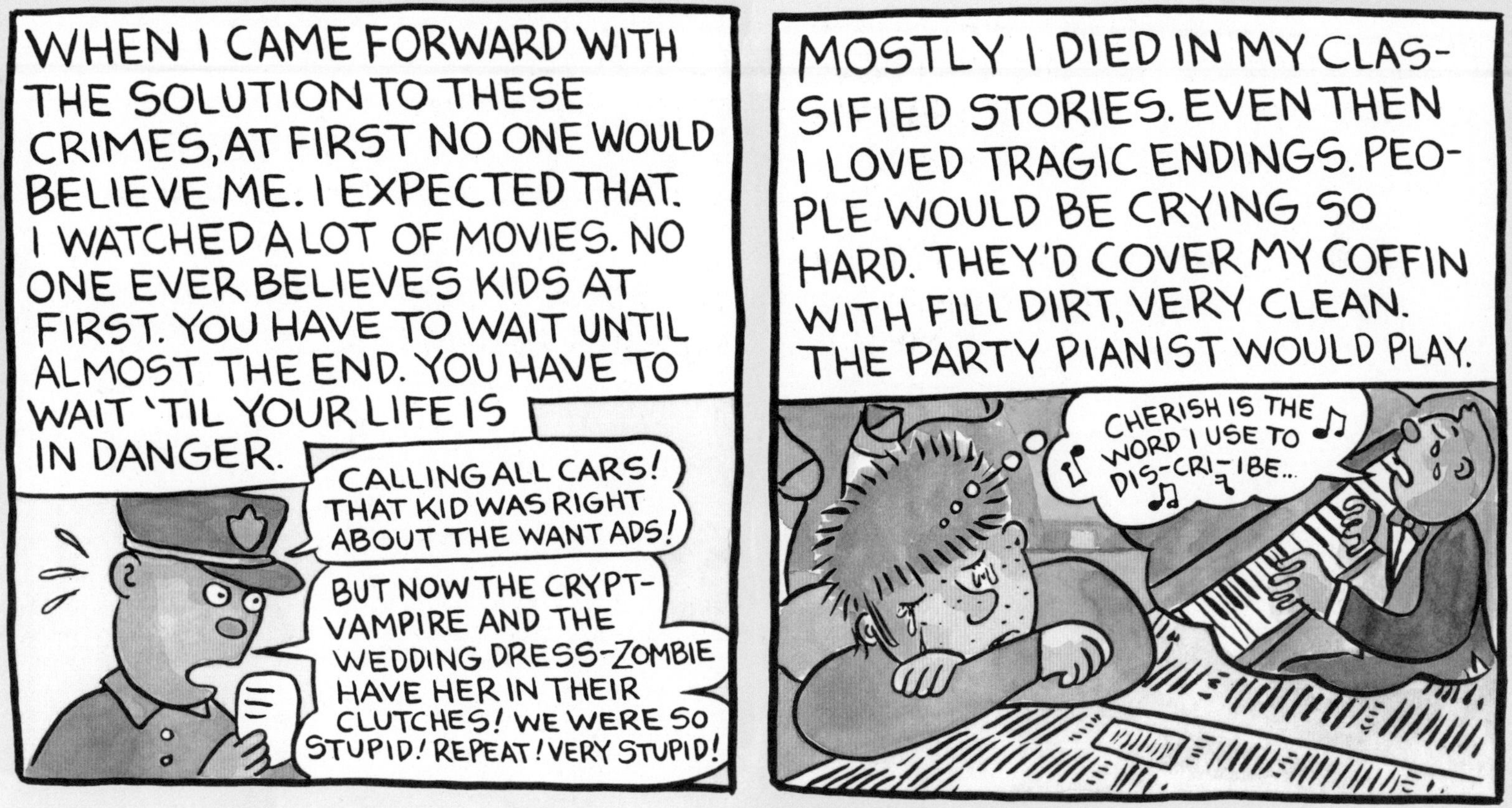
WHEN I CAME FORWARD WITH THE SOLUTION TO THESE CRIMES, AT FIRST NO ONE WOULD BELIEVE ME. I EXPECTED THAT. I WATCHED A LOT OF MOVIES. NO ONE EVER BELIEVES KIDS AT FIRST. YOU HAVE TO WAIT UNTIL ALMOST THE END. YOU HAVE TO WAIT 'TIL YOUR LIFE IS IN DANGER.
CALLING ALL CARS! THAT KID WAS RIGHT ABOUT THE WANT ADS!
BUT NOW THE CRYPT-VAMPIRE AND THE WEDDING DRESS-ZOMBIE HAVE HER IN THEIR CLUTCHES! WE WERE SO STUPID! REPEAT! VERY STUPID!
MOSTLY I DIED IN MY CLASSIFIED STORIES. EVEN THEN I LOVED TRAGIC ENDINGS. PEOPLE WOULD BE CRYING SO HARD. THEY'D COVER MY COFFIN WITH FILL DIRT, VERY CLEAN. THE PARTY PIANIST WOULD PLAY.
CHERISH IS THE WORD I USE TO DIS-CRI-IBE...

BUT ONLY CERTAIN PEOPLE WERE "ADVANCED" ENOUGH FOR WRITING AND LITERATURE. IN COLLEGE IT GOT EVEN WORSE. I LOVED THE WRONG KIND OF WRITING AND I NEVER COULD BREAK A STORY DOWN TO FIND THE SYMBOLIC MEANING, ALTHOUGH I SURE TRIED TO FAKE IT.

(3:30 AM)

In "The Bell Jar," Plath profounds her enumerated existential parthenogenesis using subvertible intramural insight on the dissimulation of her classic brummer of the 20th century.

MY TROUBLE ENDED WHEN I STARTED MAKING COMIC-STRIPS. IT'S NOT SOMETHING A PERSON HAS TO BE VERY "ADVANCED" TO DO. AT LEAST NOT IN THE MINDS OF LITERARY TYPES.

SO YOU'RE A CARTOONIST! HOW ADORABLE!

POLITICAL?

NO.

HUMOROUS?

KINDA.

WE'RE BOTH WRITERS.

SAY, MAYBE WE COULD COLLABORATE! WE WRITE IT AND YOU DRAW IT! HOW FUN!

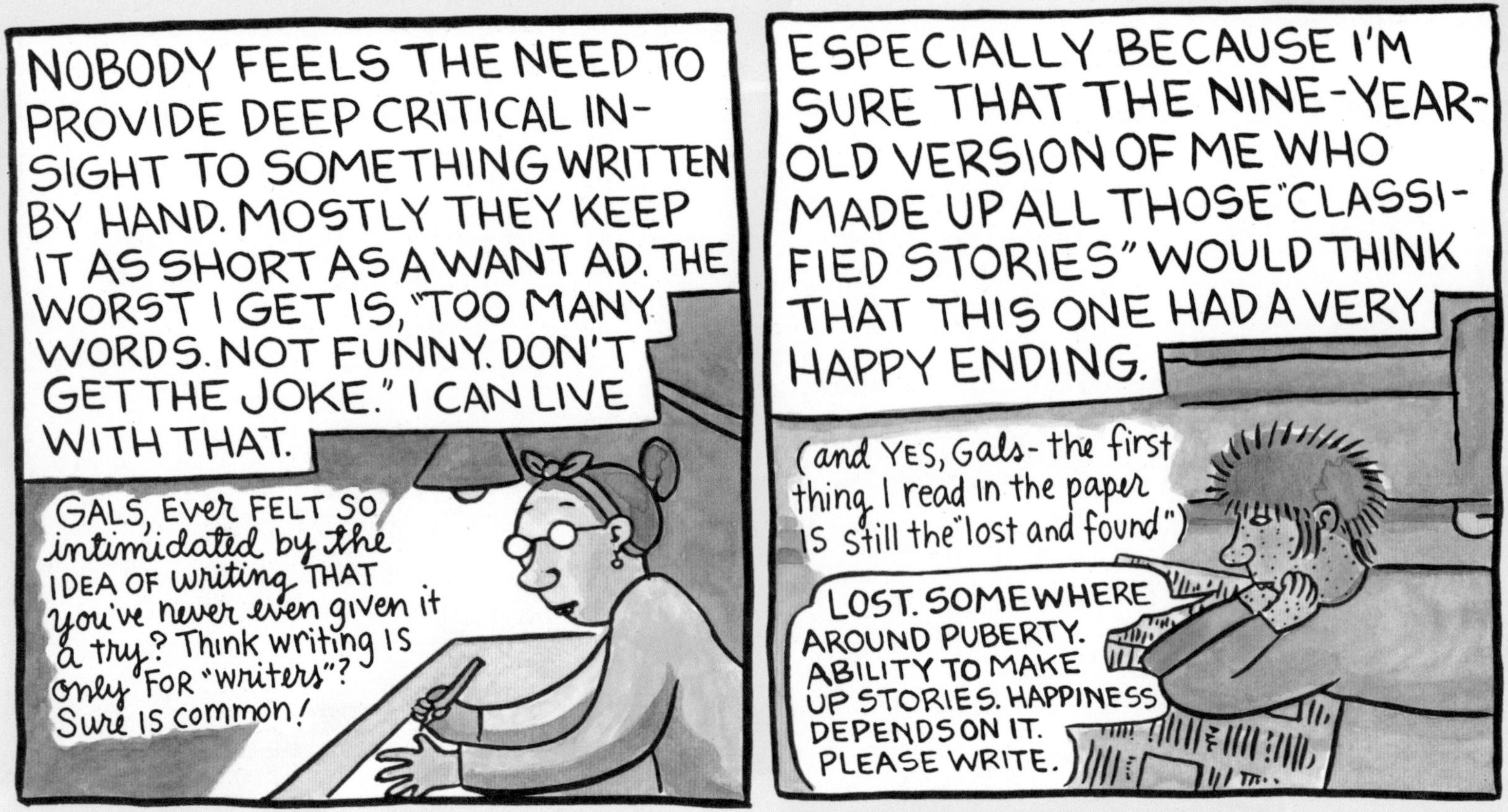
NOBODY FEELS THE NEED TO PROVIDE DEEP CRITICAL INSIGHT TO SOMETHING WRITTEN BY HAND. MOSTLY THEY KEEP IT AS SHORT AS A WANT AD. THE WORST I GET IS, "TOO MANY WORDS. NOT FUNNY. DON'T GET THE JOKE." I CAN LIVE WITH THAT.
GALS, Ever FELT SO intimidated by the IDEA OF writing THAT you've never even given it a try? Think writing IS only FOR "writers"? Sure IS common!
ESPECIALLY BECAUSE I'M SURE THAT THE NINE-YEAR-OLD VERSION OF ME WHO MADE UP ALL THOSE "CLASSIFIED STORIES" WOULD THINK THAT THIS ONE HAD A VERY HAPPY ENDING.
(and YES, Gals- the first thing I read in the paper IS still the "lost and found")
LOST. SOMEWHERE AROUND PUBERTY. ABILITY TO MAKE UP STORIES. HAPPINESS DEPENDS ON IT. PLEASE WRITE.

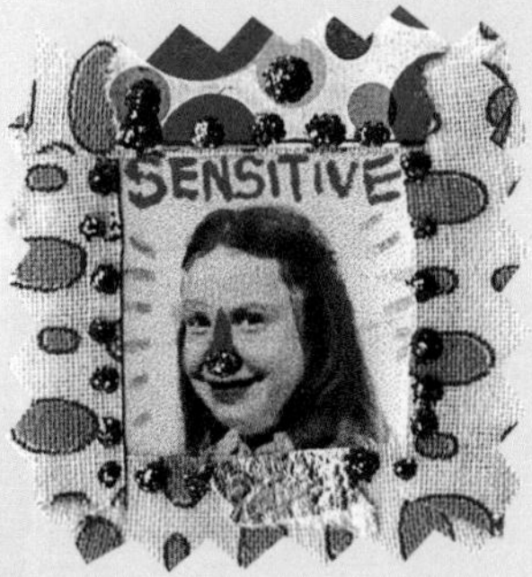
SENSITIVE

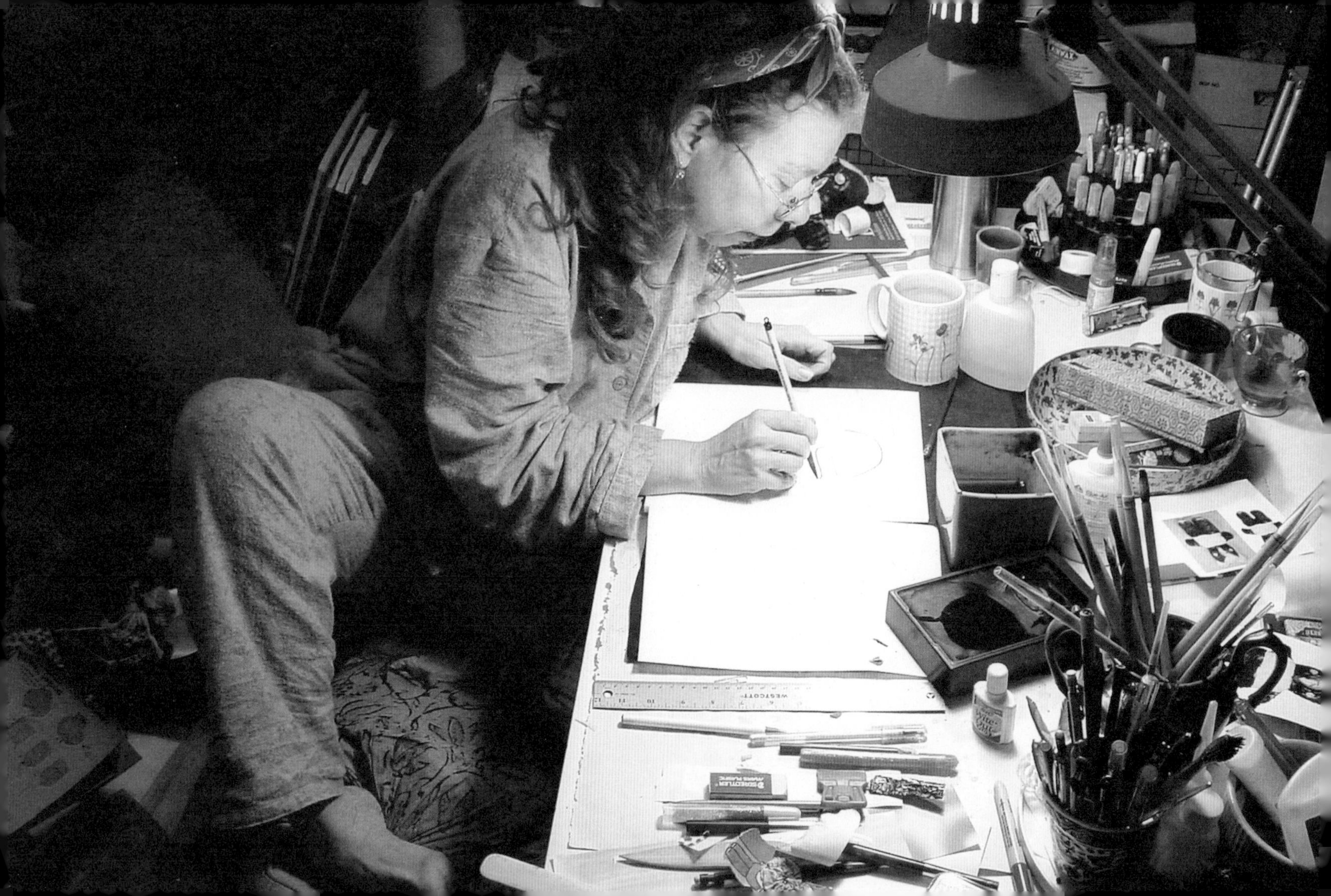
WESTCOTT

PAINT YOUR DEMON

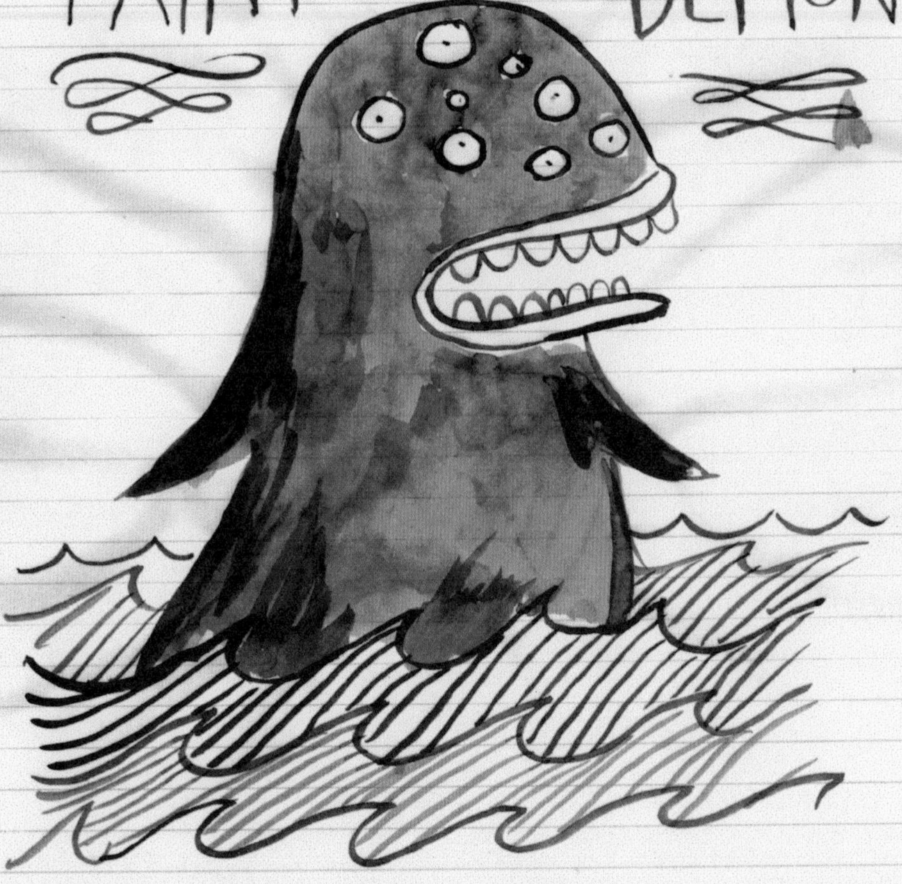

Come On!
Don't you
want to
try it??

JUST
TURN THE
PAGE →

you will need AN INKSTONE ↴

AN INKSTICK ↴

water area →

Grinding area →

(This one is hand-carved) ↴

make sure to get a NATURAL stone - the man-made ones aren't as good - at least 3 X 4 inches. you can get a good, simple one for under $20.⁰⁰

made of soot compressed into a hard stick - PERMANENT!! ARCHIVAL!! Really fantastic!! Comes in many shapes and SIZES, plain and fancy, a medium QUALITY inkstick will work just fine.

A BRUSH ↓

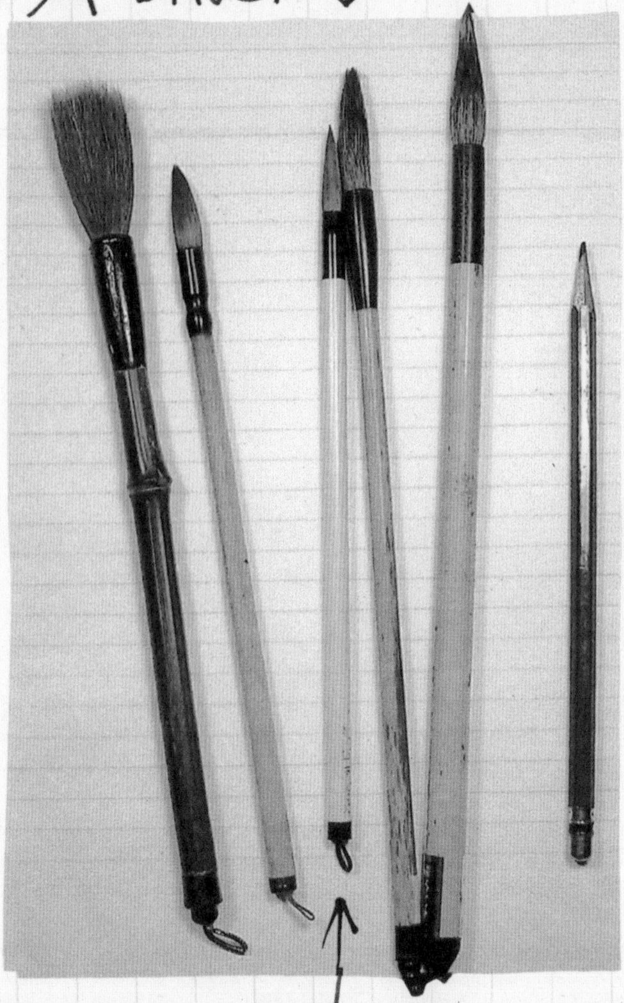

The demons came out of This one

asian style BRUSHES come in a LOT of sizes and HAIRSTYLES. The one I used for this book had a BRUSH HAIR LENGTH of 1 inch and a base diameter of 1/4 inch. The hair was pretty FIRM. For other kinds of paintings I use larger ones. A GOOD BRUSH is IMPORTANT!! But a good asian brush isn't insanely expensive! Keep them clean! Hang them to DRY!

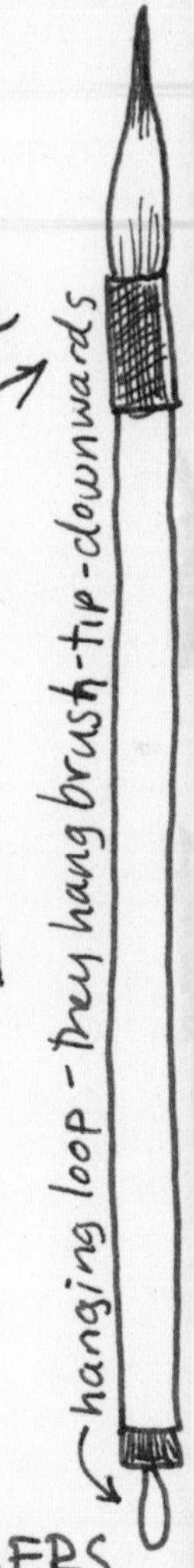
hanging loop - they hang brush-tip-downwards

I GET ALL OF MY SUPPLIES AT ACORNPLANET.COM.
YOU CAN E-MAIL THEM, ASK FOR A BEGINNERS SET-UP, AND THEY'LL Get you started!

JUST ADD water!↴

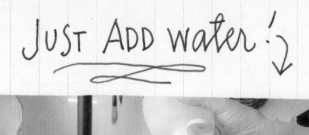

pour about a teaspoon onto the Grinding area. A plastic SQUIRT Bottle is perfect for this

and ADD INK!↴

although it's called GRINDING you actually USE Very little Pressure! Just move the INKSTICK in a light circle keeping the bottom of the INKStick Flat against the Stone. Keep on going until it looks oily. Just mess around until you get it the way You LIKE IT!! It can take 5 or 10 minutes.

now HOLD your BRUSH

Wet your Brush in water and run it across a paper-towel to get Rid of excess water, Then Dip the TIP into the INK, hold the BRUSH straight up and down and slowly pull a line across the paper. There are MUCH BETTER instructions in books on Asian-style brush work at your library.!! But mostly you can learn a lot by messing Around. I write the ALPHABET every day with a Brush.

Paint Your Demon!

↶ ↷

I like to PAINT on LEGAL paper or on the CLASSIFIED SECTION of the newspaper OR Even pages from OLD Books! I will try ANY PAPER, typing paper, wrapping paper even PAPER BAGS! ♡

MAKE FRESH INK EACH TIME YOU PAINT + keep your inkstone clean.!!

Discovering The paintbrush, inkstone, inkstick and resulting Demons has Been the most Important thing to happen to me in Years. TRY IT! YOU Will dig It!

I made a cloth pad for under my paper It's an old black T-shirt Quilted onto two layers of Flannel. IT absorbs excess water.

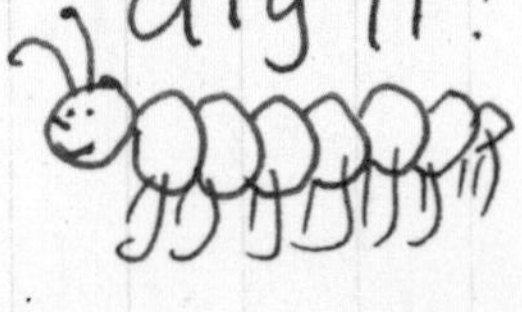

other books by LYNDA BARRY

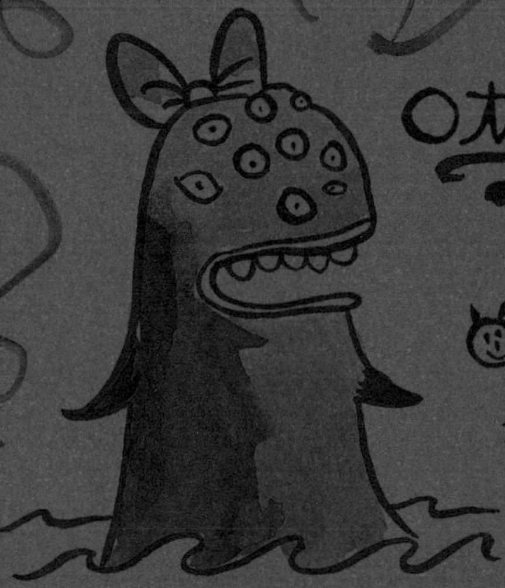

- GIRLS and BOYS ✿ Big Ideas
- naked LADIES, naked LADIES, NAKED Ladies
- EVERYTHING IN THE WORLD ♥ The GOOD TIMES ARE KILLING ME
- The Fun House ✿
- DOWN THE STREET
- My Perfect Life
- come over, come over
- It's So Magic
- THE FREDDIE STORIES
- → CRUDDY ←
- The! Greatest! OF! MARLYS!

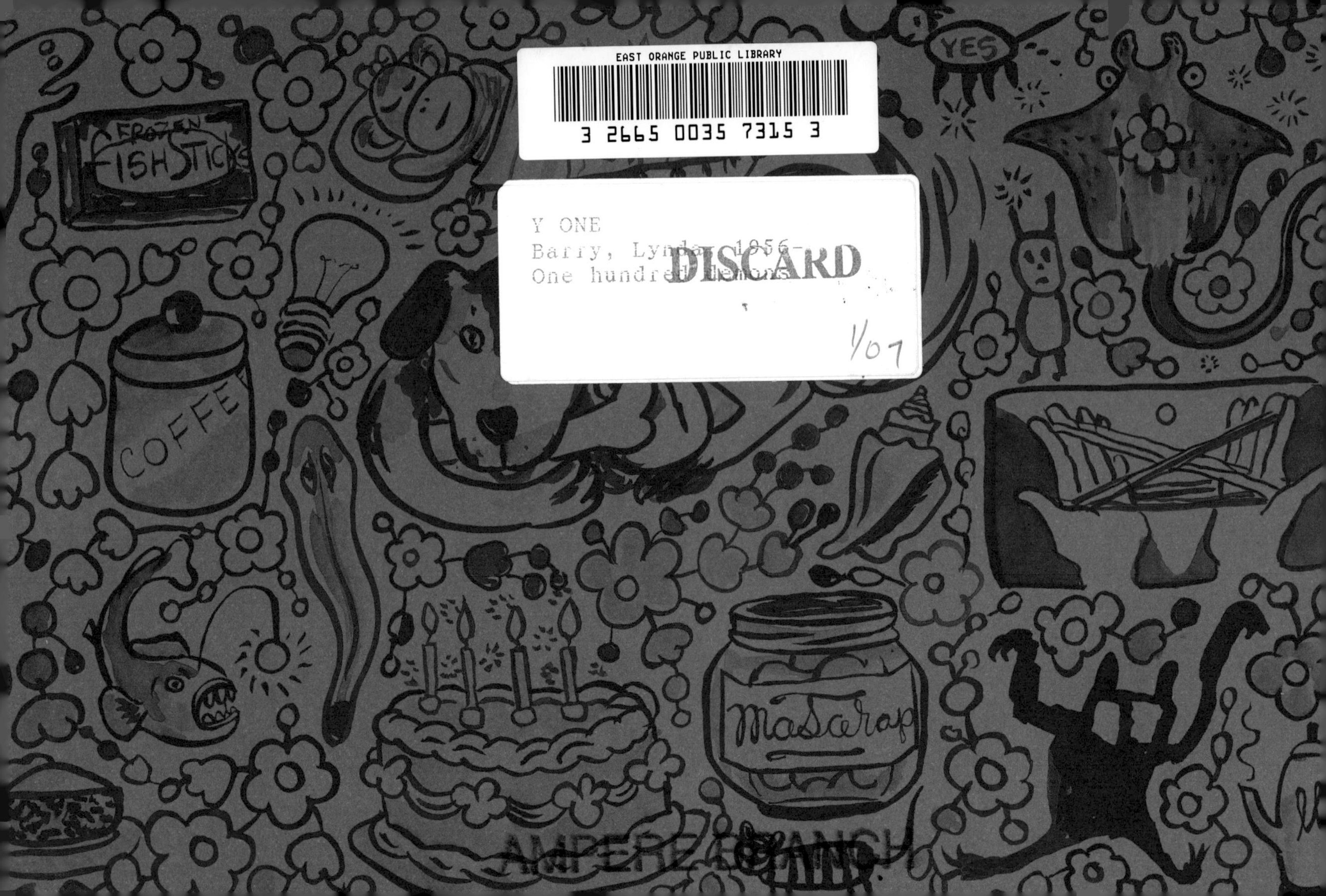
FROZEN
FISH STICKS
COFFE
YES
Masarap